Effective Church Leadership

OTHER WORKS BY KENNON L. CALLAHAN

Twelve Keys to an Effective Church
Twelve Keys to an Effective Church: The Leaders' Guide
Twelve Keys to an Effective Church: The Planning Workbook
Twelve Keys to an Effective Church: Audiocassette Tapes

Effective Church Leadership

Building on the
Twelve Keys

Kennon L. Callahan

▟ HarperSanFrancisco
A Division of HarperCollins*Publishers*

The National Institute for Church Planning and Consultation, of which Kennon L. Callahan is the founder and senior consultant, can be addressed at 15775 Hillcrest, Mailstop #455, Dallas, Texas 75248.

Library of Congress Cataloging-in-Publication Data

Callahan, Kennon L.
    Effective church leadership : building on the twelve keys / Kennon L. Callahan.—1st ed.
        p. cm.
   ISBN 0-06-061299-1
    1. Christian leadership. 2. Church management. 3. Pastoral theology. 4. Missions—Theory. I. Title.
BV652.1.C35 1990
254—dc20   89-45526
                                             CIP

95 96 97 HAD 10 9 8 7 6

This work is dedicated to my mother and father

Eileen Beatrice Arthur Callahan
and
Earl Kennon Callahan

Their wisdom and compassion, integrity and honesty,
vision and caring, have meant much across the years.
They are genuine leaders in the faith.

Contents

Preface

This book is designed to share wisdom and insights, research and experience, principles and suggestions in the areas of mission, leadership and decision making, and organization. These are the first, fifth, and sixth of the twelve central characteristics of effective churches.

May this book benefit your mission in rich, full ways in the years to come.

I want to acknowledge and thank the following persons for their direct influence in my own life: Dr. Joseph Politella, professor of philosophy and my adviser during my years at Kent State University, for helping me to see what is genuinely important in life; Dr. David Shipley, professor of historical and systematic theology during my years at Perkins School of Theology, for helping me to catch the vision of God's mission across the centuries; Dr. John Deschner, professor of systematic theology at Perkins School of Theology, for helping me to discover the church's centrality in that mission; Dr. Robert Waterman, author and consultant, for his research and contributions to the field of leadership; and the many wise, caring leaders in local churches who have touched my life across the years.

Julie McCoy Callahan has been invaluable in the development of the book. Her suggestions and direct contributions have strengthened the book greatly. It is a rich experience to share and work together with her.

I particularly want to thank John Shopp, senior editor at Harper & Row, for his major contributions to the publication of this book. His editorial work, and that of Hilary Vartanian, editorial assistant, has been extraordinary. It is a genuine joy to work with them and the many excellent persons at Harper & Row.

My thanks go to Dwayne Roberts, who typed the original manuscript and who labored long and hard to help bring the book into being.

Introduction

This book is written primarily for pastors—a valiant, extraordinary group of persons. Their contributions on behalf of God's kingdom are amazing. Their contributions to the lives and destinies of countless legions of persons are extraordinary.

Sometimes they are told they have low morale. Sometimes they are urged to work harder, and so, regrettably, they work harder. Sometimes they are told they are not doing enough, and so they try to do more. Sometimes they are blamed for their denomination's decline. Regrettably, since they are good-natured persons, they sometimes accept the blame.

This book is my gift to this extraordinary group of persons. In dark hours, it will be a source of light. In troubled times, it will help to guide the way forward. In the good times, it will be a source of confirmation and affirmation.

The book is a thoughtful book. Sometimes it will be stirring and exciting. Sometimes it will be comforting and compassionate. Sometimes it will be hard nosed and straightforward. Sometimes it will share good humor. For our troubling times, thoughtful books are the most helpful, to be read and reread, to be studied and pondered, to serve as a guide and a gift in the troubling, disturbing chaos ahead of us.

This book is, in the best sense of the term, a how-to book. It focuses on the foundational principles for developing leadership on a mission field. If you are a local church pastor—anywhere—you are on a mission field.

It is like a book on how to build a house. With these foundational principles, you will be in a position to design and build whatever specific blueprint of a home makes best sense to you. There are lots of different blueprints and floor plans for homes. The foundational how-to principles are common to all the blueprints and all the house plans.

Some will read the book and come away thinking that it is too theoretical, that what is needed is something simpler and more practical. If you are looking for one specific blueprint and floor plan, you will be disappointed. Frankly, that is the problem of many how-to books. They give you one very specific blueprint and floor plan.

Everyone does not—and should not—live in the same house. Many different blueprints and floor plans are useful and helpful. The art is to discover the foundational principles to build a variety of different houses depending on the mission terrain.

It is like a book on the foundational principles for how to play football. In football, there are lots of different ways of winning games and lots of different plays. Some how-to books for churches advocate that one play is the way forward. They have discovered that it works very well in one specific situation. They then assume that that one play will work everywhere, for everybody, on all parts of the mission field.

No football team I know of runs the same play on every down of every quarter of every game. A successful team relies on a variety of plays. But underneath all the plays is a range of sound foundational principles telling how to play the game.

This book is about the foundational how-tos. Once you know these basics, you will be in the strongest position to construct whatever home—or design whatever set of plays—will best help you in your mission on behalf of God's kingdom.

The foundational principles for leadership on a mission field do have a wide range of implications for the current practice of leadership in local churches and in denominations. In the book, I have shared some of these implications as illustrations.

You know your own setting best. You are precisely the best person to develop the applications that will be most helpful to your mission. Trust your creativity and imagination, your wisdom and insight. Confer with persons whose judgment and vision you respect. With your leadership the specific implications of these foundational principles can best grow forward in your setting.

Some of the implications are yet before me. Life is a pilgrimage, a search. Through a vast array of research, interviews, consultations, and seminars, I have discovered these foundational principles for the nature of leadership. I continue in that pilgrimage journey of discovery.

The book will be helpful for all persons in the church—both pastors and key leaders. I resist using the terms *minister* and *laity* because of the obvious caste-system connotations that those terms have come to include. Mostly, I refer to "pastors" and "key leaders." Certainly, pastors are key leaders, and the term *key leaders,* in that sense, includes all pastors.

At the same time, I find the term *key leaders* more helpful than the term *laity.* I want laity to see that they are key leaders on this mission field. The phrase "I'm just a lay person" needs to be buried and forgotten. Any quaint assumption that the minister is the leader and the laity are the followers needs to be retired.

You will discover whatever terms are most helpful to you. It will help you in reading the book to know that the terms useful to me (for now, at least) are *pastor* and *key leaders.* These terms will likely develop their own connotations and are more mutual and inclusive than the older terms *minister* and *laity.*

Likewise, you will discover a range of phrases that are distinctively my own. In my various seminars persons have been intrigued by "the way I say some things." Be at peace. I do not know quite how I have come to say certain things in certain ways. I find these phrases helpful in making the point.

Read these phrases with a good spirit. Sometimes it is the humor of the point that is at stake in the way I say it. Sometimes it is the irony of the point. Sometimes it is the straightforward analysis of the point. You will discover these phrases and, I trust, be helped by the way they are said. The context in which you discover them will help you to understand their specific meanings.

Likewise, from time to time in the book, you will discover some words in quotation marks. More often than not, the word is so marked because I am intending for that word to have some special emphasis. Sometimes, there is irony or perhaps humor. Frequently, I am using the word with a very specific focus to illustrate a very particular point. Mostly the context of the sentence and paragraph will help you to know the special meaning intended.

The book can be read at four major levels. First: *the church.* The book is primarily intended to be helpful in developing an understanding of the nature of leadership in the church. Thus, most of the examples, analogies, and illustrations relate to the church. You will discover these foundational principles most helpful in growing forward an understanding of the nature of leadership important for the church in the coming times.

Second: *your work.* The book can be read in terms of your work and vocation, to which the foundational principles of leadership can be applied directly. They apply not because these are primarily business principles but because they are primarily people principles. Wherever there is an enterprise of work or business, these principles on the nature of leadership will be helpful.

Third: *groupings.* These principles can be applied and will be helpful in whatever grouping of persons you find yourself. That may be a family, or it may be an educational, vocational, political, civic and community, recreational, or religious grouping. It is not that these are "universal" principles; it is precisely the other way around. These are primarily people principles, and they are therefore helpful wherever you find groupings of people in any sphere or sector of culture.

Fourth: *life.* These principles will be helpful in your own life. I encourage and invite you to read the book particularly at this level. We have the opportunity of this one lifetime. Mostly, we want our lives to count. There are times when we wonder whether there is any use. There are difficult times of despair, depression, and despondency as well as good times of discovery, joy, and hope.

As I have puzzled through this book, I have come to discover, in an ever-deepening manner, the ways in which these foundational principles are helpful as one lives through this life's pilgrimage. I found that I could not write about the nature of leadership without also writing about this life's pilgrimage. There is a sound reason.

Leadership is about life; life is about leadership. The two are close companions. One can best understand life as one begins to understand the nature of leadership. One can best understand the nature of leadership as one comes to understand life in ever-deepening ways.

I find writing a book a rich learning experience. As I write, I learn more about myself, people, and life. I learn about the faith and the church. I discover the enduring character of God's mission with us and for the whole earth.

This is a gentle book. I invite you to study it in a thoughtful, loving spirit. Consider these suggestions as you read.

First, before you read each chaper, gather—in your mind's eye—several persons to share the chapter with you. Think of persons close and dear to you. Think of your mentors, from whom you have learned much. Think of your best friends. Gather some of them with you. Visualize their presence around you. Surround yourself with your cloud of witnesses, that is, with persons who have nurtured you and helped you to be who you are today. Then read the chapter with their spirit in mind.

Second, be in prayer for a few minutes of quiet and reflection before you read each chapter. Recall the times when you have felt closest to God. Sense the presence of God with you. Pray that God will lead you to discover new insights and direction for your mission.

Third, immediately write down your new insights and creative ideas as they come to you. Use the margins of the book. Write them down before you lose them.

This book is a pilgrimage between the two of us. Underline the key insights that you discover in the book. In your mind the book will simultaneously stir new ideas and creative ways forward. These insights come from you. They are not in the book. Rather, the book stirs your best thinking. Write down *your* new discoveries—then act on them immediately.

With the help of this book, the spirit of your friends around you, and the presence of God close to you, look forward to rich, full new discoveries as you read. Trust your own best creativity and imagination. Discover new understandings, principles, and practices that will be for you the foundations for leadership on a mission field.

May your time with this book—and your own life—be an excellent pilgrimage.

PART ONE.

THE DAY OF MISSION

1. The Missionary Pastor

GENTLE CONFIRMATION

The day of the professional minister is over. The day of the missionary pastor has come.

These are words of gentle confirmation, not striking prophecy. A few who read these words of quiet declaration will say they are startled. They will get caught up in a futile romantic longing for a churched culture. Some may protest—and wonder out loud—if this startling, bold prophecy will come true. I can assure you that it will not come true in the future—because *it has already happened.* These two statements describe what has taken place, not what may occur.

The professional minister movement did not end with a noisy bang. It ended quietly, suitably, and decently enough a few years ago as professional ministers experienced a gridlock of meetings, desks stacked with papers, calendars filled with appointments, and declining worship attendances in their churches. There was no climactic event, no dramatic conclusion. The professional minister movement, born in the churched culture of the late 1940s, simply ceased to be functional on the mission field of the 1980s. That way of being a minister had worked for nearly forty years. But it became dysfunctional. It no longer worked.

The symptoms of its demise are self-evident in the decline of some of the "mainline" denominations of our time. It is not accidental that they are hemorrhaging and dying. The way (or essence) of being a professional minister—with its understanding of the nature of leadership and the related attenuated behavior patterns, values, and objectives—may be functional in a reasonably churched culture.

But that way of doing ministry is lost on a mission field. It is doomed. It is like sending pleasant, polite schoolboys and schoolgirls from Grover's Corners to work in the slums, the jungles, the mission field of an unchurched culture.

Professional ministers are at their best (and they do excellent work) in a churched culture. But put them in an unchurched culture, and they are lost. In an unchurched culture, they do a reasonably decent job of presiding over stable and declining and dying churches. They maintain a sense of presence, dignity, decorum, and decency—with a quietly sad regret—much like the thoughtful undertaker who sees to keeping things in good order throughout the funeral.

New understandings of being a minister are created for each new era. The professional-minister understanding, which was developed in the late forties and early fifties, served well its purpose for nearly forty years.

New understandings of doing ministry must be created with each new generation for the church's mission to move forward. When an older generation imposes its understanding on the new generation—however innocently—both groupings become dysfunctional. Each new generation must carve out an understanding of ministry that matches with its time.

The day of the professional minister is over. The day of the missionary pastor has come.

A TIME GONE BY

THE CULTURAL MOVEMENT OF PROFESSIONALISM

In the late 1940s and early 1950s, following World War II, there emerged in this country the cultural movement of professionalism. Prior to World War II, the primary focus was on vocation (from the Latin *vocare*), or calling. Following World War II, the primary focus was on profession.

Prior to World War II, doctors thought of themselves as doctors, lawyers thought of themselves as lawyers, and ministers thought of themselves as ministers. Following World War II, doctors began to think of themselves as professionals, lawyers began to think of themselves as professionals, and ministers began to think of themselves as professionals. The focus shifted from vocation to profession, from calling to professionalism.

Articles and books were written on "the minister as professional." Requirements and standards were developed for "professional ministers." Whole denominations became preoccupied with the professionalization of the ministry. Seminaries turned their attention to preparing and graduating—in the best sense of the term—"professional ministers."

The understanding of leadership, the behavior patterns, the values, and the objectives of the professional minister were widely encouraged, particularly in the so-called mainline denominations. And all of this was perfectly natural and understandable. The "professional minister movement" was a reflection, in religious circles, of the cultural movement toward professionalism in the wider society of that time.

We have always known that the church and the culture have had an interactive relationship with one another. The book *The Ministry in Historical Perspectives*, edited by H. Richard Niebuhr and Daniel Williams (New York: Harper & Brothers, 1956), traces this interactive relationship from "Ministry in the Primitive Church" to "The Protestant Ministry in America: 1850 to the Present."

In the chapter "The Ministry in the Later Patristic Period (314–450)," we find an example of this interaction described.

With the sudden cessation of imperial persecution, the ministry was obliged to accommodate itself quickly to the demands and the expectations of a patronizing magistracy. With the establishment of the church in the favor of one Emperor (by 314 in the West and 324 in the East), and the prospect of a rapid enlargement of the membership of the churches and the proliferation of new duties and opportunities and temptations, a new phase in the evolution of the ministry had dawned. (P. 60)

This developmental, interactive relationship between the church and the culture can be noted again and again across the centuries of the church's mission.

With the cessation of fighting at the end of World War II, the church again "was obliged to accommodate itself quickly to the demands and expectations" of a culture intent on rebuilding its society and leaving behind the horrors of the second war to end all wars. The church was seen as central in the reuniting and rebuilding of families, whose members had fought in battles from Berlin to Guadalcanal and beyond.

People moved from the farms and small towns to the cities and the new homes being built in the suburbs. There was a consequent rapid growth of city and suburban churches. Ministers prepared themselves for the "proliferation of new duties and opportunities and temptations."

With the acceleration of specialization, aided by the complexity of the way World War II had to be fought, the ministry prepared itself for an increasing array of specializations. And with the development of the broad cultural movement of professionalism, the church naturally began to focus on the minister as professional.

THE VALUE OF THE PROFESSIONAL MINISTER MOVEMENT

To be sure, the professional minister movement had value for its time. For many, the professionalization of the ministry was considered to be a useful corrective over against an earlier time when some felt that all that was needed to be a minister was a dose of sincerity, a dash of commitment, a little bit of good will, and a calling from God. The professional minister movement came along and decreed that a person needed training, education, professional qualifications, and even continuing education in order to be a professional minister.

It is to be observed that the professional minister movement's understanding of that earlier time is tainted by its own preoccupation with professionalism. To be sure, in that earlier time, pastors understood the importance—indeed, the centrality—of their calling, but there was also a widespread, very strong emphasis on intellect and research, study and learning, growth and development.

The professional minister movement has not completely overlooked the value of a calling to ministry. But its primary contribution has been to advance—for better or worse—the formal educational and degree requirements among the mainline denominations. In other words, the church was experiencing the direct influence of the culture's movement toward professionalism.

At this juncture, I am not proposing whether that influence was good or bad. I am simply noting that the professional minister movement constitutes one component of the broader movement toward professionalism in many aspects of the culture. In time, it will likely be judged as both a reflection of and understandable for its time.

At a recent seminar for pastors and their spouses, I was sharing my thoughts about this interrelationship of the movement toward professionalism in the culture at large and the movement toward professionalism in the ministry. During one of the breaks, a pastor's wife (whose father had also been a pastor) offered the suggestion that a further factor may have driven the professional minister movement.

She remembered a time when pastors were "placed on a pedestal" by the culture. Then, more recently, she could remember a time when pastors were no longer held in high regard by the culture. She suggested that the professional minister movement may have partly evolved as a way in which some ministers sought to regain a position of high regard in the culture.

These are my words, not hers. As pastors discovered they were no longer placed on a pedestal by the culture, they sought to regain the pedestal through the credentials of professionalism. *We went from pedestal to professional.* And we must confess that the culture's preoccupation with credentials has frequently been the church's preoccupation as well.

As the educational training and resultant number of degrees required to enter various professions were increased in the culture at large, the church likewise upped the ante and matched the culture degree-for-degree. When a college degree became important in the culture, a number of denominations said a college degree was virtually essential to enter the ministry in their denomination.

When a master's degree became important in the culture, various denominations—particularly mainline ones—said a master's degree was now important. As various doctoral degrees became more common in the culture, the doctor of ministry degree was invented.

The professional minister movement was a cultural reflection of the broader cultural movement toward professionalism. To be

sure, much was gained. And it worked as long as the culture was
a churched culture.

FOCUS INSIDE THE CHURCH

**For the professional minister, the understanding of the nature
of leadership is *inside* the community of faith.** The foundational
leadership perspective of the professional minister is a focus *inside* the church. For the professional minister, leadership is en-
acted *inside* the church.

In *The Purpose of the Church and Its Ministry* (New York: Harper
& Brothers, 1956), Richard Niebuhr wrote that the minister's
"first function is that of building or 'edifying' the church. . . . The
work that lays the greatest claim to his time and thought is the
care of a church, the administration of a community" (pp. 82–
83). The churched culture in the United States during the late
forties and fifties, which continued in some parts of the culture
into the sixties and, to a lesser extent, into the seventies, was
distinguished by a ministerial focus inside the church.

Within the broad-based culture after World War II, people
held the value that church was important. There was a commonly
held belief that participation in church helped one to live a good
life. Newcomers, when they moved into a community, were asked,
"What church do you belong to? We want to invite you to visit
our church." People sought the church out and self-initiated their
own participation. It was "the thing to do" to go to church.

It would be well to note that a churched culture is not so much
defined as a culture in which a certain statistical percentage of
the population is actively participating in church work, although
the level of participation is likely to be higher than in an unchurched culture. Rather, a churched culture is a culture marked
by the presence of a persistent, pervasive, major feeling among
the people that the church is important.

Richard Niebuhr's statement "The church is becoming the minister with the world and its 'minister' is its servant, directing it in
its service," (*The Purpose of the Church and Its Ministry*, p. 83) can
be easily made and understood in the context of a churched culture where:

1. The value of church is among the major values of the culture.
2. A substantial number of persons are seeking out churches on their own initiative.
3. These persons are readily and actively participating in church work.

The busy suburban churches of the 1950s illustrate these three integral factors of the churched culture. Within this environment, more and more ministers and key leaders became preoccupied *inside* the church. And they got away with it because *the world was coming to the church.*

Since people were seeking out churches of their own initiative, the understanding of the nature of leadership could focus inside the church. Committee and organizational structures were developed to administer the busy programs and activities "for all ages"—"something for everyone"—in bustling suburban and city churches. Only modest efforts of evangelism and outreach by ministers and key leaders were needed to win enough persons to swell the membership numbers and fill the sanctuaries to a comfortable fullness.

Within this culture, the notion naturally arose that administration was a significant part of the minister's work. The minister was to care for and administer a church. A proliferation of studies reported the vast amounts of time pastors spent in administration inside the church.

Niebuhr's work was both a culmination of and a foundation for the professional minister's preoccupation *inside* the church. As a culmination, his work is best seen as a summary of a trend that had been developing in the late forties and early fifties. At the same time, his work became part of the foundation for the professional minister movement of the years since then.

In a certain sense, Niebuhr's original understanding became subverted to mean administrative and institutional care. In fairness to Niebuhr, one must note that he was reporting the developing understanding of ministry for that time. That concern for the "care of a church, the administration of a community" became subsequently a preoccupation with the institutional care of the church. And as the mainline denominations began to decline, the preoccupation with institutional survival increased.

At rock bottom, the understanding of the nature of leadership inherent in the view of that time was:

1. The minister serves inside the church.
2. The laity ministers in the world.
3. The world is seeking out the church.

The premise worked as long as it was a churched culture. In short, #1 and #2 could work as long as #3 held true. In such a setting the minister could focus the understanding of leadership *inside* the church, and the laity in turn would minister with the world. This pleasant premise creates "inside the church" ministerial leaders, as over against "outside, in the world" ministerial leaders.

But what happens when the world quits seeking out the church? We are left with well-intentioned, "inside the church" ministers, whose understanding of the nature of leadership—with its related behavior patterns, values, and objectives—works best in a churched culture.

It is one thing to say, "The *world* is my parish." It is another thing to say, "The *church* is my parish." The former is decisive on a mission field. The latter works only in a churched culture.

It was understandable that an intense churched culture would emerge following World War II. The tragedies and horrors of the war, the family disruptions and deaths (families die during a war, as well as individuals), the psychological disorientation, and the societal dislocation of the times all created a profound drive toward the rebuilding of society.

New housing developments rapidly expanded the suburbs. New suburban communities were increasingly built. Among the factors that contributed to the proliferation of the suburbs was the yearning to recreate the quiet, pleasant, small-town atmosphere—like Grover's Corners of Thornton Wilder's play *Our Town*—in which much of the culture had lived prior to the war. In a certain sense, the rapid suburban growth was an aftermath of World War II, and the busy suburban church became a concomitant result of that churched culture.

The Christian mission had moved forward for nineteen hundred years without ever knowing what a busy suburban church looked like. And suddenly the busy programs and activities of bustling suburban churches filled the land. Many a minister sought to be the pastor of one of these lively suburban churches. Sure, the pace was hectic. But life was essentially safe and secure.

The people were reasonably decent, church-going types who sought the church out and wanted to work in it. Remember that much of the church-growth boom of that time was based on "letter of transfer." That is, churched people moved in from rural areas to the cities and suburbs. They filled those suburban churches to brimming over.

And they brought with them a range of "church skills." They knew how church committees were supposed to work. They knew something of the Bible and the Christian faith. They had taught Sunday school. They knew how to participate in adult Sunday school classes. And they were comfortable with an "inside the church" pastor.

It is not accidental that in his chapter "The Emerging New Conception of the Ministry," Niebuhr wrote, "Our problem is to describe the theory that seems to be emerging and to be gaining ground in the thought as well as the practice of ministers. For want of a better phrase, we may name it the conception of the minister as a pastoral director" (pp. 79–81). "Pastoral," à la the emerging pastoral counseling movement of that time; "director," meaning administrator of the many programs and activities of a busy, churched-culture church.

To be sure, professional ministers were either primarily pastoral directors (à la Niebuhr) or preaching administrators. In smaller busy suburban churches, professional ministers tended to be pastoral directors. In city churches and the larger busy suburban churches, professional ministers tended to focus on preaching and administration. These two typologies became the dominant behavior patterns of professional ministers. While the pastoral director and the preaching administrator had distinctive functional focal points, the understanding of the nature of leadership that they shared in common was an inside-the-church perspective.

Given the churched culture of the times, the leadership value set that emerged from this inside-the-church understanding of the nature of leadership can best be described as:

- reactive
- passive
- organizational
- institutional

This leadership value set will be discussed in greater depth in conjunction with the leadership value set of a missionary pastor.

For now, it is sufficient to note that this leadership value set functioned reasonably well in a churched culture. *But it has not worked in the unchurched culture of the 1980s and will not work in the 1990s and beyond.*

THE MINISTRY AS PROFESSION

In a technical sense, the ministry as profession will continue. That is, the ordained clergy will continue to live out the best characteristics of a professional society that sets its own standards for:

- academic and technical preparation
- admission
- collegiality
- ethical conduct
- evaluation

In this sense, the ministry as profession will continue to have all of the marks of a professional craft or trade. The ministry as profession will continue. The professional minister, however, is finished.

That is not to say the professional minister will disappear. Some professional ministers will simply continue in their present understanding of leadership with its behavior patterns, values, and objectives until they retire. Some will "find work" as the thoughtful, polite undertakers of stable and declining or dying churches.

The professional-minister focus inside the church is no longer an effective functional understanding of the nature of leadership. The day of the missionary pastor has come.

2. The Mission Field

The day of the churched culture is over. The day of the mission field has come.

It feels strange to me to write these words. Indeed, it has felt strange to say these words in the many seminars I have led in recent years. Yet, on all sides, it is self-evident that we are no longer in the churched culture that existed in the late 1940s and the 1950s.

Statistical research, analyses of this culture, and long-range projections all clearly indicate that ours is no longer a churched culture. Study after study and the steady decline of many mainline denominations confirm this fact. We are clearly and decisively entering the mission field of the 1990s.

It feels strange to me, therefore, to declare what, in fact, is obvious to so many people. Yet we have many churches behaving and acting as though ours was still a churched culture. Their understanding of leadership, their behavior patterns, the values that they nurture, and the objectives that they set all suggest that they still believe we are living in a churched culture.

It may well be that we were lured into a false sense of security by the snug comfortableness of the churched culture. It has happened before—it will happen again. It is not unique, nor is it unusual. From time to time, across the history of the church's mission, there have been distinctive occasions in which the church came to love too much the culture in which it found itself.

Think of the period of time after Constantine declared Christianity to be one of the legal religions of the Roman Empire. Think of the height of the papacy and its relation to the culture of the Middle Ages. Think of some of the early colonies of this country where church and state were virtually synonymous one with another. There have been a number of occasions when the church has loved a culture too much.

Yet it is precisely because so many churches continue to believe and act as though this were a churched culture that we have as many stable and declining and dying churches as we do. The understanding of leadership and the behavior patterns that were helpful in the churched culture of the 1950s are not well adapted for the unchurched culture of the 1980s and 1990s.

OLD WAYS DIE HARD

SELECTIVE PERCEPTION

Old ways die hard—and one reason is selective perception. We see what we look for.

In churches all across this land, when I have asked, "What is one of the things you like best about your church?" people immediately respond by saying, "Dr. Callahan, one of the things we like best about our church is that it is a friendly church." By definition, virtually all churches are friendly churches.

By definition, the only people who are *not* in a given church are the people who did *not* find that church friendly. Obviously, the people who did not find that church friendly departed quickly. They are not there. Usually the only people who stay in a given church are those people who have found it friendly. I have yet to have a single person raise their hand and say, "Dr. Callahan, one of the things I like best about my church is that it is the most unfriendly group of people with whom I have ever had the privilege of associating." The only people who might say that are not there. They have already left. We see what we look for. Our selective perception works extraordinarily well.

There are many good pastors who are attempting to do effective shepherding work who frequently visit in the homes of their members. But they develop selective perception too. Once they have become familiar with their members and where they live, these pastors' selective perception takes over, and they do not "see" the other people—the other homes—in their community.

For them, their community consists primarily of their church's members and their homes. They illustrate this selective viewpoint as they show a consultant around—they point meaningfully to this house or that house of members of their church, hardly seeing the other homes on the block or in the community.

Church leaders frequently spend substantial amounts of their available time with one another inside their church. But when they begin to extrapolate and assume that there are many other persons investing major volunteer hours in the other churches in the community, they end up making unrealistic assumptions about their community. They see their community as more churched than it really is. Selective perception helps old ways die hard.

FAMILIAR AND HABITUAL

Old ways die hard—and the second reason is that they are familiar and habitual. Behavior patterns of any kind that have been ingrained and repeated for years upon years are not easily extinguished. It is not simply that these behavior patterns have been consistently rewarded over and over during the past nearly forty years. The rewards may have been diminishing over a long period of time. But as long as the familiar and habitual behavior receives even occasional rewards or intermittent reinforcement, it will persist.

Many of our current pastors and many key leaders were originally trained to focus their work primarily inside the local church. And in simple day-to-day ways, familiar and habitual behavior patterns have reinforced that focus inside the local church.

To be sure, excellent seminars on societal issues have been bravely sponsored by and boldly held inside local churches. To be sure, there have been occasional forays "outside the fort" into the world. And from time to time there have been striking examples of courage out in the world.

However, in interviews when I have asked pastors, "Share with me how your week begins," they typically report that they usually go to their office first thing on Monday morning and hold a staff meeting. If there is no staff, they go to their office on Monday morning and open the mail.

The initial locus and primary focus of their work is in their offices. Time-management studies again and again have confirmed that pastors invest a large percentage of their time in their offices—in meetings, in doing administrative work, and in taking care of administrative details.

The anxiety level noticeably rises whenever I have proposed that a pastor might serve as a missionary pastor without necessarily investing so much of their work week inside the church. I am not proposing that pastors eliminate their offices. That would miss the central point. Pastors continue to spend so much time in their offices simply because it is a familiar and habitual behavior pattern that has been nurtured and reinforced for many, many years. And the foundation underlying that behavior pattern is an understanding of the nature of leadership that is no longer helpful.

PEACEFUL AND SECURE

Old ways die hard—and a third reason is that they have been peaceful and secure. It is more peaceful to stay in one's office than to venture out into the world. It is more secure in a committee meeting than it is in the world.

To be sure, there have been moments of unrest and insecurity inside the church, too. We remember the counseling session where someone became angry and upset. We remember the meeting where an individual became stridently hostile. We even remember the bitter division in a building committee over the colors for the carpet in the new church school rooms.

Taken on balance, however, working out in the world on emerging trends important to this time—working with persons and groups who do not immediately acquiesce to the church's leadership, working in the terrain of the unchurched culture—is less peaceful and a whole lot less secure. And sometimes, after we have tried venturing into the world, we so strongly sensed the unrest and insecurity that we were glad to be able to retreat to our churches.

Reflecting back on the long-lost churched culture of the 1940s and 1950s in the United States, we view it as a relatively peaceful and secure time. We are much too fond of those years. We can fantasize about the old days of the 1940s and 1950s. "If only life were like it was then, it would certainly be more peaceful and secure." But the reality is that it is a mission field now.

Think what it meant to be a Christian during the 1940s and 1950s in some other parts of the planet—we probably would not be using the words *peaceful* and *secure* to describe those mission fields. A mission field is neither peaceful nor secure. A mission field is frequently noisy, disturbing, challenging, uncertain, chaotic, and hostile.

A TIME FOR REJOICING

REALISTS AND ROMANTICISTS

Some persons might suggest that the invitation to be a missionary pastor has the ring of romanticism about it. To the contrary, the fact that we now live in an unchurched culture is not a romantic perspective, it is realistic.

The romanticists are those who behave as though it were still the churched culture of the 1950s, who still long for the busy, bustling suburban churches of the 1940s and 1950s. The romanticists look back to those grand times when their sanctuaries were full and long for that bygone era when people sought out the church on their own initiative. The romanticists are those who continue to spend most of their time in their offices, committee meetings, and administrative sessions, believing that this will somehow help.

The realist is the one who knows that this is a mission field and who behaves as a missionary pastor.

A TIME FOR MISSION

This is a time for rejoicing, not a time for a churched-culture romanticism. God has given to us a great new day. This is not a time for despair. This is an Easter time—a time for great rejoicing and excitement. God has planted us on one of the richest mission fields on the planet.

Just when many of the best-trained professional ministers have reached a point of moderate success, they are recognizing that their familiar way of ministry is not working as it used to do. Just when life is about half over and all we have to do is stay out of major trouble until the end—just then, God calls us to a new day.

Remember your yearnings, your longings in years gone by? You almost felt it might be your calling to be a missionary in some distant part of the world—southern China, central India, northern Africa, somewhere in Central or South America? This day,

God has planted you on one of the richest mission fields on the planet.

Most people want their lives to count for something. And to be sure, one's life did count in the churched culture. But life counted then as though on a pleasant merry-go-round, where the music was charming, the company was congenial, and the activities were cheery and convivial.

Now God calls you to be a missionary pastor, not a professional minister. Your life will count—in an extraordinary way. It will not always be pleasant. Life will be complex, ambiguous, and tenuous. There will be occasions when you will feel more battle fatigued and burned out than ever before.

And there will be times when you draw deeply on your best creativity, strongest competencies, and deepest compassion. God invites your life to count in fresh, new ways. It *is* a time for rejoicing!

THE "GOOD NEWS BOYS"

The "Good News Boys" are now trying to reassure us that things are not as bad as they had seemed. Here I refer not to the strong evangelical wing found in some churches but to the bureaucratic brontosaurs who have begun to whimper—in the best pip-squeak fashion—about statistics of a mild turnaround.

In previous years, they spoke of the hemorrhaging of the mainline denomination churches as members were being lost at the frightful pace of a runaway train. And now, alarmed to realize the flimsy priorities with which they have been preoccupied (for even they know the foolishness of them), they are beginning to try to reassure us that a mild turnaround is in the works. How pathetic.

The problem is not *in* the system. The problem *is* the system. We need a turnover, not a turnaround.

Preoccupied with the institutional welfare of our denominations, we have developed a "squozilogical" understanding of leadership (our thinking has become squeezed, tiny, and frozen), rather than an eschatological and missional understanding of the nature of leadership.

We have been preoccupied with whether our churches are growing; we should be preoccupied with whether our mission is dying. We have been preoccupied with whether we are yet alive; we should be preoccupied with whether we are yet in the world.

When we become concerned with whether our institution is yet alive, we have already died. And that is excellent—for the resurrection is to come.

BEYOND CHURCH GROWTH

In recent times, the church growth movement has had an important influence in church life. And it has done us a good service in helping us to be *outside* in the world. The church growth movement has accurately assessed that this is a mission field. It has drawn on the biblical and theological understandings of evangelism to point toward the fundamental concern for witness and outreach on a mission field.

And it has done us a disservice as well; namely, it has reduced the issue to growth alone. Our current problems cannot be conveniently reduced to whether the church membership statistics are growing or declining. Our current problems have more to do with mission than membership, more with service than survival, more with the planet than the church plant, more with the human hurts and hopes of the world than the hemorrhaging of a denomination.

The church is called to mission for the integrity of mission, not for the sake of church growth. We are called to share the kingdom, not to grow churches. The fundamental category for this time is *mission*, not *church*. What we need is mission growth.

THE MISSION FIELD OF OUR TIME

THE UNCHURCHED CULTURE

Some would be harshly critical of an unchurched culture. At the extreme, they would charge that an unchurched culture is marked by gross atheism, sheer secularism, and morbid materialism. Actually, a more objective understanding indicates that an unchurched culture is marked by three factors:

1. The value of church is not among the major values of the culture.

2. A substantial number of persons are not seeking out churches on their own initiative.
3. By and large, persons live life through as though the church did not substantially matter.

To be sure, atheism, secularism, and materialism are strongly present in an unchurched culture. But these are present in a churched culture as well. It is not so much that these are *more* present in an unchurched culture. More to the point, no major cultural value says that the church is important.

In an unchurched culture, people do not necessarily view the church as harmful or hurtful. Rather, people simply view the church as not particularly relevant or helpful.

NOT A SAFE, PLEASANT PLACE

An unchurched culture is not a peaceful and secure place to be for professional ministers, for two reasons. First, their understanding of leadership inside the church is no longer operationally functional in an unchurched culture. Professional ministers were trained to deal with matters *inside* the church. Now, they are called to move out and deal with matters *outside* in the culture.

Second, life out in the world becomes more ambiguous and complex. There is much that is tragic, dark, and sinful in this time. To be sure, some elements of life on a mission field are celebrative and hopeful. At the same time, there is substantial chaos, confusion, commotion, disturbance, disorder, and disarray with which missionary pastors are called to work.

THE NATURE OF LEADERSHIP—NEWLY UNDERSTOOD

Precisely this state of affairs invites all of us—pastors, key leaders, and grass roots—to a new understanding of the nature of leadership. **People lead in direct relation to the way they experience being led. When the minister's focus is inside the church, that creates laity whose focus remains inside as well.**

On a mission field, leadership is best understood as focusing *outside, in the world*—not inside, in the church. The missionary pastor will participate actively among the leaders of the mission—outside, in the world. No longer does the minister train the laity, who, in turn, do the mission in the world. No longer does the pastor serve inside the church and the laity serve outside in the world.

In our time, a new understanding of the nature of leadership needs to be grown forward. We need a foundational understanding that the focus of leadership will be *in the world*, not in the church.

We need an understanding of the nature of leadership that is more proactive and less reactive. We need an understanding of leadership that is more intentional and less passive, more relational and less organizational, more missional and less institutional.

The day of the churched culture is over. The day of the mission field has come.

3. The Mission Outpost

A RESILIENT ENTITY

The day of the local church is over. The day of the mission outpost has come. More precisely, the day of the *churched-culture* local church is over. I do not mean to suggest, obviously, that there will no longer be local churches. For yet a generation and more to come, local churches will survive. Yea, we will discover a hundred years hence that there are many, many local churches continuing in existence.

A local church is a tough, resilient entity. In thirty-plus years as a consultant and researcher, professor, pastor, and author, I have seen many churches. I have helped in some churches where, many years before, a reputedly knowledgeable person had predicted the impending death of that church within five years. And yet ten, fifteen, twenty years later, that church was continuing to survive.

I am not, therefore, predicting the imminent or even long-term demise of local churches. They will be with us for many, many decades to come. What I am suggesting is that the way in which local churches have done business, conducted leadership, and developed administration is no longer functional in our time. Churches that cling to the old ways that worked so well in the churched culture will survive for a number of years. Their people will grow old together, and many of those churches will eventually die.

Changes are needed in the way a local church thinks of itself and in the way it operates. As a way of illustrating this, think of yourself right now as a pastor of a mission outpost. Imagine you are in mission work somewhere—in southern China, central India, northern Africa, or somewhere in Central or South America. Consider the radically different setting in which you would find yourself. Consider how many of the practices and principles that used to work in local churches during the 1940s and 1950s in the United States would not work on that foreign mission field.

Recall your earlier longings and yearnings to be a missionary somewhere on our planet. Relive the spirit of affinity and kinship you once felt with the missionaries who have gone out to strange, new places.

Now see your present community as your mission field. Do well here the same mission work you would do somewhere else on the planet.

The nature of leadership of a mission outpost takes seriously the distinctive qualities of that mission outpost. Leadership of a mission outpost is practiced with faithfulness and compassion, knowing that the congregation may, for many years to come, happily be a mission outpost. Leadership of a mission outpost does not have a goal of becoming a churched-culture local church.

Mission outposts may be of any size—small, medium, or large. What counts is not their size but their spirit. The spirit of a mission outpost is one of mission, whereas the spirit of a churched-culture local church is one of maintenance.

A WISTFUL WISHFULNESS

MEMBERSHIP

It is regrettable that many pastors, key leaders, and denominational personnel, whose fond early-life experience was within a churched culture, have a wistful wishfulness for the return of those good old days. It is even more tragic that they sometimes behave and act as though those good old days were still with us. One of the simple destructive influences upon local churches in our time is precisely this wistful wishfulness for bygone "better times."

In a number of the mainline denominations there is a nervous, strident preoccupation with membership decline. Bureaucratic leaders of boards and agencies hark to the statistics each year within their particular denomination.

It is most important, at this point, to note that the focus on membership is a characteristic mark of a churched culture. When the nature of leadership is understood to be focused *inside* the church and when people in the culture are self-initiating their activity in the church, then membership becomes a mark of a "successful church." Statistics reporting membership numbers are pleasingly noted.

And to be sure, the Christian church across the centuries has been interested in the dynamic of membership. And yet the pronounced emphasis on membership becomes too easily the significant statistical measure in a churched culture. The focus on membership is a mark of an *associational* understanding of the church.

By contrast, on a mission field the characteristic mark that is of predominant concern for the Christian church is salvation, not membership. On a mission field, the focus is on sharing the good news of the kingdom and on winning persons to Christ. The central concern is helping persons to claim "Jesus is Lord" in their lives, whether they become members of a specific denominational entity or not.

To be sure, salvation implies membership in the body of Christ. Certainly it is understood that they will look forward to being a part of some local congregation. But the focus is in the world more than in the church. The predominant focus is on mission, not on membership.

MAINTENANCE

The tragic dilemma of the wistful wishfulness for the return of those good old days of a churched culture is also evident in the current preoccupation with the maintenance of the institution rather than the mission of the congregations.

There is a correlation between the focus on membership and the focus on maintenance. Watch what happens in many of the declining denominations when the basis for determining the amount of money to be sent to the headquarters has something to do with the number of members a local church has. As the number of members declines, the amount of money that is sent to the headquarters for the maintenance of the institutional church also diminishes. As a result, the central headquarters periodically increases the proportional rate per member that each local church is asked to send to the headquarters in order to pay the denominational expenses.

Yet it would seem to be self-apparent that those increases can only continue for so long. Eventually the maintenance of the bureaucratic structures of the institution will be in jeopardy; and this ties in directly with the strong preoccupation with membership goals. The cry becomes, We need more members.

A concomitant development is the preoccupation of local church leaders and pastors with "clearing the rolls" so they will be "more accurate" (and so they will have to send less money to the central headquarters). I have often wondered what would happen if the energy and time invested in clearing the rolls was invested in mission?

The whole preoccupation with maintenance is a deceptive merry-go-round. The more concerned we are with maintenance, the less vital in mission we become. The less vital our mission, the more the institution declines. The more the institution declines, the higher the priority of maintenance rises. The more concerned we are with maintenance, the less vital in mission we become. It becomes a never-ending carousel of self-suffocation and death.

MONEY

One of the marks of the churched culture of that bygone time was the notion that mission primarily constituted the sending of monies to do good elsewhere on the planet. The current preoccupation with money constitutes another telling sign of that wistful wishfulness for those happy days. Indeed, in hundreds upon hundreds of churches when asked the question "What specific, concrete, missional objectives are central to your church?" members frequently and immediately responded by saying, "We pay our apportionments each year."

A primary concern expressed by many of the area supervisors in one of the stable and declining denominations is whether the local churches in their district or region have "paid out" their proportional allotted giving to the headquarters. Certainly, these adjudicatory personnel also have other profound and comprehensive interests. Yet during the closing months of the fiscal year, their behavior pattern is predominantly focused on ensuring that each of the churches in their region or district will "pay out in full." "Send in your money" is the message they communicate.

Many bureaucratic leaders will correctly point out that the issues of membership, maintenance, and money are directly related
to salvation, outreach, and mission. But what the local churches
hear coming from those leaders is language that focuses more on
membership than on salvation, more on institutional maintenance
than on societal outreach, more on concerns for lost dollars of
giving than on mission with specific human hurts and hopes.

What the local churches need to be about, what they *need to
hear* from their denominational leaders, is how to be effectively in
mission with the vast numbers of unchurched persons in their
community, with the focus on salvation, outreach, and mission.

GOD'S WAY OF HELPING

DECLINE AND DEMISE

Be at peace. The current decline and demise of the mainline
denominations is God's way of helping.

I am not proposing to blame God for the loss of members in
these denominations. God is not at fault. But it is also clear that
God has not intervened to stop the loss and the decline.

We should be wiser and more thoughtful than we have been.
The loss and the decline should be teaching us something. The
ways in which we have been doing leadership are no longer working on this mission field on which we now find ourselves. In a
clear sense, I think this is God's way of teaching us that what we
have been doing no longer works. Ultimately, we will continue to
lose members until we finally figure that out.

Unfortunately, up to this point, as we have tried to stem the
loss of members, we have primarily focused on doing the things
that used to work in the old days. And when it has not worked,
we have simply tried harder. We have assumed that if we throw
enough hard work at the declining numbers—if we throw enough
commitment, brochures and newsletters, and personnel—the situation will somehow turn itself around.

We have assumed that if we work longer hours, take more
courses in time management, participate in enough continuing
education seminars, and focus on more and more work, then
somehow things will get better. But all of these valiant, last-ditch

efforts will not work because they are based on an understanding of the nature of leadership that no longer works.

We could learn many, many beneficial lessons from our efforts of these recent years. Our recent efforts have not worked because they will not work on a mission field. This is a radically new setting. We need new ways of leadership that match with the mission field on which we serve.

Best on a Mission Field

I am convinced the church is at its best on a mission field. Do not long for the return of a churched culture. The peace and tranquility, the pleasant programs and endless committee meetings of a churched-culture church is not where the church is at its best.

The church is always at its best on a mission field. One can look to the early church and discover this. One can look to the mission field on which the church found itself in Augustine's time following the fall of Rome in A.D. 410 and discover this. One can discover this in the time of Luther or in the extraordinary expansion of the church through the missionaries of the eighteenth, nineteenth, and twentieth centuries. One can see it in the confessing church of Germany during the rise of the Nazi regime. And one can see it—*now*—on the many, many mission fields across the planet.

On a mission field the church is lean and strong and has courage and vision. In a churched culture the church becomes lazy and weak, timid and cautious, bloated and bureaucratic. The understanding of the nature of leadership is reduced to the principle of coordination. And coordination becomes the front—the code word—for caution.

On a mission field the church is at its blazing best. God has blessed us greatly by planting us on this mission field.

Leadership

This new day of mission calls for a new understanding of the nature of leadership for our time. And there are decisive signs that this new understanding is emerging.

It will not hurt to save some of the books on leadership that were published in the churched culture of the 1950s. They will still have some value. It is useful to note that many of these resources primarily paralleled and reflected the then-current trend in the understanding of leadership by business management—a parallel that was frequently most constructive. Some of the best breakthroughs in understanding the nature of leadership have come through research in business and industry.

At the same time, those resources and materials primarily mirror the culture of that bygone time. Those resources point to and assume an understanding of leadership that can best be productive only in a churched culture. The intent of the material that follows is to carve out the foundations for an understanding of the nature of leadership that will be productive in our time of mission.

THE MARKS OF A MISSION OUTPOST TEAM

A mission outpost is more a people than a place. It is a grouping—a team of people—gathered at the front lines of human hurts and hopes.

A mission outpost is now here, now there. The mission team is more like a M*A*S*H unit that moves flexibly and quickly to where the needs are, close to the front lines. A mission outpost may have a tent, but it does not have a fort. A mission team is more like a pilgrimage people. The team's permanence is its compassion for mission, not its commitment to mortar.

The nature of leadership of a mission outpost team takes seriously six distinguishing marks.

RELATIONAL CHARACTERISTICS

The first distinguishing mark of a mission outpost is that it delivers the relational characteristics of an effective congregation. The relational characteristics are:

1. specific, concrete missional objectives
2. pastoral and lay visitation in the community
3. corporate, dynamic worship
4. groupings of significant relationships of sharing and caring; roots, place, and belonging
5. strong leadership resources
6. a solid, participatory decision-making process in a streamlined organizational structure

There are also six functional characteristics:

7. several competent programs and activities
8. open accessibility
9. high visibility
10. adequate parking
11. adequate space and facilities
12. solid financial resources

A mission outpost delivers five out of the six person-centered, people-centered relational characteristics of effective churches. A mission outpost may also deliver several (three or four) of the functional characteristics.

By contrast, churched-culture local churches tend to be preoccupied with the functional characteristics. They tend to deliver most of these six functional, institutional, organizational characteristics reasonably well, but only one, two, or three of the relational characteristics. (In *Twelve Keys to an Effective Church* [San Francisco: Harper & Row, 1983], you will find a full discussion of each of these central characteristics, as well as help in rating your own church's strengths, using rating guides and a chart like the one illustrated here.)

The Central Characteristics of Successful Churches

Relational Characteristics	Functional Characteristics
1. Specific, Concrete Missional Objectives 1 2 3 4 5 6 7 8 9 10	7. Several Competent Programs and Activities 1 2 3 4 5 6 7 8 9 10
2. Pastoral/Lay Visitation in Community 1 2 3 4 5 6 7 8 9 10	8. Open Accessibility 1 2 3 4 5 6 7 8 9 10
3. Corporate, Dynamic Worship 1 2 3 4 5 6 7 8 9 10	9. High Visibility 1 2 3 4 5 6 7 8 9 10
4. Significant Relational Groups 1 2 3 4 5 6 7 8 9 10	10. Adequate Parking 1 2 3 4 5 6 7 8 9 10
5. Strong Leadership Resources 1 2 3 4 5 6 7 8 9 10	11. Adequate Space and Facilities 1 2 3 4 5 6 7 8 9 10
6. Solid, Participatory Decision Making 1 2 3 4 5 6 7 8 9 10	12. Solid Financial Resources 1 2 3 4 5 6 7 8 9 10

A characteristic is well in place—it is a strength—if your church rates itself as an 8, 9, or 10 for that particular characteristic. An *effective* church delivers at least nine out of twelve; that is, it has nine characteristics well in place and these are primarily the relational characteristics.

RESOURCES

The second distinguishing mark of a mission outpost is that it is always living at the edge of its resources. That is to say, on a mission outpost, there will always be a shortage of personnel, inadequate supplies, and hardly enough of anything. A mission outpost is always investing its leadership, resources, and money to the outermost limits. It is always stretching to the limit of its means.

As a consequence, a mission outpost will have its fair share of battle-fatigued, bleary-eyed, sometimes-worn-out leaders and pastors. That goes with the terrain. By contrast, churched-culture denominations usually have extensive bureaucracies and ample resources. They usually have much institutional baggage that must be tended and carried.

IN THE WORLD

The third distinguishing mark of a mission outpost is that its leaders and pastors "live out" much of their leadership and work in the world. By contrast, in the local church of the churched culture, leaders and pastors live out much of their work and leadership inside the safety and security of the local church.

This is not accidental. With the best of intentions, good people in the church—pastors and leaders—have worked from the assumption that they must first tend to the needs of the church before they can tend to the needs of the world. They must first tidy up their room before they can go outside. The problem comes when they seldom or never get outside.

The hook is this: God is in the world. Whenever the church is in the world, God is in the church. Whenever the church is not in the world, God is in the world. God sent his only Son to save the world, not the church. In John 3:16, the text clearly states, "For God so loved the *world*"—not "the church."

On a mission outpost, the leaders and pastor have an abiding compassion for the human hurts and hopes of people in the world. They invest the driving focus of their leadership and work in mission, in the world.

FULFILLMENT

A fourth distinguishing mark of a mission outpost is that it helps people to find fulfillment of their foundational life searches. These foundational life searches are the searches for individuality, community, meaning, and hope. By contrast, a local church in a churched culture delivers a pleasant merry-go-round of programs and activities, meetings and committees, and just enough religiosity that participants can develop a pleasant piety that immunizes them from any real religious feeling.

The relationship between the nature of leadership and these four foundational life searches will be discussed in depth in part 2 of the book. For now, it is important to note that fulfillment of these foundational life searches is central to the understanding of leadership with a mission team.

VALUE OF THE POST

The fifth distinguishing mark of a mission outpost is that it grows forward mission team leaders more than it does lay leaders. The day of the lay leader is over. The day of the mission team leader has come. That is the best way to describe the decisive change that takes place on a mission outpost.

In a churched culture, leaders focus on activities that are important inside the local church. The leadership posts that had value were inside the local church. A person would become chair of the Finance Campaign, then chair of the Finance Committee, and then chair of the Administrative Board, the Session, or the Board of Deacons. To be a trustee was to hold one of the posts of greatest value in a local church.

Not all positions are seen to have equal value and weight in a local church. Local church nominating committees are frequently concerned to put their very best leadership in the Finance Committee, the Trustees, the posts of the Board or the Session. Local churches draw up lists of the activities for which they need volunteers. The majority of the posts on the list are for tasks inside the church.

Where an organization places its best leaders describes the central values of the organization. When the best leaders are placed on the finance committee, solid financial resources (the twelfth central characteristic) become the center of values. When the best leaders are put on the trustees, adequate space and facilities (the eleventh central characteristic) become the center of values. When the best leaders are placed on the Program Council, several competent programs (the seventh central characteristic) become the center of values.

By contrast, on a mission field there is a decisive reversal in terms of the value of the posts. Positions that now have greatest value, premium, and importance are those that take place outside the local church—*in the world*. In a mission outpost, the best leaders are put on mission teams (the first central characteristic), on visitation and shepherding teams (the second central characteristic), on worship and prayer teams (the third central characteristic), or on grouping teams (the fourth central characteristic) that are starting new significant relational groupings.

You can tell the difference between a mission outpost and a local church by the way in which the nominating committee functions each year. In a mission outpost, the greatest care, thought, and deliberation is given to putting the very best of all possible leaders into the mission, visitation, worship, and grouping posts. Only after those mission positions are filled are the leadership posts inside the mission outpost also filled as best one can.

GAP, CHASM, GULF

A sixth distinguishing mark of a mission outpost is the extraordinary sense of commonality and mutuality as God's missionaries. On a mission outpost, there is no gap, there is no chasm, there is no gulf between the mission team and the missionary pastor. There is no caste system.

During the Middle Ages, there developed a gap, a chasm, a gulf between priests and people. In Luther's time the polarization between the priests and the people was pronounced. In his theses, Luther declared the priesthood of all believers.

What was at stake for Luther was considerably more important than the declaration of a priesthood of all believers. Luther used the dominant theological category important to his time—namely, the category of priest—to declare with a ringing finality that there is no gap, no chasm, no gulf. *We are together God's people.* We are together priests.

During the past forty years, we have successfully widened an enormous separation between professional ministers and laity. With considerable pomp and circumstance we have highlighted the centrality of the role of the professional minister. We have nurtured our own caste system between professional ministers and laity.

Examples abound. Again and again I have heard, "I am just a layman." The caste system is further evidenced by the various "perks" professional ministers have assumed to belong to them: the special titles, the reserved parking space, the private bathroom, the polite deference. What is worse, the inference is that to be an ordained minister is to have a "higher calling." And we hardly ever find laypersons involved in the regular leadership of the services of worship in a local church. The service of worship is led by "those persons who have been trained," the ordained elders.

During recent years, we have developed quaint theologies of the laity to bridge this gulf. But these theologies of the laity have functioned more like swinging vines that break halfway across the chasm. They have not functioned as rich, full bridges to the other side.

On the mission field, the way forward is to give up the caste system. The way forward in our time is to declare, "We are together God's people, missionary pastors and the mission team."

The central theological category important to Luther's time was the category of priesthood. The central theological category important to this time is the category of mission. There is no gap, there is no chasm, there is no gulf. We are no longer professional ministers and laity. We are together God's missionaries on one of the richest mission fields on the planet.

SUMMARY

DISTINGUISHING MARKS

Mission Outpost	*Churched-Culture Local Church*
1. focus on the relational characteristics	1. focus on the functional characteristics
2. living at the edge of its resources	2. conserving and holding its resources
3. in the world	3. in the church
4. fulfillment of foundational life searches	4. pleasant programs and activities
5. value of leadership posts: external and missional	5. value of leadership posts: internal and institutional
6. God's missionaries	6. a caste system of professional ministers and laity

It is helpful to see, side by side, the distinguishing marks of both. To be sure, the list illustrates the *primary emphasis* of each, not an exclusive separation. For example, a churched-culture local church would have an interest in the relational characteristics, but its primary emphasis is on the functional characteristics. Likewise, the mission outpost will have some interest in the functional characteristics, but not a primary interest. Be at peace. The list is not overstated. It identifies the primary emphasis of each.

The distinguishing marks of a churched-culture local church may well have served a real and important function in that churched culture of the 1940s and the 1950s. In that environment, those distinguishing marks would be an excellent match, and the churches would flourish well. Indeed, they did.

In the environment of the eighties and nineties and beyond, they are not helpful. They are counterproductive and dysfunctional. As soon as we come to realize this, we will be in a strong position to develop the foundations for a missional understanding of the nature of leadership that will be decisive for the times to come.

PART TWO

THE NATURE OF LEADERSHIP

4. Life and Leadership

A DIRECT CORRELATION

There is a direct correlation between one's philosophy of life and one's understanding of the nature of leadership. One's philosophy of life influences one's understanding of the nature of leadership; one's understanding of leadership influences one's philosophy of life.

This correlation has not always been recognized. Some, in developing their philosophy of life, have overlooked or ignored its implications for an understanding of the nature of leadership. And in recent times, some have developed their understanding of the nature of leadership without explicitly thinking through its interrelationship with one's philosophy of life.

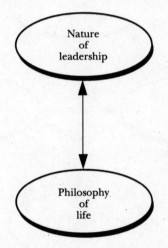

Much has been written on the subject of leadership. Some works have reflected a current fad—or foolishness—in the culture or the church. Worse, some works have dealt with the nature of leadership as though some system or sequence of steps, some graph or chart, some gimmick or gadget, or some trick or triviality would hold the secret to leadership. Overall, much of what has been written has failed to take seriously the direct correlation between leadership and one's philosophy of life.

Indeed, in a fuller sense, an expanded view includes two additional interactive components that have an extraordinary influence. In addition to one's philosophy of life and one's understanding of the nature of leadership, I would also include one's perspective on the emerging trends within the culture and one's theology of the church. Our understanding of the nature of leadership does not develop in a vacuum.

Each understanding of the nature of leadership draws on an underlying philosophy of life, is affected by its perception of the major trends emerging in the culture, and is influenced by a distinctive theology of the church.

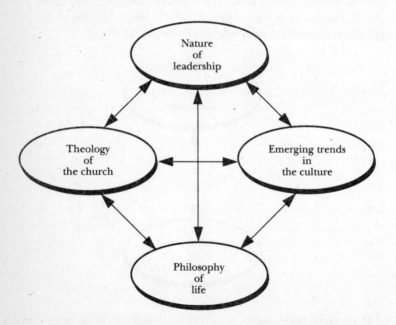

Finally, you cannot have one component without the other. Each component has implications for all. All have impact on each other.

UNDERSTANDINGS OF LEADERSHIP: "OCCASIONAL" ALTERNATIVES

Four alternative understandings of the nature of leadership have had a pervasive influence in the culture and in the church. I refer to these four as "occasional" alternative understandings because no one of these alternatives remains constantly predominant. One tends to come to the forefront, to be in vogue for a time, and then to recede into the background when another comes to the fore.

It can be said that all four are always present to a greater or lesser extent. At any given time, one of the four will usually be the popular focus of much research, training, and usage. Then that one will recede as another comes strongly forward to occupy "center stage" in research, training, and widespread practice.

These four occasional alternative understandings of the nature of leadership are:

- manager (or administrator)
- boss (or benevolent, authoritarian dictator)
- enabler (or developmental process planner)
- charismatic inspirer (or motivator)

Persons usually adopt one primary leadership perspective and yet occasionally find themselves enacting now one, now another. We do find that each understanding on occasion applies best to some particular situation because of the central truth implicit in that understanding of the nature of leadership.

THE MINISTER AS MANAGER

Life is material. Leadership is being a manager. A philosophy of life based on materialism tends to create an understanding of leadership that focuses on the functional and economic well-being of the organization. The more successful the manager is at achieving a strong bottom line and profit dollar, the more fully that understanding of the nature of leadership nurtures a philosophy of life built on materialism.

It is important to distinguish between a philosophy of materialism, on the one hand, and an extremist, crass materialism, on the other hand. In its simplest form, materialism, as Webster

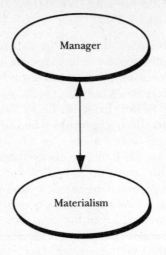

notes, is a philosophy grounded in the premise "that the highest values or objectives lie in material well-being and the furtherance of material progress." There is ample evidence to suggest that materialism is one of the dominant philosophies in our culture.

In many, many organizations, the understanding of leadership, the behavior patterns, the central values, and the predominant objectives focus on the material welfare and economic well-being of the institution. We tend to spotlight the instances of extremist, crass materialism, with its rampant greed and avaricious lustfulness for material and economic gain.

But a philosophy of materialism is perhaps less noticeable. In quiet, steady ways it works its influence in the culture—and in the church. Decent, thoughtful organizations find themselves primarily concerned with economic welfare and institutional survival. And the understanding of the nature of leadership that emerges is that of the efficient manager who conserves and holds, protects and preserves the material welfare and economic well-being of the institution.

Furthermore, in the manager/materialism perspective, the important trends of the culture are seen as primarily economic in nature. Social and economic change are materially caused. The polarities between scarcity and affluence become an overriding preoccupation.

This philosophy of materialism is so ingrained in the culture that it has an enormous influence in the church. It creeps in seemingly by osmosis. To be sure, the church rails against the obvious, extremist crass materialism of the culture. But the simpler, almost quiet form of materialism develops an insidious influence in the church.

With such a philosophy of materialism, one's theology of the church tends to gravitate to a theology of institutionalism. The issues of survival, maintenance, membership, and money become the preoccupations in times of scarcity. The issues of growth and institutional success become the goals in times of affluence.

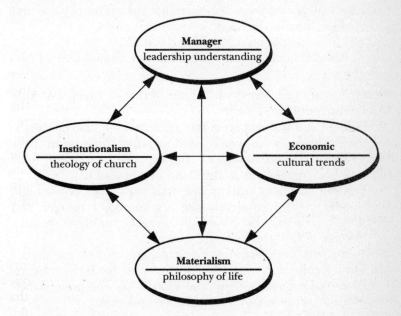

The church has frequently been drawn to a managerial understanding of leadership. Following the fall of Rome in A.D. 410, the bishop of Rome increasingly became the manager of the material resources of the Italian peninsula. In the thirteenth century, the various popes sought to manage the material resources of the church and the nation-states in Europe. In the early colonies of this country, the minister frequently served as manager of the colony's material resources.

In more recent times, a variety of popular writings have been published on "the minister as manager." Indeed, the understanding of leadership for key leaders and ministers alike has frequently focused on the role of manager. The statement has been reiterated more than once that "what we need is a minister who can be a good manager."

What is wanted is a minister, as manager, who will focus on:

- property management: see that the buildings and grounds are looked after
- financial management: be sure that the books balance and that we "stay in the black"
- office management: administer the staff
- personnel management: organize the committees of the church

These areas are concerned with the material, or functional, side of the church's life and work.

In times of cultural and economic affluence, the manager manages the institution's burgeoning and growing affluence in these areas. Managerial bureaucracies are expanded as added staff members find their places in the chain of command.

In times of economic scarcity, the manager's task becomes one of trying to control prudently the organization's meager and dwindling resources. The effort is to conserve and hold, protect and preserve as best the manager can.

One can best understand some denominations' recent preoccupation with the decline of their institutions—with the concern for maintenance, membership, and money—as one understands the influence of these four interactive components:

1. The nature of leadership is understood primarily as being a manager.
2. One's philosophy of life is focused on material things.
3. One's perspective on the culture is a preoccupation with economic trends, identifying priorities primarily in terms of the polarities of affluence and scarcity.

4. One's theology of the church is primarily a theology of institutionalism.

Underlying an understanding of leadership as being a manager and a related philosophy of materialism is a central truth: *we are beings who live in a world of matter, space, and time.* Hence, it is natural and reasonable that we give *some* consideration to material and economic matters.

But an excessive preoccupation with material things quickly becomes an extreme, crass materialism. There is a difference between a philosophy of materialism that has a modest perspective on material and economic objectives and an extremist preoccupation that leads to a self-consuming, crass materialism. Such an extremist materialistic philosophy cannot finally sustain an enduring, full perspective on life. It is hollow and empty of meaning.

The church is not without sin here. The church has allowed itself to be caught up with its fair share of shining buildings and materialistic projects. To be sure, the church has historically preached against materialism from time to time. And frequently the church has described itself—rightfully so—as a movement. But it has built its fair share of monuments. Here and there, the church has lavished upon itself "the things of this world." Most particularly, the church has been too preoccupied with its own institutionalism—a telling sign as to how influential a philosophy of materialism has been in the church in recent years.

To be sure, we as persons are likewise attracted to these material things as potential sources of recognition, power, belonging, meaning, self-worth, or hope. The hook is that these *things* provide only momentary, fleeting value to the person and to the church.

Management without mission becomes crass materialism. Church management without an overriding theology of mission becomes a preoccupation with this world's symbols of growth and success. The minister, as manager, ends up focusing on:

1. property, financial, office, and personnel management
2. the development and administration of policies and procedures for the stability and well-being of the institution

3. ensuring and advancing the institutional success of the organization, by:

- increasing the membership
- keeping the yearly budget in balance
- "paying out" on apportionments

The preponderance of the field of management, in the culture and in the church, has brought a preoccupation with these kinds of concerns. The philosophical influence is materialism, sometimes taken to the extreme.

There are strong signs of hope. Two movements show considerable promise. In the business circles of the culture, recent years have seen a growing movement that is focusing more on "people, service, and quality" and less on the bottom line and profit dollar. Earlier precursors of this movement have drawn on the work and research of Tead, Drucker, and MacGregor. More recent leaders have depended on the research of Waterman and Peters. The emphasis is on human resources and the important value of persons to the organization. This particular understanding of the manager relies more on a philosophy of humanism and less on a philosophy of materialism. The focus is more on service than on survival, more on people than on profits.

The second promising movement can be found in the church. Many are working to link the manager understanding of leadership with a strong theology of mission. The whole church administration movement has become increasingly strong in recent years. The very useful post of church business manager, or church business administrator, is found increasingly within many local churches in a wide range of denominations. In the best of seminaries, solid courses on church management have been added to the curriculum in recent years. All in all, these developments in both the business circles of the culture and in the church suggest genuine signs of hope. Both efforts are solid improvements on a materialistic understanding of manager.

But both movements are frequently influenced and distorted by the more pervasive understanding in the culture that links the manager with a philosophy of materialism. The human resources movement is sometimes distorted into "develop your people so your profits will be bigger." Then the goal of human development becomes a new means to an old end—economic profit. The emphasis on human resources development is made, not for its own sake, but to ensure the well-being of the institution.

Even in the church, the emphasis on the minister as manager frequently has had more to do with the institutional well-being of the local church or the denomination. The influence of the culture weighs heavy on the church. The focus has been too much on survival, not service; money, not mission.

Note that hardly ever has management been thought of as "mission management." Why not? In our culture, a philosophy of materialism and a theology of institutionalism constitute the major components of a manager understanding of leadership.

The "mission manager" would be willing to risk the well-being—even the very existence—of the institution. Seldom does the minister, as manager, ever run such a risk. It is difficult to reconcile mission management with the philosophy of materialism, preponderant in the culture, that so fully influences the manager perspective. For all their efforts, some denominations are too much influenced by the materialism of this culture.

The Minister as Boss

Life is a hierarchy. Leadership is being the boss. In an effort to propose something more to life than a world of matter, space, and time, some have adopted a philosophy of hierarchicalism. A philosophy of life based on a hierarchy tends to create an understanding of leadership that focuses on "being the boss." The more drastic the hierarchical perspective, the more readily the boss's understanding of leadership progresses to that of benevolent, authoritarian dictator.

The two components mutually reinforce one another. The more successful the boss becomes in acquiring power, the more convinced this person becomes of a hierarchical philosophy of life.

Furthermore, in such a philosophy of life, the trends in the culture are seen primarily as historic and destiny driven—usually toward the further accumulation of power by the authoritarian leader. It is interesting to note that authoritarian bosses always assume they know "what is best" for the common person.

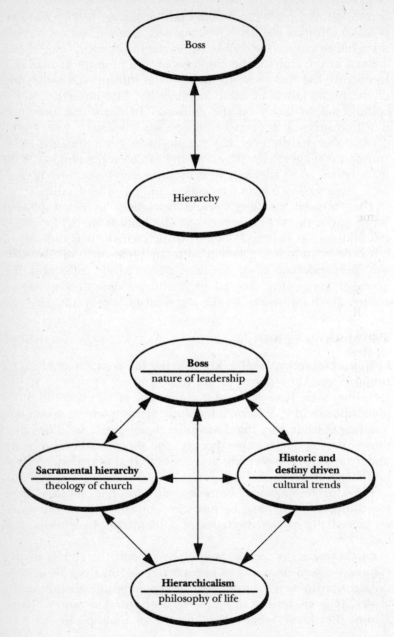

Moreover, in this hierarchical perspective, one's theology of the church tends to gravitate to a sacramental hierarchy of the church's nature and mission. It is not accidental that this perspective *always* builds a caste system in the church.

In earlier centuries, this hierarchical philosophy took the shape of a Platonic philosophy of a world of forms and ideas. From this perspective, there *is* a hierarchy of what is worthwhile in life: the forms of this life are merely fleeting shapes—shadows on the wall of a cave—of that which is enduringly real, namely, the "ideas" of these forms. There is a hierarchy of forms and ideas. It is not accidental that an understanding of the nature of leadership as that of philosopher-king emerged.

In later Neoplatonic thought, this hierarchical perspective came to be a dualism between a world of the flesh and a world of the spirit. This gnosticism created a hierarchy of values in which the world of the flesh was seen as evil, and the world of the spirit was seen as the way of salvation:

spirit = good

flesh = evil

Across the centuries, with varying degrees of force, this dualism of flesh and spirit has been emphasized.

Indeed, some elements of the church have from time to time adopted this hierarchical dualism, equating:

spirit = good = church

flesh = evil = world

Taken a step further, this subtle dualism has created an enormous caste system in the church. The statement "I am just a layman" is a reflection of that dualistic caste system:

spirit = good = church = minister

flesh = evil = world = laity

Some churches delineate their staff into "professional staff" and "support staff." This is a further example. Frequently, my response to them is, "Are you trying to teach me that your support staff are not pros?"

spirit = good = church = minister = professional staff

flesh = evil = world = laity = support staff

I often see evidence of this hierarchical-caste perspective in the parking lots of many churches, where the only marked parking space is reserved for the pastor. Sometimes pastors reveal their real theology of the church in their "theology of parking."

A more tragic example of the dualism of the caste system in churches is the benefits package. How many churches do you know that provide equivalent hospitalization, retirement, and other compensation benefits to pastors *and* to persons on the support staff? They often hardly think of providing comprehensive benefits for all staff members; they work out of a philosophy of life and an understanding of the nature of leadership that is primarily hierarchical and dualistic.

Many ministers take comfort in a hierarchical perspective. Worn out from serving on a very complex, tough mission field, they take solace in the thought that at least they are about "spiritual matters." They take comfort in the notion that they are the "boss" of the church. I am amazed at how many different ways pastors say in staff meetings, directly and indirectly, "We will do it my way. I am the boss."

Sometimes the repetition of those words is to reassure themselves, to build up their low self-esteem and lack of confidence. Anyone who has a genuine sense of confidence, however, does not need to keep reminding people who the boss is. And sometimes, these words are the minister's telling way of claiming a view of life that is hierarchical and an understanding of leadership based on being the boss.

In more recent times, there has emerged the concept of a hierarchy of needs. The Platonic hierarchy of forms and ideas passed out of use. In the view of some circles, the Neo-platonic dualism of flesh and spirit collapsed.

And so, a new hierarchical principle was conceived as a hierarchy of human needs. There were basic physical needs that must be fulfilled, and then the individual advanced to the fulfillment of higher needs, eventually to that of self-actualization.

A hierarchical implication for ministers was clear: those who "ministered to" the higher needs of the person were more important than those who ministered to the lesser, more basic needs. Thus, ministers found a new kind of authoritarianism as they counseled their parishioners on the higher needs of self-actualization.

Some pastors preach a priesthood of all believers, and yet their day-to-day lives evidence a belief in a caste system, a "boss" understanding of the nature of leadership. A number of pastors carry such a perspective a bit further and end up seeing themselves as the "strong leader" (translation: a benevolent, authoritarian dictator).

To be sure, the term *dictator* is hardly ever used, at least not by them. They see themselves as primarily benevolent, wishing for "the good of the whole"—according to their own definition of *good*. They see themselves exercising "strong leadership," meaning that they insist on things being done *their* way. It is not accidental that any hierarchical philosophy leads primarily to an authoritarian understanding of the nature of leadership. To be sure, this understanding is sometimes thought of as a "benevolent authoritarianism" (generally, as seen through the eyes of the one having the power).

One can best understand some pastors' recent concern with the diminishing of their prestige and authority in the culture and the church as one understands the influence of these four interactive components:

1. The nature of leadership is understood as being an authoritarian boss.
2. One's philosophy of life is focused on a principle of hierarchicalism.
3. One's perspective on the culture is primarily historic and destiny driven, generally toward the acquisition of more influence and power.
4. One's theology of the church is primarily a theology of sacramental hierarchicalism.

Underlying an "authoritarian boss" understanding of leadership and its related philosophy of hierarchicalism is a central truth: *some things are more important than others*. Some values, principles, and ideas are, in fact, more significant than others. But an excessive preoccupation with this central truth becomes a desire for domination. When this central truth is pushed to excess, who decides what is of greater or lesser importance? It frequently ends up being "might makes right." That is, the one who has the power decides.

There is a second concern. Although some *things* are more important than others, we cannot say that some *persons* are more important than others. Some values, principles, and ideas are indeed more important in this life's pilgrimage, but there is no central truth that says that some persons are more important than others.

Authority without mission becomes authoritarianism. Church authority without a theology of mission becomes bossism and dictatorship. The minister as authoritarian boss focuses on:

1. the development and administration of a "top down" organizational structure, using words like *coordination, cooperation*, and *centralization*
2. policies of accountability and evaluation, usually by the boss
3. the acquisition of additional power—usually, in a very beneficent way
4. the reduction or elimination of differing values, principles, ideas, and persons

The central influence is hierarchicalism, with its concomitant drive for influence and power.

THE MINISTER AS ENABLER

Life is a process. Leadership is being an enabler. A philosophy of life based on developmental stages tends to create an understanding of the nature of leadership that focuses on an enabling and developmental-process approach. A developmental philosophy views life as a series of sequential stages. This perspective views leadership as a matter of enablement.

A philosophy of developmentalism rejects the materialism of this world. Furthermore, such a philosophy rejects any rigid hierarchy of life. Rather, this perspective proposes that each person moves through a series of appropriate, constructive stages in this life's pilgrimage, each stage building sequentially on those that have gone before. It is understandable, therefore, that the nature of leadership is viewed as enablement—the leader is the enabler.

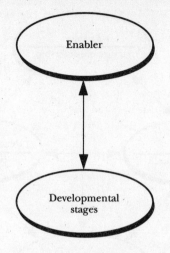

It is further understandable that the emerging trends in the culture are seen as a series of processive, developmental stages, with the corollary that there are primitive cultures and more advanced cultures.

The theology of the church, important to this perspective of enablement, is a theology of process. The church (each local church, as well as the denominational entities) is seen to be moving through a series of developmental stages.

In recent times, the church seems to have been attracted to an "enabler" understanding of leadership. Adherents to this perspective have rejected any manager understanding of leadership, built on a philosophy of materialism and committed to a theology of institutionalism.

Furthermore, these adherents have rejected the role of an "authoritarian boss" with the related caste-system theology of sacramental hierarchicalism. Indeed, the abuses of authoritarian bosses have prompted the growth and advancement of an understanding of leadership as enabler. The more excessive the abuses of authoritarian dictatorial pastors, the more fully the enabler understanding moved forward.

One should not stereotype authoritarian pastors as belligerently insisting on their own way in a loud, noisy manner. Most au-

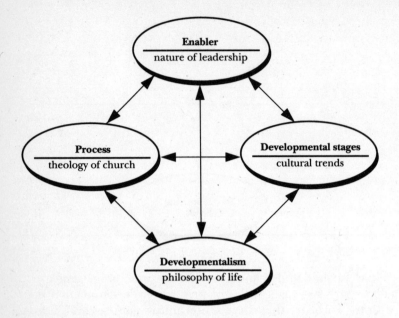

thoritarian pastors are quiet and firm, gently demanding that things be done their way. Most "boss" pastors bring off their understanding of leadership in subtle, dignified ways. They count on an implicit hierarchical dualism to provide them with all the authority they want.

Such pastors are generally kind and thoughtful and go out of their way to be helpful. And once you are obligated to them, you will also grant them the authority that they claim. Now that you have experienced the "helpfulness" that their authority delivers, you will support the value of their hierarchical leadership authority.

Over against the manipulative and quietly coercive tendencies of an authoritarian understanding of leadership, we see the enabler committed to focusing on the process more than the solution. The manager proposes to follow the policies. The authoritarian boss declares it *will* be done "my way." The enabler seeks to facilitate a process whereby a constructive solution can be found.

In times of cultural stability, the enabler's leadership understanding comes to the fore to "enable" the church to develop a sense of purpose and to process goals for the future. Indeed, some of these enabler planning processes move leisurely onward, consuming enormous amounts of time. Frequently, the results are a very complex set of goals displayed in extraordinarily elaborate charts.

In times of cultural instability, the enabler's leadership understanding perceives the crisis as a "threshold" or "transition." Influenced by a Rogerian psychology, the enabler—particularly in times of crisis—blithely repeats, "I hear you saying. . . ."

I often hear leaders and grass-roots members of local churches express their deep frustration and longing to have a pastor who will *lead* them, not be an enabler. One can understand their frustration in the light of the influence of these four interactive components:

1. The nature of leadership is understood as being an enabler.
2. One's philosophy of life is focused on an analysis and development of successive life stages.
3. One's perspective on the culture is viewed as a series of developmental stages.
4. One's theology of the church is primarily a theology of process.

A central truth underlies an understanding of leadership as being an enabler and the related philosophy of developmentalism: *life does appear to be a series of successive stages, each leading to the next.* But an excessive preoccupation with these developmental stages leads to minimizing the distinctive particularity and individuality of each person.

The tragic mistake of a developmental approach is the generalization that any given set of stages can best describe the human condition and the human pilgrimage. People are not simply at different stages. Nor is it as simple as saying there are distinctive stages for differing people. Life is a matter of crises as well as stages.

For enablers, life is pleasant and polite. One must trust "the process." Tragedies and calamities are viewed as "thresholds" and "growth experiences." The dark side of life is not taken seriously.

Dire apocalyptic events are simply a little rain on an otherwise clear, sunny day in the park.

The darker and more apocalyptic life becomes, the more the enabler develops yet more complex processes (with the alleged purpose of broadening the base of ownership for the process) and, by inference, the resultant goals. On occasion, some accomplishments and achievements appear. As a matter of fact, however, even the most elaborate planning processes, with their long lists of variables, cannot account for cataclysmic events.

There is a further problem. In actual practice, many enablers are not really enablers, they are covert manipulators. They use the techniques of process, coupled with a pseudo-pastoral psychology, to manipulate the group toward an already self-ordained conclusion. With either the manager or the authoritarian boss, the position of the pastor is reasonably clear, straightforward, and up-front. With enablers, the difficulty is that a manipulative direction may be present, but it is covert and well hidden.

Another serious problem for the developmental-enabler perspective is that frequently the enabler is so faithful to the *process* that the group does not get the benefit of the enabler's own wisdom, judgment, vision, and common sense. Indeed, I have observed many groups where an "enabler pastor" has been asked by someone in the group, "Pastor, what do you think?" And the enabler pastor has dutifully responded with, "I hear you saying. . . ."

In such instances, the group would have benefited, more often than not, by hearing the pastor's best thinking. The enabler would not need to try to influence the group toward that specific solution. Rather, the group would have had available, for its own best consideration, the additional ideas and suggestions from their pastor.

I sometimes refer to the "I hear you saying" enabling pastor as the "echo enabler." They primarily echo what someone else has just said. To be sure, the manager pastor is always reminding the group of this policy or that procedure. And the boss pastor is always informing the group of the decision that has been made. Regrettably, the enabler pastor focuses too much on the process and not enough on where we are headed and what we plan to achieve in mission.

The Minister as Charismatic Inspirer

Life is a crisis. Leadership is being a charismatic inspirer. A philosophy of life based on apocalyptic crises tends to create an understanding of the nature of leadership that focuses on being a charismatic inspirer or motivator. The more severe the apocalyptic crises, the more charisma the charismatic inspirer must project.

Seen from this perspective, the manager, boss, and enabler simply do not understand the apocalyptic nature of the times. The manager pastor focuses on the institutionalism of the church. The boss pastor is preoccupied with issues of power. The enabler pastor is merrily walking us through a new process. And all the while, the world is crumbling around us.

Thus, in an effort to take seriously the calamitous, tragic, and dramatic upheavals in life, some pastors have adopted a philosophy of apocalypticism. In earlier centuries, this took the form of millenarianism, with strong prophecies concerning the end of one age and the beginning of a new one. In our time we also have our fair share of apocalyptic philosophies of life.

Given the crisis perspective of an apocalyptic philosophy of life, it is not surprising that the understanding of the nature of lead-

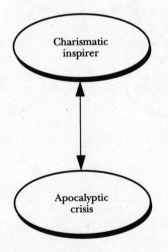

ership that ensues is inevitably charismatic. Crisis times necessitate charismatic leaders who point the way to the new age, even as the old age has collapsed around us.

Furthermore, from an apocalyptic perspective, the culture is viewed as having fallen, with a new community rising from the ashes. Hence, the theology of the church is built on a covenant community—a remnant—that is faithful until the new age has come into its fullness.

Across the centuries of the church's mission, movements have emerged that have announced or decried the apocalypticism of that time. Each movement has raised up its charismatic inspirer to provide a sense of direction and inspiration, even as they see the world to be crumbling down around the faithful remnant.

It should not be surprising that such a theology of the church is that of a covenant community. It is precisely the decay, sinfulness, and collapse of the world that necessitates a remnant that is pure, whole, and faithful. That remnant can best achieve its destiny as it follows its charismatic inspirer.

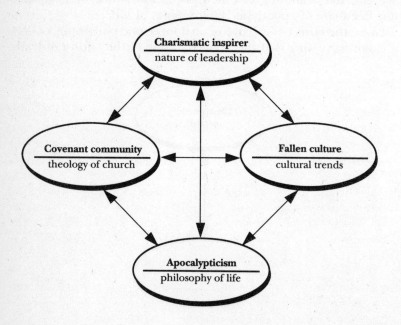

One can best understand the difficult quest of leaders and grass-roots members of local churches—as they yearn for a blameless, saintly, inspiring leader—by understanding these four interactive components:

1. The nature of leadership is understood as being a charismatic inspirer.
2. One's philosophy of life is focused on dealing with whatever apocalyptic event is currently decisive.
3. One's perspective of the culture is that it is essentially fallen.
4. One's theology of the church is basically that of a covenant community.

Underlying an understanding of leadership as charismatic inspirer and a related philosophy of apocalypticism is a central truth: namely, *life does have its upheavals and resultant new ages.* Civilizations do rise and fall. Ages do come and go. Major crises and disasters do happen.

This perspective quite rightly points out that the manager pastor, with his or her policies and procedures, is inadequate to the crisis. Furthermore, the authoritarian pastor, with a philosophy of hierarchicalism, will not last. The hierarchies that the world invents always "come tumbling down." This charismatic view recognizes the fact that life cannot be understood as simply a set of developmental stages, processed politely by an enabler pastor.

But taken to excess, the charismatic inspirer position has its own unique problems. Pride gets in the way. Belief in "one's own press" leads to vanity and delusions of grandeur. Sin shows its ugly head. Greed and power become fascinations. Lust sometimes slips in.

As this happens, leaders and grass-roots members in local churches frequently feel a sense of betrayal when they discover their charismatic inspirer has "feet of clay." The more severe the apocalypticism, the more blameless, saintly, and charismatic they expect their leader must be.

The problem is that there are very few persons in this life's pilgrimage who can survive the pressures of being the charismatic leader without incurring some major misstep along the way. It is hard to find a charismatic inspirer who can sustain the expectations of the covenant community for very long. The fall of that charismatic inspirer then becomes an apocalyptic event in itself.

A second problem for the apocalyptic perspective is the energy required to sustain the fanaticism against a culture that is seen as essentially fallen. There is much sinfulness, estrangement, alienation, and injustice in the culture. And as such, it must be brought to a sense of reconciliation, wholeness, caring, and justice.

But some elements in the culture are constructive and creative, even as others are destructive and sinful. It is not simply a matter of black and white. An "identity crisis" develops in the covenant community as it seeks both to remain apart from the evils of the culture and, at the same time, to benefit from the constructive elements within the culture. That identity crisis creates a sense of "internal betrayal" in the covenant community.

This leads to a third problem for the faithful remnant. It is not easy to stay "faithful." Just as it is difficult to find a charismatic inspirer who is without sin, it is hard to maintain a covenant community that is "unsullied and without sin." Indeed, the effort to do so creates all sorts of rules, regulations, rites, and practices to keep the community safe from the world and, frankly, from itself.

Try as the community may, however, sin creeps in. Sometimes the realization of sin's presence in the community provokes an apocalyptic purification. Sometimes sin's presence precipitates an abrupt flight by the community to a new, safer place. And sometimes the community looks for a new and even more charismatic inspirer.

But perhaps the most severe problem of an apocalyptic philosophy is simply that it becomes a tiring way of life. Finally, one gets tired of living from one crisis to the next. It takes considerable effort to maintain one's level of energy in an apocalyptic world. Finally, one longs for something more than just the next tragic upheaval.

5. Life Is a Search

THE MISSIONARY PASTOR AS LEADER

Life is a search. Leadership is being a missionary pastor. A pilgrimage philosophy of life based on search tends to create an understanding of leadership that focuses on discovery and fulfillment. In our time, it is the missionary pastor as leader who best helps persons in their search and discovery.

Certainly, the missionary pastor is *not* the only leader in the church's mission. There are many leaders in that work. The key point is that the missionary pastor functions primarily as a leader and more than simply as a manager, boss, enabler, or charismatic inspirer. The professional minister may have been able to func-

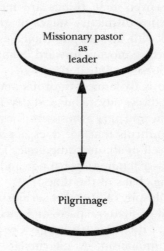

tion as a manager, boss, enabler, or charismatic inspirer. In our time, the missionary pastor is a leader.

SEARCH

Life is a search. Leadership is discovery and fulfillment. Life is a search that is dynamic and random, not processive and progressive. Life is a wandering in the desert and sometimes along flowered hillsides and through gentle forests. Sometimes through dark valleys. There are times when we find ourselves caught up in bizarre events, desperate anger, and eruptive violence. Sometimes we find gentle laughter, peaceful silence, and a deep closeness.

The search does not follow a clear path to a promised future. Life is not always processively and progressively "onward and upward." Our source of confidence and hope is that *God is with us,* not that everything will always be better. Our God goes before us as a cloud by day and a fire by night, leading us toward the future that God has both promised and prepared. That path leads us up from slavery, across a sea, and on a wandering pilgrimage through a desert. It is not a clearly mapped, paved highway, with "no worries."

The search is a pilgrimage—in matter, space, and time. In this pilgrimage, we discover some things are more important than others. We experience distinctive stages of growth and development. We struggle with apocalyptic tragedies and crises. Sometimes it feels like we are moving forward. Sometimes, like we have been thrown off course or defeated.

Life's pilgrimage is dynamic—vigorous and active. That does not mean that it is always advancing and developing or that there is a kind of rhythm and flow (thesis-antithesis-synthesis) to life. The word *dynamic* affirms that life does not simply stand still or inevitably repeat itself in an unending cycle. This life's pilgrimage is a *dynamic search*—a longing, yearning, and movement toward fulfillment amid the chaos of the times.

A pilgrimage philosphy of life takes seriously that we are beings who live in a world of matter, space, and time. But a pilgrimage perspective does not turn this truth into a crass materialism or a preoccupied institutionalism. A pilgrimage philosophy affirms that some things in life are more important than others, but it does not conclude, therefore, that some persons are more important than others and go on to create a rigid, hierarchical caste system.

A pilgrimage philosophy understands that life has its stages of development, but it also understands that these stages cannot be codified or established as fixed generalities and that any notion of stages is highly distinctive from one individual to the next. A pilgrimage philosophy of life takes seriously the tragedies and despair of this life, but it refuses to reduce life to one apocalyptic crisis after another.

DISCOVERY AND FULFILLMENT

In life's search, there is discovery. There are minor disappointments, and there is sadness. But life is not simply a matter of a never-ending, never-fulfilled search. Life is also discovery and fulfillment.

Discovery comes—now here, now there—in relationships with persons and groupings. This fulfillment is discovered in decisive events. Life is not simply a matter that we are born, we suffer, and then we die. There *are* relationships and events of discovery and fulfillment.

These experiences of fulfillment are for the moment and are not enduring. They do not have the character of an unending presence in our pilgrimage. We discover a sense of fulfillment for this moment, and we move on. We discover a sense of fulfillment for yet another moment, and then we move on.

Life does not guarantee that we will have a sense of fulfillment for every moment of every day. There will be deep, dark times of despair, depression, and despondency. There will be times of:

- powerlessness
- alienation and loneliness
- meaninglessness
- hopelessness

Through it all, we cling to the fragile confidence that somewhere ahead there will be relationships and events of discovery and fulfillment—brief, for the moment, *and* for the time to come.

We live with the expectancy that there will be future events of fulfillment, even as we have already experienced some in our past and are experiencing some in our present. But this sense of ful-fillment is now here, now there, and not yet in its fullness.

A FOUNDATIONAL VIEW

My basic, fundamental view of life is that *life is a search.* This pilgrimage view of life is foundational to the development of an understanding of the nature of leadership.

Some have sought to view life as primarily materialistic and have given us such slogans as "You only go around once"; "Enjoy the things of this life while you can"; and "A person is measured by their means." After a time, people discover the poverty of this philosophy of life.

Some have sought to view life from a hierarchical perspective, with all its caste systems. Some have sought to describe life as a series of developmental stages, chapters, and passages, but the singularity and particularity of each person's pilgrimage is such that one can make only the most general statements about developmental stages.

Some have sought to describe life from an apocalyptic perspective. For them, life is a series of one apocalyptic event after another. Indeed, the word *series* overstates the apocalyptic perspective. Life is a matter of experiencing this apocalyptic event, and then that apocalyptic event, and then yet another apocalyptic event.

Each of these perspectives has a grain of truth in it. We certainly are beings in matter, space, and time. Some things in life clearly are more important than others—that is the central genius of the hierarchical view. Likewise, life does have its distinctive stages—that is the central core to which all developmental understandings cling. Furthermore, life does have its share of apocalyptic events. Decisive events do change our lives and shape our destinies. You are invited to see the central truth in those philosophies that view life in materialistic, hierarchical, developmental, or apocalyptic ways.

Even more basically, I view life fundamentally as a pilgrimage search. Some may frame that pilgrimage in materialistic fashion, some in hierarchical ways, some in developmental stages, and some in apocalyptic events. I am not suggesting an encompassing view that embraces these other philosophical views. What I am simply suggesting is a foundational view: life is a pilgrimage of search and discovery.

FOUR FOUNDATIONAL SEARCHES

Four foundational life searches are decisive in this life's pilgrimage and for the mission field on which we now live and serve:

1. the search for individuality
2. the search for community
3. the search for meaning
4. the search for hope

Any number of life searches may persist through the whole of our lives. This is neither an exclusive nor an exhaustive list. These four are basic, however, and provide the foundation upon which we build our philosophy and perspective of life.

These foundational life searches are dynamic and interactive, not sequential and linear. The best way to illustrate this interaction is as follows:

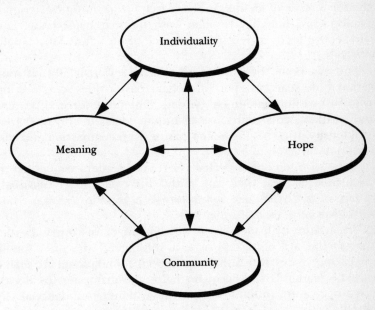

Interaction of Four Life Searches

The search for individuality is interactive with the search for community, meaning, and hope. And each of the others is interactive with the remaining three. No one search stands alone at any given point in time. All four are present, interrelated and dynamic, at any given moment in our lives.

One search may be more predominant and pervasive at a given point in this life's pilgrimage. Another will be predominant a day, a week, or a year later. The precise interaction of the four will be distinctive from one person to the next. There is no fixed hierarchy among these four searches. All four are always present.

A pilgrimage philosophy of life takes seriously all four of these life searches. The four "occasional" alternative perspectives do not do so. They may identify with one or another, but not with all four searches.

Bosses, with their identification with power, resonate with the search for individuality. Enablers, with their emphasis on developmental process, resonate with the search for community. Managers claim that the policies and purposes of the institution provide a sense of identity in the search for meaning. Charismatic inspirers say that they resonate with the search for hope. Each perspective tends to resonate with one of life's four foundational searches.

The missionary pastor, as leader, takes seriously all four foundational life searches. The missionary pastor does so as best one can, with wisdom, judgment, vision, common sense, and prayer— and with an occasional sense of humor, detachment, relaxation, or intensity. It is the missionary pastor, with compassion and community, who *serves as a leader*.

To be sure, no one is perfect. Certainly, leaders are not. At the same time, as best they can in this life's pilgrimage, *missionary pastors, as leaders, do seek to help persons to the discovery of individuality, community, meaning, and hope.*

The nature of leadership is to lead toward discovery. Leadership is the art of discovery and fulfillment, the art of helping people to discover fulfillment in their foundational life searches. The leader is the one who helps the grouping toward the discovery and fulfillment of these four foundational life searches.

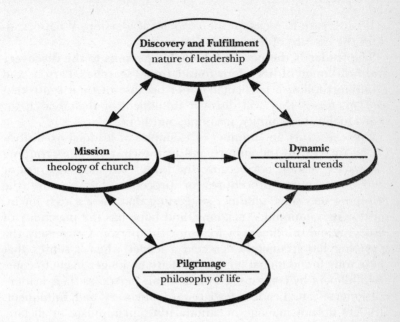

For the missionary pastor:

1. The nature of leadership is one of discovery and fulfillment.
2. One's philosophy of life is that of a pilgrimage.
3. One's perspective on the culture is a focus on the dynamic, emerging trends of the time.
4. One's theology of the church is primarily a theology of mission.

Note well: The focus is on the *nature* of leadership. Some people confuse the attributes and traits of leadership with its nature. Its nature is discovery. The attributes and traits vary from one leader to the next.

Some people even confuse the nature of leadership with various skills and styles of leadership. Long lists of skills are drawn up. Serious discussions are held concerning styles of leadership. How-to books focus on the techniques, tactics, and tricks of leadership. The skills and techniques vary widely from one leader to the next.

It is decisive to focus on the *nature* of leadership. What constitutes the essence of leadership?

The leader is the person who helps persons to the discovery and fulfillment of life's four foundational searches. Persons and groupings follow a particular leader because of their sense that *with this person* they will discover fulfillment of their search for individuality, community, meaning, and hope.

One can study any number of examples of leadership, historical or current, in the culture and in the church. The grouping follows the leader, not because the leader has more degrees or credentials, more procedures or processes, but because the grouping sees some glimmer suggesting that their search for individuality, community, meaning, and hope has the possibility of discovery and fulfillment by following this person. Conversely, the grouping has frequently deserted a leader when it senses that these four foundational life searches are no longer likely to come to fulfillment by continuing to follow this person as their leader.

Leaders lead. Leaders lead toward discovery and fulfillment. Leaders do not manage or administrate, manipulate or dictate, process or enable, mandate or command, threaten or scare. They do not push, prod, or poke—they lead. Leaders lead. And the grouping—whether a local church, a subcultural grouping, a movement, or a nation—senses that *this person* is helping them toward discovery and fulfillment.

DISTINCTIVE COMPETENCIES

MORE THAN ONE

God gives us many kinds of special abilities (1 Cor. 12:4). There is more than one competency. It is *not* true that leadership is a competency and that management, bossism, enablement, and charismatic inspiration are forms of incompetencies. No. The biblical principle is clear: There are many distinctive competencies.

Some persons have developed the competency of being a leader. Some have developed the competency of being a manager or a boss or an enabler or a charismatic inspirer. Each is a distinctive competency, a distinctive gift.

A competency is a gift that the individual must then develop. Leaders are not born leaders. For that matter, managers, bosses, enablers, and inspirers are not born. These distinctive competencies cannot be reduced to genetics, hormones, heredity, and birth. Pastors grow forward and develop each of these distinctive competencies.

Observers may say, "Oh, what an amazing leader. She surely has the gift of leadership." That may be their way of sharing their admiration and appreciation for excellent work. But pastors with a gift for leadership have not "rested on the laurels" of their gift. They have grown and developed that particular competency.

They know, perhaps better than anyone, what they have invested in advancing that particular competency to its fullest, and they view it as a *gift,* as what they do best. They know it was not handed to them "on a silver platter"; they see it as a gift from God.

The biblical principle is clear. There is a diversity of gifts, and they come from God.

NONE GREATER

There is no hierarchy of greater or lesser competencies. To be sure, the pastor, as leader, touches more of the whole person or grouping than the manager, the boss, the enabler or the charismatic inspirer do. This does not make the competency of leadership "better." Some would be tempted to hold it in higher esteem. Please, "give up for Lent" any temptation in that direction.

There are *no* caste systems. The minute someone succumbs to the gently insidious temptation of thinking that leadership is a better competency than that of management, bossism, enablement, or charismatic inspiration, that very minute he or she is headed toward creating a hierarchical caste system.

"Leader" positions would immediately become thought of as better than positions as managers, bosses, enablers, or inspirers. Seminars on "leadership" would quickly become thought of as better than courses on management, and so on. An elitism would slowly develop, much as it did around the earlier myth of the "professional minister." Caste systems have a way of creeping in.

God gives us many kinds of special abilities. God calls—invites—some to be missionary leaders, some managers, some bosses, some enablers, and some inspirers. God gives each the abilities needed for their calling. All are blessed in the sight of God. All are *equally* blessed in the sight of God.

VALUE

CONSTRUCTIVE ROLE

Each of these competencies has a rightful place—a constructive role—in the mission of God. As we saw earlier, each is based on a central truth about this life's pilgrimage. Each can contribute a distinctive value to the advancement of the mission.

The manager can organize the resources of the grouping. The boss can provide specific, assured authority and direction. The enabler can contribute the planning process. The inspirer can motivate the grouping. The missionary pastor, as leader, leads.

A team of five persons representing all of these competencies will accomplish more than a team composed entirely of five enablers, or a team of five managers, and so forth. A *balanced* mission team will have the best opportunity to succeed because of the complementary strengths that each member brings to the team.

A team of five managers will create an excellent policy and procedures manual, being sure to gather every policy and procedure the church has ever had. What a weight that manual will become!

Five bosses will issue more directives than the grouping can follow. They will end up saying among themselves, "There are too many chiefs and not enough Indians in this church." Really, there are too many directives and objectives. Or sometimes five bosses will engage in a power struggle among themselves to determine who is really *the* boss. That power struggle may do positive harm to the organization.

A team of five enablers contributes only one competency and, importantly, evidences only one of the central truths about life. They will create an amazing process, but that is all.

A team of all inspirers will surely motivate us, stimulate us, scare us, and stir us. But while there may be some vague, shared vision—off in the distance—it will be unclear as to how we get from here to there.

DISTINCTIVE TIME

Each of these competencies flourishes and serves well in its own distinctive cultural time. In times of cultural affluence, the manager understanding comes to the fore to administer the church's burgeoning and growing affluence. In times of desperate cultural scarcity, the manager seeks to conserve, hold, protect, and preserve the church's meager and dwindling resources.

In times of confusion in cultural identity, with its attendant shifts in power *and* powerlessness, the boss understanding comes to the fore. Sometimes the authoritarianism is on the side of those seeking to *retain* power. Sometimes it is on the side of those seeking to *attain* power. Whichever may be the case, the focus is on the strong boss understanding of leadership.

In times of cultural transition, the enabler understanding rises to prominence. It is not a time marked by dire economic poverty or extravagant plenty. It is not a time of major shifts in power. Rather, the cultural transition is more developmental. It is in this "soil," this environment, that the enabler flourishes.

And there are times of cultural crisis, when what used to be is no more. The thunder crashes. The lightning strikes. The former things have passed away—suddenly, swiftly, in less time than a single breath of air or blink of one's eye. Amid these cataclysmic events and apocalyptic disasters, the charismatic leader arises to save the day. The more cataclysmic the events, the greater the charisma of the leader. The events themselves almost seem to provide the charisma.

In all these cultural times—whether affluence/scarcity, identity confusion, transition, or crisis—the missionary pastor, as leader, is the one who understands (as best one can) the dynamics of the times. It is precisely the missionary pastor, as leader, who has a "distance" on the time at hand and can appreciate fully the current cultural context. The missionary leader does not absolutize one current time as though all times are like that.

By contrast, the charismatic inspirer "needs" every time to be apocalyptic—he or she will turn a time of cultural transition into the "apocalypticism of the ages." Likewise, the enabler "needs" every time to be one of cultural transition. Even in a time of genuine cultural catastrophe, he or she will press forward with newsprint and developmental planning process, as the city "burns all around him."

This missionary pastor, as leader, values the distinctive competency important for that specific time. It is precisely the missionary pastor, as leader, who gives encouragement to all of the others, just when their "gift" can best be helpful. The missionary pastor understands the way in which each cultural time invites a specific competency.

Life is not so neat and tidy that one can say that each of these cultural times is distinctive and totally separate from the others, in a kind of linear sequence such as the following diagram:

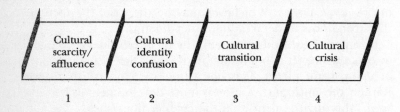

The relation of the times is more like the following diagram:

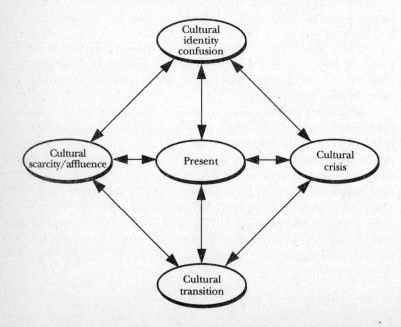

To be sure, one of these is predominant in any given "present." But all four are interactive and overlapping. The missionary pastor, as leader, seeks to understand this interaction and refuses to perceive time from any one of the four cultural time perspectives.

Furthermore, the missionary pastor refuses to perceive one of these cultural times as a more "churched" time. For example, the enabler's affinity to a time of cultural transition sometimes causes the enabler to see that time as churched (better, more desirable, more "ripe" for the church). The charismatic inspirer, however, with an affinity to a time of cultural crisis, will have a tendency inadvertently to "sanctify" that time. The missionary pastor sees finally that *each* of these times—indeed, all of them—are, in the end, "the day of mission."

Missionary pastors have a perspective of the whole, not the parts. It is exactly missionary pastors, as leaders, who can appreciate both the value and the limitations of each perspective. Sometimes the other views have a better sense of their own value and the others' limitations. Indeed, missionary pastors have enough sense to appreciate the relative (not absolute) nature of their own understanding.

LIMITATIONS

Absolute View

There are limitations. First, each of the four "occasional" perspectives tends to make its own understanding of leadership *absolute*. Each perspective, whether manager, boss, enabler, or charismatic inspirer, tends to see itself as separate from and better than the others.

Managers tout their "bottom line"; bosses, their directives; enablers, their process; charismatic motivators, their new inspiration. All up the ante in "results" to prove that their perspective is correct, absolute, and unshakably the only way—the "right understanding." With the knowledge that even missionary pastors are sometimes tempted to absolutize their own understanding, the missionary pastor, as leader, chuckles with a sense of gentle understanding of how all of us seek some sense of identity and certainty and how sometimes in so doing, we tend to absolutize our own perspective.

END IN ITSELF

The second limitation in each of the four perspectives is the tendency to lose sight of its implicit central truth, allowing the perspective to become an end in itself. Thus, the central truth that we are creatures of matter, space, and time gets lost in a management zeal to perpetuate an institution. The central truth that some things are, in fact, more important than others gets lost in the boss's demand for more power. The central truth that life is sometimes developmental gets lost in the insistence that the process must be followed exactly. The central truth that life does have its fair share of apocalyptic events gets lost in the need of the charismatic inspirer to provide new sources of motivation and inspiration. In each case, the means becomes an end in itself.

EXCESS

The third limitation occurs when the strength in each of the four "occasional" perpectives becomes present *in excess*. What gets each perspective in trouble is not so much a weakness as an excess.

What gets the manager in difficulty is not, finally, a focus on policies and procedures. They are appropriate and have their rightful place. What gets the manager in difficulty is the excessive preoccupation with every jot and tittle. The manager becomes a bean counter. Hardly anyone follows a bean counter.

Likewise, what gets the boss in difficulty is authoritarianism present in excess—the boss becomes dictator. An autocratic authoritarianism prevails. One directive after another comes down from on high, creating passive behavior in the grouping.

The enabler gets in difficulty with the excessive preoccupation with the process, almost to the exclusion of the solutions, the people, or the mission. With charismatic inspirers, the excess emerges when they become enamored with their own publicity and charismatic fame, eventually becoming spiritual tyrants and manipulators.

Ironically, with each of these perspectives, the weakness is the presence of that strength *in excess*. It is not the absence or lack of something. Rather, it is the excessiveness of the area of focus that is the difficulty.

With the missionary pastor as leader, two things are true:

1. The leader understands the danger of "excessiveness" in relation to any perspective.
2. The leader shares his or her distinctive strength with a sense of balance.

6. Leadership, Discovery, Fulfillment

THE NATURE OF LEADERSHIP

In the fullest sense, the understanding of the nature of leadership important on a mission field includes six components. The missionary pastor, as leader, takes each seriously:

1. Life is a search.
2. Leadership is discovery and fulfillment.
3. Leadership is distinct from management, bossism, enablement, and charismatic inspiration.
4. The missionary pastor draws on the major resources for leadership.
5. The missionary pastor takes advantage of the occasional resources for leadership.
6. The missionary pastor advances the three central qualities of missional leadership.

We have already discussed components 1 and 2. With respect to the third, several factors distinguish the leader from the manager, boss, enabler, or charismatic inspirer. First, look at each one's "preoccupation." The missionary pastor, as leader, is "preoccupied" with helping the grouping to discover fulfillment in its foundational searches.

The manager is preoccupied with administration and policies. Leadership, however, is not a matter of policies and procedures, neatly and tidily developed, printed, bound, and distributed to all concerned. Leadership is not lived out by being a busy bureaucrat or by being a systems person with complex charts and graphs.

The boss is preoccupied with control and power. The leader, however strong willed and driving, is not the boss. Leadership is not a matter of having one's own way, of saying, "we'll do it my way, or else." The leader is not the benevolent, authoritarian dictator—however authoritarian or benevolent he or she may be.

The enabler is preoccupied with developmental process. The leader is not the enabler, with polite process and tidy planning charts. The leader is not the reactive, enabling-process person with a quiet, persistent echo of "I hear you saying. . . ." The leader is not the person with the newsprint and markers.

The charismatic inspirer is preoccupied with apocalyptic events. The leader is not the charismatic inspirer with a thunder of prophecy and flashes of charisma. Leadership is more than good public relations, slogans, or prophetic chastisements.

All the while the manager is preoccupied with policies, the boss with power, the enabler with process, and the charismatic inspirer with the next apocalyptic event, the leader is "preoccupied" with helping the grouping toward fulfillment of the foundational life searches.

Second, in helping the grouping to discover and fulfill the four foundational searches in this life's pilgrimage, the missionary pastor, as leader, is the one who is primarily:

- proactive
- relational
- missional
- intentional

The leader is not basically reactive, responsive, organizational, or institutional. Given their human failings, doubts, and misgivings, however, leaders continue forward with a consistent sense of direction and work at being increasingly proactive, intentional, relational, and missional.

Third, with the help of the leader, the grouping does discover the fulfillment—for the moment—of the four foundational life searches. The leader is the one whose ability leads the grouping toward discovery and fulfillment. Leadership is more an art than a skill.

Managers can get away with studied efficiency toward improving the bottom line, with the endless development of burgeoning policies and detailed procedures, *only* when one of the four foundational life searches is being at least partially delivered to their people. They, therefore put up with the policies and procedures.

Likewise, bosses (frequently, to the extreme of being benevolent, authoritarian dictators) can get away with issuing ultimatums and directives and having tantrums only when one of the four foundational life searches is being at least partially fulfilled for their people. That promise of fulfillment, in fact, gives bosses, "power" over the grouping, not their striding up and down, shouting orders.

Enablers can get away with the endless steps of the cumbersome process methodology, but not because people have "ownership" for the process—they put up with it only as they have discovered some fulfillment in one of the four foundational searches.

Charismatic inspirers can get away with the dark thunder of prophecies and the shining brilliance of inspirations only as one of the four foundational searches is fulfilled for their people, who almost know the charisma is more style than substance, more cheerleader than content.

Some missionary pastors, as leaders, may be tough-minded; some may be gentle. Leaders may be sarcastic or humorless; they may be good fun or a pain-in-the-neck. Leaders are sinful and saintly—frequently more the former than the latter.

The nature of their leadership is in their ability to help the grouping discover fulfillment in their foundational life searches. And note that the grouping discovers a sense of fulfillment in more than one—sometimes all four—of life's foundational searches. This "wholeness" of fulfillment, not partial, distinguishes the leader from the manager, boss, enabler, and charismatic inspirer.

Leadership is a matter of philosophy of life. Leadership is not a matter of skills and strategies, tricks and gimmicks, newsprint and reports. Leadership is not a matter of a "good first impression," styling, or protocol.

Leadership is more than management, bossism, enablement, or charismatic direction. To be a leader is to be more than any of these. "More" here is not to be understood as "better." It is simply that the leader resonates with the whole of life; others resonate only with part of life. That is why the leader is the leader.

To be sure, some leaders are also good managers, but leadership is more than management. To be a leader is to be more than a manager. The same can be said for the boss, enabler, and charismatic inspirer—to be a leader is to be more than these. The manager manages. The boss controls. The enabler processes. The charismatic inspires. The leader leads. In our time, we need more leaders.

MAJOR RESOURCES FOR LEADERSHIP

The missionary pastor, as leader, draws on the major qualitative resources for leadership of wisdom, judgment, vision, common sense, and prayer.

The first major qualitative resource that helps the missionary pastor fulfill the role as leader is wisdom. Wisdom has more to do with insight than information. Wisdom is the capacity to discern and understand the meaning and value in the grouping's foundational searches.

The second resource is judgment—the ability to discern, compare, and decide among various opinions and possibilities. The missionary pastor does not deal primarily in procedures, power,

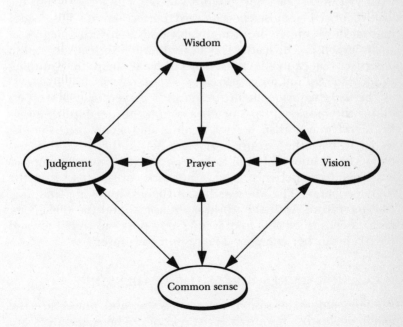

process, or charisma. The missionary pastor does not focus on generalizations, sentimental notions, or doom-and-gloom. As leader, he does not traffic in long hesitations or snap answers. The leader's judgment includes a sense of timing and a sense of fairness. The missionary pastor does not insist on always being "right." As leader, he or she uses his or her judgment to delegate and share authority and does not abuse it. Over the long haul, the judgment of the leader has a sense of soundness and integrity.

The third resource is vision. The missionary pastor has a sense of vision that draws on powerful imagination, unusual discernment, and foresight. As leader, his vision is responsible and realistic, not naive and idealistic. His vision is courageous and compassionate, not timid and calculating. The missionary pastor's vision is prayerful and powerful, not self-centered and weak. Most important, his vision is constant. To be sure, it is now and then wavering and uncertain, but overall steady and constant.

The fourth resource is common sense. In everyday, ordinary life, the missionary pastor, as leader, has the ability to understand what will work, not what "ought to work." The leader is not the captive of a compulsiveness toward perfectionism. The leader may tackle seemingly insurmountable odds, but with a degree of common sense. The leader is not caught up in unrealistic, foolish objectives that cannot be achieved. The leader helps the grouping to succeed, not fail, in its search.

The fifth major qualitative resource is prayer. One of the best things the missionary pastor does is pray. Leadership is more a matter of prayer than it is of legalism and techniques. For the leader to have the resources to share help rather than condemnation, the leader will want to be a person of prayer. Leadership is a draining experience. The complexities of the task drain the leader's energy. The life searches of the grouping are draining. The interacting with the world is draining. And the missionary pastor needs to be able to draw on God's power to "rebolster and refuel" his or her energies. The resource is prayer.

"OCCASIONAL" RESOURCES FOR LEADERSHIP

Wisdom, judgment, vision, common sense, and prayer are the major qualitative resources for the leader. These resources are important to be consistently present with the missionary pastor. From time to time, several other resources will be helpful. These occasional resources may be drawn on, as needed, by the leader.

The first is humor—not a silly humor or a sarcastic, "put down" humor, but the ability, in good-natured ways, to see the humor in life and events and to see the humor in one's own mistakes and failures. Humor heals.

The second resource is detachment—from bias or prejudice. From time to time, the leader will experience a sense of incongruity with persons or events. Sometimes he or she will feel a sense of betrayal. The missionary pastor is not so naive, when betrayal occurs, to take it too personally or too seriously. Not that the leader expects or counts on betrayal. But he or she occasionally needs to have the ability to draw on a gentle detachment that understands such events.

The third is the capacity to relax. Some persons in positions of leadership are too tense and tight, which only causes the grouping to become tense and tight. The art is from time to time to relax, enjoy life, and have fun. The baseball player who is deter-

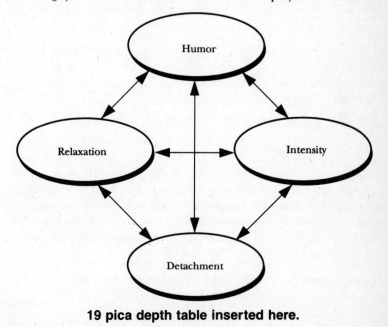

19 pica depth table inserted here.

mined to hit a home run every time at bat does one thing very well—strikes out! The player who goes to bat relaxed may hit a single one time, may bunt down the first-base line the next time, and may strike out. Another strike out. Then a hard grounder to the shortstop, beating the throw. Take a walk. Hit a double.

Players are more likely to do better when they go to the plate with a relaxed intentionality. Good baseball is not a matter of home runs every time at bat. Neither is leadership. You are more likely to be a stronger leader as you, from time to time, relax, enjoy life, have fun with the grouping, and live in Christ.

The fourth occasional resource is intensity. There are times when being intense will help, and there are times when it will be counterproductive. Leadership is not the result of intensity. Leadership is the art of knowing when intensity will help. To be sure, some "very intense" persons become leaders. Indeed, some conclude that the stronger the intensity, the stronger the leader. The myth is that "type A" persons make excellent leaders. But constant intensity wears thin with the grouping. Over the long haul, it has a marginal return. It wears down the grouping and eventually burns out the leader. Some people imagine that the way to become a leader is to be very intensive. No, that is simply the way to be intense.

Leadership is the art of drawing on each of these "occasional" resources at the most helpful time.

CENTRAL QUALITIES OF MISSIONAL LEADERSHIP

THEOLOGY OF MISSION

Three central qualities are present in the missionary pastor's understanding of the nature of leadership. **The first is a theology of the church that is a theology of mission, not a theology of institutionalism.** In traditional theological circles, it has been customary to speak of three theological streams of thought about the nature and purpose of the church:

1. sacramental—Roman Catholic, Eastern Orthodox
2. prophetic—Lutheran, Presbyterian
3. covenantal—Baptist, Assemblies of God

On occasion, some theological circles also speak of a dialectical, or process theology of the church. But in the main, the focus has been on these three theological streams of thought about the nature and purpose of the church. Considerable important effort has gone into tracing out the implications of each of the three for the life and work of the church in our time.

Over against this, there is a genuine sense in which it is fitting to say that there are really two major theologies of the church— a *missional* and an *institutional* theology of the church—which, in fact, "live themselves out" in sacramental, prophetic, or covenantal ways. That is, through the sacramental tradition, some persons live out a theology of mission, some a theology of institutionalism. Through the prophetic tradition, some persons live out a theology of mission, some a theology of institutionalism. The same is true through the covenental tradition.

Some persons in one theological camp are fond of smugly deriding the theology of institutionalism in the other two camps, while pointing with pride at their own theology of mission. All three camps, though, fall victim to a preoccupation with a theology of institutionalism, especially among denominations that are now stable and declining or dying.

These two theological understandings apply to our understanding of leadership. The truth is that missionary pastors, as leaders, develop a missional theology of leadership, and professional ministers an institutional theology of leadership. We need more missional leaders.

Tradition	Theology of Mission	Theology of Institutionalism
Sacramental		
Prophetic		
Covenantal		

An institutional theology of leadership lives itself out as in the following diagram:

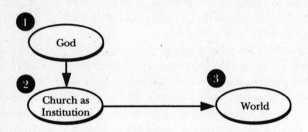

Professional ministers, as institutional leaders, thus focus first on the stability and well-being of the institution, then on the church's mission in the world. "We take care of our own, then we take care of others."

Missionary pastors, as leaders, by contrast understand that God is in the world. Whenever the church is in the world, God is in the church. Whenever the church is not in the world, God is still in the world. God does not forsake the world for the church.

The missional leader first has a concern for "people, service, and quality." The missional leader's focus is first on the mission, not the maintenance. *The focus is on service,* not survival.

To be a missionary pastor, as leader, is to be a servant *with people,* not of institutions. To be a servant is to be a strong, wise,

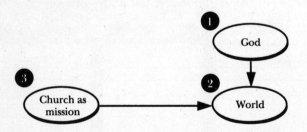

caring, initiating person. To be a servant is to be prophetic. We need a strong sense of what it means to be a servant.

To be a servant is not to be subservient. It is not a passive, responsive, "I hear you saying. . ." sense. Christ is servant in prophetic and dynamic ways, rather than in passive and dormant ways. That is a strong sense of what it means to be servant.

Being a servant is not the same as having vulnerability. Leaders frequently are vulnerable, make mistakes, have things wrong with themselves. But the source of leadership is not the leader's vulnerability. The source of leadership is the leader's capacity to move beyond the stark mistakes, sinfulness, and corruption. Amid such failings, the missionary pastor moves on toward the vision of the future that God has both promised and prepared.

Missional leaders serve the mission, not the institution. The sense of institution is strong. The sense of the mission is stronger.

FAITHFUL AND SUCCESSFUL

The second central quality present in missional leadership is an adequate understanding of the relationship of faithfulness and success in terms of the mission. Note:

1. Some churches are faithful and successful.
2. Some churches are faithful, not successful.
3. Some churches are not faithful yet are successful.
4. Some churches are not faithful and not successful.
5. Some churches use "faithfulness" as their excuse for not being successful.
6. Some churches use "success" as their excuse for not being faithful.

The missional leader understands that to be faithful is "to be faithful to the *mission*," not to success. Indeed, the missional leader redefines success as mission. For the missional leader, one does the mission for the sake of the mission. If, as a happy by-product, there is success (as the world defines success, such as church growth), the missional leader praises God and continues in faithfulness to the mission. The leader does not allow the success of growth to alter his or her mission.

The missional leader understands that *both #1 and #2 are responsible possibilities*. The missional leader rejects possibilities #3–#6 outright, as terrible misunderstandings of responsible missional leadership.

To be faithful is to be proactively, intentionally faithful *in mission*, not passive amid declining membership numbers. I hear too frequently in stable and declining churches, "Well, at least we are being faithful." No, all too often they are simply being passive.

COMPASSION AND COMMUNITY

The third quality present in missional leadership is the confidence that compassion and community are more helpful motivations than challenge, reasonability, and commitment. To be sure, five major motivational resources are important in missional leadership:

1. *compassion:* sharing, caring, loving, giving, serving, supporting
2. *community:* good fun, good times, fellowship, affiliation, belonging, family, home
3. *challenge:* accomplishment, achievement, goals, objectives
4. *reasonability:* logic, data, "it makes good sense," analysis
5. *commitment:* dedication, loyalty, duty, obligation, vows

All five of these motivational resources are present in any given congregation and in any given community. Two of the five will be the predominant motivations among the key leaders. Two of the five will be the predominant motivations among the grass roots. And two of the five will be the predominant motivations among the unchurched in the community. And it is not necessarily the same two.

Again and again, when I tabulate the motivations reported among church leaders, grass-roots members, and unchurched within a community, the results look like the following:

I have the privilege, frequently, of being asked to help dying churches. Inevitably, their motivational analysis looks like this chart. Why? By definition, in a dying church, the key leaders—the only people who are left—are the people *committed* to the *challenge* of "keeping the blooming doors open." Everybody else has gone somewhere else.

Motivational Resources

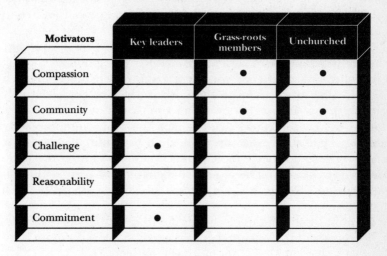

Motivators	Key leaders	Grass-roots members	Unchurched
Compassion		●	●
Community		●	●
Challenge	●		
Reasonability			
Commitment	●		

But when I ask those key leaders what drew them to that church thirty-five and forty years before, they talk about a *compassionate,* shepherding pastor and the fellowship and *community* of potluck suppers, family, and friends. But over the years that have come and gone, the motivational resources of compassion and community have been less well tended. Key leaders, weighed down by the institutional baggage of the church, have nurtured the motivations of challenge and commitment.

The difficulty is that the grass roots and the unchurched are best reached by the motivations of compassion and community. Think of radio-wave signals. The key leaders send out messages on the "radio-wave frequencies" of challenge and commitment, but both the grass-roots members and the unchurched are tuned in on the radio-wave frequencies of compassion and community. The messages are not being received. There is no resonance. There is no match. There is a *motivational gap.*

In a churched culture where many people self-initiated their participation in church, the motivation of commitment worked very well. A church could get away with focusing primarily on commitment to attract new people in a culture where it was "the thing to do" to go to church and where there was a reasonable density of long time "pro" Christians. But on a mission field the motivational resources that work best are compassion and community.

When someone says to me, "Dr. Callahan, what we need in our church is people with more *commitment*," I respond by saying, "You have just taught me you are a longtime Christian." Then I will ask what drew them to the faith in the first place. Usually their response focuses on events of compassion and community. Then I will gently remark that if compassion and community were the two motivations that drew them to the church in the first place, why would they expect to reach new persons on the radio frequencies of commitment and challenge? And then I will quietly conclude, "What we *really* need in this church are people with more compassion."

In most communities, in order for the church to reach the grass roots and the unchurched, we need people with more compassion and community, not more commitment.

I am not knocking commitment. Note that it made the list. But commitment is a motivational resource developed over time—as one lives in the Christian life over ten, fifteen, and twenty years. It is not an effective motivator with new unchurched persons.

The initial motivational resources that draw new persons to the faith are compassion and community. Regrettably, many of the people who write books on renewing the church (or on leadership or on stewardship) have lost sight of the early motivations that drew them into the church in the first place. They are long time "pro" Christians. Hence, their misguided emphasis has been on commitment.

We learn as much from what the New Testament does not say as from what it does say. The text does not say, "We are committed to Jesus because Jesus was first committed to us." It reads, "We love Jesus because Jesus first loved us."

The text does not say, "For God was so *committed* to the world. . . ." Rather, "For God so loved the world. . . ."

It was not said of the early Christians, "Look how they are committed to one another." It was said of them, "Look how they love one another."

These are texts of compassion, not commitment. Yet during the bygone years of the churched culture, we turned the God of compassion into the God of commitment. We turned the community of compassion into an institution of commitment. It may have "worked" in a churched culture. It no longer works on a mission field.

The missionary pastor understands well the motivational resources that are most helpful on a mission field.

The missionary pastor develops a *motivational match* with the key leaders grass roots and the unchurched. The missionary pastor does not forsake the grass roots and the unchurched for a brief peace solely with the key leaders.

The missionary pastor can take two important steps to bring the key leaders on board. First, he or she can build a *motivational bridge* by inviting key leaders to being committed to the challenge of doing whatever they do out of the motivations of compassion and community. It is amazing how many key leaders rise to that challenge and accept that commitment.

The Missionary Pastor and Motivational Resources

Motivators	Key leaders	Missionary pastor	Grass-roots members	Unchurched
Compassion		●	●	●
Community		●	●	●
Challenge	●			
Reasonability				
Commitment	●			

Second, the missional leader can build a *motivational match* between the key leaders and the grass roots and unchurched by helping the key leaders to rediscover the motivations that drew them to the church in the first place, namely, compassion and community. (See *Twelve Keys to an Effective Church: The Leaders' Guide*, 76–83, for additional material on these five major motivational resources.)

For now, it is important to note that these are *motivational* resources. Motivation is internal, not external. These are the resources within individuals that they draw on to motivate themselves. The missional leader and the individual, whether grass roots or unchurched, "resonate"—communicate—with one another on the same motivational wave frequency. That is what creates a motivational match.

In teaching Sunday school a number of years ago, I came to this conclusion: children care what the teacher knows when they know the teacher cares. By extension, on a mission field, people care where the leader is leading when they know the leader cares.

Compassion is more important than committees. Leaders who share their compassion with the grouping will lead the group forward faster than those who organize the group into a network of committees.

To be sure, people develop ownership for an organization when they participate in ways that help to shape the future of the organization. But as a matter of fact, people develop an even stronger ownership for the mission when the leader evidences tangibly a compassion for the persons in the grouping. The more the leader cares, the faster the grouping will move forward. The missionary pastor values the motivational resources of compassion and community as being more helpful on a mission field.

PART THREE.

FOUNDATIONAL SEARCHES, EMERGING TRENDS, AND CONSEQUENCES

7. The Search for Individuality

FOUR CENTRAL LEADERSHIP TASKS

Four tasks are central to understanding the nature of leadership important on a mission field. These four leadership tasks are decisive in the work of missionary pastors. Part 3 describes how these four central tasks come into being in relation to life's foundational searches, the emerging trends in the culture, and the consequences of those trends.

The four central leadership tasks on this mission field are:

1. to help persons rediscover power in their own lives and destinies
2. to construct new communities of reconciliation, wholeness, caring, and justice—in the name of Christ
3. to create a new theological direction and specific, shared purposes
4. to launch and lead intentional missional teams to meet specific, concrete human hurts and hopes—both societal and individual—in the world.

Each of these central tasks is related to one of life's foundational searches—individuality, community, meaning, hope. These four central tasks are the ways in which missonary pastors best help persons to advance their life searches.

In our time, each foundational life search lives itself out in relation to one of the major emerging trends in the culture—dislocation of power, cultural heterogeneity, theological pluralism, and societal specialization. These emerging trends are having considerable impact on people's lives and destinies.

Each trend brings with it an array of consequences. Some of these consequences are constructive and creative. Some are destructive and debilitating. Nevertheless, they are the consequences with which missionary pastors wrestle on this mission field.

Thus, part 3 develops the correlations between the task, search, trend, and consequences. Understanding these correlations is most important. Missionary pastors best understand the four central tasks of leadership in this time as they see the correlations between these tasks and the searches, trends, and consequences.

Certainly, each of these four central tasks will "live themselves out" distinctively from one mission terrain to the next. Count on your creativity and imagination to focus these four leadership tasks in ways that are useful, from one setting to the next.

Two principles are important for now. First, understand that there are not forty or twenty or ten central tasks for a missionary pastor. There are four. To be sure, we will do our fair share of other things in a given year. Focus on these four.

The mistake on a mission field would be to focus on too many tasks. Some people make the mistake of assuming, "The more tasks on which I focus, the more effective I will be." No, the more tasks on which you focus, the tireder you will be. And the more diffused and dispersed will be your impact. Focus on the four central leadership tasks.

Second, understand that leadership is a matter of perspective. Leadership is not a matter of busy activities and a flurry of projects. It is a matter of perspective. Most important, notice the correlation between these four central tasks, life's foundational searches, the emerging trends in the culture, and the consequences of those trends.

Leadership is not tricks and techniques, styles and strategies. Leadership is a matter of focus and perspective, understanding and direction. The perspective in part 3 will help, with its focus and direction on the four central leadership tasks for missionary pastors.

CENTRAL LEADERSHIP TASK: POWER

The first task for missionary pastors is, in a proactive way, to help persons rediscover power in their own lives and destinies.

IDENTITY AND INTEGRITY

Who am I? Three words sometimes said in wonder, sometimes in despair, sometimes in discovery. The psalmist wrote, "Who is man, that thou art mindful of him?" In each century, in each generation—indeed, in each day of our lives—we ask in fresh, new ways, "Who am I?"

From psalmist to philosopher, from adolescent to aging person, from four-year-old to forty-year-old, from cynic to sentimentalist, from agnostic to Christian, these three words represent a persistent, pervasive search for individuality. This search for individuality is the search for identity and integrity, responsible autonomy and power over one's own life and destiny.

The search for individuality is the search for identity. Finally, each of us wants some sense of selfhood. We want some sense of knowing that we are a distinctive personality. While we frequently

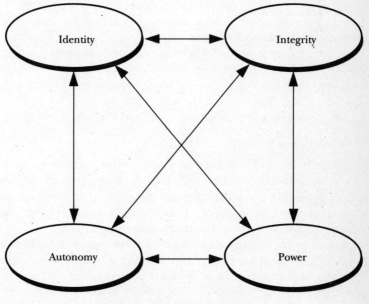

The Search for Individuality

succumb to the pressures of whatever grouping has our loyalties for the moment, nonetheless each of us has a drive toward singularity. It is not simply that we want to have our own name; more profoundly, we want to have our own sense of personhood.

Likewise, the search for individuality is the search for integrity. We are constantly shaping our value system. Each of us longs for some sense of stability and soundness about ourselves. We want some sense of grit, of honor, and of character.

Identity and integrity go hand in hand. Integrity gives a sense of cohesiveness to one's identity. Without the benefit of some sense of integrity, one's identity becomes fragmented, inconsistent, widely variable, "slippery."

This is not to say that integrity is instantaneous. Frequently, persons come to the moment of integrity with fierce struggle and deep travail. There is considerable doubt, much misgiving, and many temptations to "go an easier way"—and then, there is the act of commitment to integrity.

Nor is integrity ironclad. There are "second thoughts" and moments of doubts. There are questions of "what might have been." There are sleepless nights and turmoil. Sometimes there is almost a turning back. But the quiet resolve stays steady. One's sense of identity grows forward in the decision and the act of integrity.

AUTONOMY AND POWER

The search for individuality is a search for autonomy. It is a search for a sense of freedom, of being independent, of being one's own self. It is a search for an autonomy that is responsible, not manipulative or egotistic. It is a search for a sense of one's own being, not an individualistic excessiveness.

Some persons, in their effort toward autonomy, wrestle between the polarities of dependence and isolated self-sufficiency. Sometimes the "significant others" in their life communicate the message that "life will be safer and surer if you continue to be dependent on us." Such significant others can be identified as "codependents." These codependents frequently define their own individuality by continually arranging to have others dependent on them.

At times, persons in their struggle toward autonomy erupt in rebellion against a dependent pattern of life and head toward gross self-centeredness. They define autonomy not as responsible self-direction but as "having their own way." Their sense of self-ishness, hedonism, and self-centeredness becomes an overcompensation for their earlier state of dependency. But autonomy, at its best, is responsible moral independence.

The search for individuality is a search for power. It is a search for the ability and the authority to shape one's own life and destiny. This search for power is not always a gentle, polite search. People frequently have a desperate struggle to obtain some control over their own lives and destinies. One cannot understand some bizarre forms of behavior that occur in us from time to time, apart from this profound search for power. The more pervasive the sense of powerlessness, the more bizarre and desperate the forms of behavior.

Most people do not have an insatiable thirst for power. Most people do not want the kind of power held by dictators. Most people simply want some sense that they have some power over their own life and destiny, that they are not victims of the manipulations of others, that they are not the discards on the garbage heap of the galaxies.

The search for individuality is thus the search for identity, integrity, autonomy, and power. And this search for individuality is currently being lived out in the midst of the emerging trend toward dislocation of power in our times.

THE TREND TOWARD THE DISLOCATION OF POWER

The dislocation of power is the process whereby power and decision making have been increasingly centralized at national and international levels. In the earlier part of this century, many of the decisions that affected people's lives and destinies were made individually and locally within their own community.

Over the course of a number of years, there has been a movement for many of those decisions to be made not individually and locally but in the county and the state, then regionally, then nationally, then internationally. As a result, people increasingly have felt that many of the decisions that affect their lives and shape their destinies are made somewhere else by someone else, and they cannot quite find out who or why or when.

Just try to track them down! You pick up the phone to call some government office or service agency. And even as you dial the number, you already begin to dread the number of times you will have to repeat your story—and the number of people you will be referred to—before you get to talk to the right person.

The dislocation of power is pervasively felt and desperately present. World War II was the first major war that was really conducted on an international basis. If one looks closely at World War I, one realizes that it was fought by more of a confederation of military units that were sent by various states and countries. With the advent of World War II, decisive, decision-making power occurred internationally. From World War II on, there has increasingly been the sense that the real decisions are made nationally and internationally, not individually and locally.

We see international leaders on the nightly news. The visual impact of daily television news conveys what the real "movers and shakers" have been doing. The local news may be only a passing comment if something else does not upstage it. This has quite a different impact from the impact of the news that was heard on the radio and occasionally seen in brief clips between movies at a double feature picture show years ago. The individual in today's world has learned to take his or her place as more of a casual observer or victim and less as an interested decision maker.

To some extent, the sheer density of people and the sheer mass of the population on the planet have created compromises over decision making and power. Sometimes those compromises are fortuitous and happy. Sometimes they are stifling and demeaning.

THE CONSEQUENCES

An Acceleration toward Centralization

The first consequence of the dislocation of power is an increased acceleration toward centralization. Once there is a movement toward decision making at national and international levels, and once a bureaucratic system is well in place, there is an acceleration of the dislocation of local power—an acceleration toward centralization.

Bureaucrats breed bureaucrats, and do so extraordinarily well. Bureaucratic structures increase geometrically, not arithmetically. Perhaps they innately sense the tenuousness of their position and the limitations of their meager contributions. Their instinct toward self-preservation, their defense against extinction, is the rapid multiplication of the breed.

One has only to look in educational, business, governmental, political, and religious circles to discover glaring examples of this rapid increase of bureaucracy and also to note that bureaucracy and centralization are symbiotic, mutually interrelated dynamics. The more rapid the acceleration toward centralization, the more geometrically the bureaucracy increases itself. The faster the bureaucracy increases itself, the stronger the rate of acceleration toward centralization.

A Pervasive Sense of Powerlessness

The second consequence of the dislocation of power is a pervasive sense of powerlessness. The more centralization and the more bureaucratization, the more deeply people feel a pervasive sense of powerlessness. The dread of bureaucracy is an increasingly pervasive tendency in the culture. It is not that people finally dread the bureaucracy—they know that bureaucracy can serve their interests as well as suppress them. What they dread is the sense of powerlessness that they feel when an entrenched, self-interested, noncaring bureaucratic structure increases its power over them.

Much attention is given to the percentages of people who vote and who do not vote in our culture. There are a variety of reasons for declining turnouts at the polls, but certainly one of the reasons is the widely held perception that not much will change, regardless of who is elected, because of an entrenched, immovable bureaucracy.

This same sense of powerlessness is found in the church. The perception is clearly present. People say, "Why become active? The bureaucracy and politics are entrenched. My being there will make very little difference."

Apathy and Anonymity

The third consequence is apathy and anonymity. People again and again ask me, "Could you please help us with the apathy among our church members?" It is not as simple as apathy in the church. One of the decisive clues that helps to identify the trend toward dislocation of power is a pervasive sense of apathy *throughout* people's lives. It is a sort of inevitable, passive indifference in life—an impassive listlessness.

If you look below the surface of church apathy, you will discover that apathy is strongly present in all spheres and sectors of people's lives, whether family, educational, vocational, political, civic and community, recreational, or religious spheres. In all sectors of life, many people are living out a pervasive apathy, a feeling that they are now anonymous, a sense that they *do not count*.

ANGER AND DEPRESSION

A fourth consequence of the dislocation of power is anger and depression. You will better understand the picayune, petty arguments that occur in administrative board meetings when you discern that some of them are the results of dislocated power. These petty arguments are frequently an expression of displaced anger. People eventually resist a continued state of apathy, and one way people break out of apathy is through the expression of their anger.

They frequently express their displaced anger at church, hoping that in the church we will love and care and understand. It is a whole lot easier and safer to express one's anger over apportionments in the church than it is to express one's anger over things at work or taxes to the Internal Revenue Service.

You can better understand some of the anger that is expressed in the church toward apportionments when you also understand that it may very well be displaced anger over mismanagement at work or the economic issues in the country, including taxes and the IRS. Many people feel taxed to death in this country. They feel powerless to control Congress or taxes or church apportionments.

The more persons experience the trend toward dislocation of power, the more some of them will erupt in anger or live out a state of depression. Depression is finally anger turned inward toward one's self.

SUBMISSIVE INACTIVITY

The fifth consequence of the trend toward dislocation of power is submissive inactivity. I had originally thought of this as quiet inactivity. But the word *quiet* is not the word to describe the state of this inactivity. It is not simply quiet, it is submissive. There is finally the inevitable sense that one can do nothing about one's plight. One can do nothing about having power in relation to those matters that shape one's own life and destiny. That brings about a state of almost catatonic submissiveness.

All of these consequences are both sequential and interrelated. As people experience the acceleration toward centralization, one of the early responses is a feeling of powerlessness, then apathy. Next, many people move to anger. Anger is an aggressive effort to declare one's individuality, autonomy, and power. Having failed there, people move to a state of submissive inactivity.

THE DEMAND FOR POWER

After inactivity, generally there occurs a sixth consequence: an increased demand and drive for power, for taking control, in the decisions that affect people's lives and destinies. Sometimes this demand for power is healthy, constructive, and vigorous. Very frequently, this drive for power can be chaotic, destructive, and deadly.

We are at an important crossroads in this regard. Countless thousands upon thousands of persons have nearly reached the end of their rope. Too many of the decisions that affect their lives and shape their destinies have, in fact, been made somewhere else, by someone else. They will not let it go on indefinitely.

It thus becomes decisive for the missionary pastor to help persons—constructively and courageously—to rediscover power in their own lives and destinies. That means helping persons to recover power in *all* spheres of their lives—family, educational, vocational, political, civic and community, recreational, and religious. Not simply in the religious sphere.

The missionary task is not simply helping persons rediscover power in their own church. The missionary pastor is more interested in helping persons recover power in their whole lives, not solely their "religious life."

This missionary task is crucial. People do not lie dormant in submissive inactivity forever. The whirlwinds gather. The forces of chaos and strife arise on the horizon. The demand for power is strong and growing stronger. And this demand will not be satisfied by the "pretty parlor games of process" practiced in many churches, while a few still make the key decisions behind the scenes. It will take real power, in all spheres and sectors of life. The missionary pastor is crucial and decisive for this foundational life search.

8. The Search for Community

CENTRAL LEADERSHIP TASK: COMMUNITY

The missionary pastor's second task is, in a relational way, to construct new communities of reconciliation, wholeness, caring, and justice.

Who do I belong with? The search for community is the second of the four foundational searches that are decisive in this life's pilgrimage. Individuality is discovered *in* community. In our time, the search for community is living itself out in the emerging trend of cultural heterogeneity.

In *Our Town*, Thornton Wilder portrays a strong sense of belonging, continuity, certainty, and community. George and Emily live side by side, grow up together, fall in love, and get married. The train goes through "regular" every night at 11:00, and most folk are in bed. And that is the way life has been lived for years.

But sudden, dark tragedy happens even there. Even in Grover's Corners, Emily dies in childbirth. She learns, after her death, that she can go back and relive one day in her life. Against the advice of the others already buried in the cemetery, she chooses to go back for a day.

She chooses her twelfth birthday. The Stage Manager takes her back so she can watch the events of that day unfold. She sees the hustle and bustle, the baking of the birthday cake, the busyness and hurriedness, the wrapping of the presents, and people living in the same house but hardly noticing one another.

Finally, in desperate pleading, she cries out, "Mama, just look at me one minute as though you really saw me. . . . Just for a moment now we're all together. Mama, just for a moment we're happy. *Let's look at one another.*" In tears, she is led back to the cemetery by the Stage Manager. Arriving there, she hears Simon Stimson, the organist and town drunkard, gently and cynically say, "Yes, now you know. Now you know! That's what it was like to be alive . . . to spend and waste time as though you had a million years. . . . That's the happy existence you wanted to go back to. Ignorance and blindness."

The search for community is the search for roots, place, and belonging. It is the search for sharing and caring, for family and friends.

ROOTS

The search for roots is the search for heritage and history amid the cultural apocalypticism of our time. There are simply too many primary groupings being terminated. We have too many "endangered species" in *both* nature and humankind. Too many families are breaking up. Many extended families are no more.

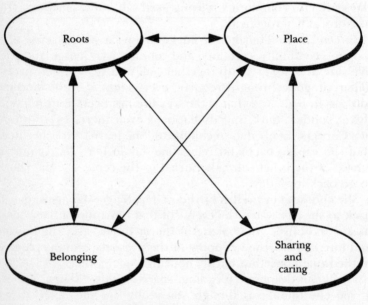

The Search for Community

Some people seek out their ancestors, develop family genealogies, and track down their distant relatives. It is neither accidental nor simply a hobby. It is a profound search for roots in a larger, complex, heterogeneous community.

The search for roots is the search for continuity and certainty. We seek the sense of an enduring character to our pilgrimage— that we are not some brief nanosecond, a momentary blip in the cosmos—that we are part of a community that has more of an everlasting continuity than threescore years and ten.

The search for roots is the search for participation in a community that has a future and a past, not only a present. The assumption—yea, the abiding hope—is that if this community has had a long-term continuity in generations gone by, it will have the possibility of long-term continuity for generations yet to come. We will therefore endure—"live on" in that community—as a cloud of witnesses even after we have crossed over the river.

Place

The search for place is spatial and territorial amid the societal dislocation of this time. It is the search not simply for space but for a space one can call one's own. That sense of space may live itself out as a home, a piece of land, an apartment, an office, or even as a "moving space" in the form of a car. Driving around town, one has the sense that the space of this car, albeit moving, is one's own space.

And this search for some space is profoundly territorial and possessive. It is not simply that some other creatures are territorial and humankind is not. We see territoriality exhibited in nations, groupings, and individuals. Family clans gather for reunions at "their" place. High school groupings develop "their sacred place of meeting." Ditchdiggers develop "their gathering place." Business and professional groupings meet at "their special place."

Individuals seek some sense of their own place as well. It may be a room with two dresser drawers and a closet. It may be a "hiding place" for retreat and sanctuary. People resist violation of "their space." As best they can, they seek to keep their space inviolable. They do the best they can to insulate their sense of place from encroachment and intrusion. We can thank Norman Lear for immortalizing this in Archie Bunker's favorite chair.

This search for place is societal and spiritual, as well as spatial and territorial. This search is clearly societal. Individuals invest considerable energy in achieving and securing their place in the societal groupings important to them. Sometimes they lie in bed at night awake with worry and anxiety, fearful as to whether they have achieved "their place" in the group. This is true of teenagers, but it is also evident at other ages as well. Indeed, this concern for place in the grouping—this sense of role, niche, image, position—is persistent throughout one's life.

This search for place is spiritual. It is the search to secure a place with God. To be sure, it is puzzling that we search for that place. God has already assured us of our place, through the life, death, resurrection, and continuing presence of Jesus Christ. The incredibility of the gift must be what overwhelms us. We search frantically, with good deeds and righteousness, for the place that God has already given to us. How amazing the gift! How assuming that we seek to earn what we have already been given!

This search for place is pilgrimage, as well as something permanent. We seek to find a sense of place on the journey along the way. We work hard for the sense of place to be permanent, fixed, certain, sure. Yet the apocalypticism of our time makes that most difficult. There are simply too many abrupt, drastic changes and too many upheavals. There are too many microtrends and too many megatrends. Most of us settle for—long for, hope for— a sense of place *for now,* and a series of places during our life's pilgrimage. And perhaps yet one more beyond the river.

BELONGING

The search for belonging is the search for family and friends amid the psychological disorientation of our time. People live in four "neighborhoods"—relational, sociological, geographical, and genealogical. The first neighborhood many people experience is their genealogical family. There was a time when the genealogical neighborhood was synonymous with the relational, sociological, and geographical neighborhoods. But for many, many persons, the original genealogical neighborhood seldom continues to be the primary source of belonging.

Their sense of belonging is discovered and, as best it can be, fulfilled in a relational neighborhood of acquaintances, work associates, and friends—the new "extended family" of relationships. Sometimes this relational neighborhood of friends overlaps with the sociological neighborhood in which one lives. And thus the sociological neighborhood becomes also a source of belonging.

Seldom does the relational neighborhood overlap with the geographical neighborhood. In some small towns and some rural areas the relational neighborhood and the geographical neighborhood may yet overlap. But the geographical neighborhood has receded as a primary source of belonging. The search for belonging is primarily lived out in the relational neighborhood—the network linkages of our time.

Frequently, this relational neighborhood is primarily derived from associates in one's vocation. Increasingly, people find their sense of community in what I call the "vocational villages" of our time. Whether it be the company, the ditchdigging crew, the shift at the plant, the office building, the local chapter of the National Secretaries Association, the fleet of fishing boats, and so on, people have found their "new extended family" increasingly in such vocationally related communities.

When life was simpler, the people who lived in Grover's Corners were like an extended family. Even with occasional bizarre events back then, there was still a sense of certainty about roots, place, and belonging. Now we live in a pilgrimage time, not a home-base time. The challenge of our time is to find home along the way.

SHARING AND CARING

The search for community is the search for sharing and caring amid the alienation and loneliness of our time. People seek to participate in sharing and caring. They want to be both on the receiving end and on the giving end of sharing and caring. People are not primarily interested in only receiving sharing and caring—that would be a one-sided relationship. Intuitively, people know that that type of relationship will wither on the vine, decline, and decay. Instinctively, most people shy away from that type of relationship, which would place them in a pattern of dependency.

At the same time, people search for relationships of mutuality in which they can both give and receive sharing and caring. They want to share mutually, collegially with the other persons in the grouping. They want to care deeply, fully, and wholly, for and with the other persons in the grouping. It is important to them that this sense of sharing and caring have a grass-roots, collegial spirit, not a top-down, paternalistic spirit.

This sense of sharing and caring helps people through the difficult twists and turns of this life's pilgrimage. Not everything in this life is understandable or explainable. Tragic events scar our lives. Sinful events trouble us deeply. Apocalyptic events disrupt and disturb what fragile sense of well-being we have almost achieved. Amid all of this, what sees us through is the sense of sharing and caring that we have discovered within the relational neighborhoods that we have helped to create as "our family."

People come to a church longing for, yearning for, hoping for this sense of roots, place, belonging, sharing, and caring. People come to a church in our time with a search for community, not committee.

We make the mistake of assuming that, by putting people on a committee, they will develop ownership for the objectives of the church. People are not looking for ownership of objectives or for functional, organizational, institutional goals.

Their search is far more profound and desperate than that. They are looking for home, for relationships. They are looking for the profound depths of community. They are not looking for transitory, temporary, annual goals, hurriedly sketched on newsprint or butcher paper at a planning retreat.

Amid the alienation and loneliness of this time, they bring to our churches a desperate search for community. They almost put up with the silliness of our brochures, the institutionalized new-member orientations, the self-serving nature of our membership hustling. Their search is that desperate.

About now, you should be asking, "If there are so many out there searching, how come our church isn't full?" Some of them have probably visited your church. Eventually—and inevitably in some churches—the visitor discovers that the perspective is so institutional, the mentality and values are so organizational, and the behavior patterns are so functional that the people of that church are simply too preoccupied with their own busyness to welcome them, to share some personal warmth with them.

Jesus said, "I must be about my Father's business." He did not say "busyness." But within some churches the people are so intent on their own busy activities and programs (birthday cakes and pleasant presents) that they cannot see or hear the desperation and profundity of another person's search for community. Visitors see, with Emily, the "blessed busyness" of the church. And so they continue the search elsewhere for the community they want and need.

THE TREND TOWARD CULTURAL HETEROGENEITY

The second emerging trend that is having a strong influence in the culture and the church is the emergence of significant cultural heterogeneity. This cultural heterogeneity (as compared with the more homogeneous character of nineteenth-century rural society), coupled with increased population mobility, has resulted in historical-societal disorientation for many persons.

A wide divergence of subcultural groupings has developed in contemporary society. Each of these subcultural groupings has its own:

- goals and values system
- life-style of customs, habits, and traditions
- language and communications network
- leadership, authority, and decision-making process
- sacred places of meeting
- vision of the future

The rampant proliferation of subcultural groupings can be understood, in part, as the drive to recreate roots, place, and a sense of belonging, all of which were available in the "tribal extended family" society of the nineteenth and early twentieth centuries. But roots, place, and belonging have become increasingly difficult to find amid the loneliness of the nuclear family and the cultural fragmentation and mobility of both urban and rural society.

The local church has, to a large extent, increasingly mirrored this cultural heterogeneity in its own life and work. The character of the local church as tribal extended family has largely disappeared, except in some more remote and rural areas. More often than not, the contemporary local church is a collection of subcultural groupings and isolated families, with only the barest thread of commonality to bind them together.

It is ironic that the program emphasis on small groups in many local churches has further contributed to this heterogeneous diffusion. Frequently, these programs and activity groupings have represented the epitome of socioeconomic exclusiveness. There is considerable need for local churches to create new communities of reconciliation, wholeness, caring, and justice.

Cultural heterogeneity has resulted from the diversification of the rural and town culture of the late 1800s and early 1900s. Grover's Corners is no more. In an earlier time, we mostly lived in communities of cultural homogeneity, where most folk were like us. We liked most folks because they were like us.

We now live in a time of extraordinary cultural heterogeneity. To some extent, this emerging trend toward rapidly developing cultural heterogeneity is explainable in terms of the in-migrations, out-migrations, and trans-migrations of distinctive groupings across the planet. What drives the rapid pace of that cultural heterogeneity is the search for community.

The old groupings in which people had found some fulfillment of roots, place, belonging, sharing, and caring have split asunder—they have disbanded and been scattered across the landscape. Some people have thus found themselves in a desperate search for new sources of community.

Some people have found themselves in a loud and absurd behavior pattern, searching for community. Some have done the best they could to hold on and hope that some sense of home will soon be found. The primordial engine that drives the trend of cultural heterogeneity is this profound, desperate search for community.

THE CONSEQUENCES

THE PROLIFERATION OF GROUPINGS

We can see four consequences of this trend toward cultural heterogeneity. The first is the proliferation of groupings. There was a time when the available groupings in a culture could be graphically displayed in a reasonably simple chart. If you attempt now to illustrate the available groupings in a given culture, the chart would be many times bigger and much more complex. There is an ongoing proliferation of the range of available groupings. People search for their roots, place, and belonging with one group and may not quite find it there. So they move to another or even start yet another new grouping in their unfulfilled search for community.

SOCIOCULTURAL EXCLUSIVENESS

The second consequence of the trend toward cultural heterogeneity is that the more groupings available, the more likely they are to become exclusive. Think about high schools. Some of us went to high schools that had two or three groupings, and one of them was sort of exclusive, a clique.

But as high schools have grown and enlarged, a number of distinguishable subcultural groupings can be identified among the heterogeneous student body:

- athletes
- intellectuals
- extracurricular club members
- socials
- "trendies," who follow the current fad of the moment
- outcasts
- independents

Each of these subcultural groupings has its own (1) goals and values system; (2) customs, habits, and traditions; (3) language and communications network; (4) leadership, authority, and decision-making process; (5) sacred places of meeting; and (6) vision of the future. Generally speaking, the larger the high school, the more numerous and definitive the subcultural groupings.

The phenomenon of overlap does occur. That is, on occasion an individual or a small grouping may successfully participate in more than one of these distinctive, subcultural groupings. It is the rare student who belongs in more than one grouping.

There is also the phenomenon of interchange. That is, some persons participate for a period of their high school life in one subcultural grouping, and then, for whatever reasons, they successfully shift to become a participant in another subcultural grouping. Sometimes the person who is cut from the football team makes the shift from the athletic subcultural grouping to the social or extracurricular subcultural grouping.

But by and large, most youth live out their high school years in one subcultural grouping or another. Typically we see students fitting in and defining themselves uniquely with one grouping. There is very little mobility between them. The larger the high school, the more rigid the sociocultural exclusiveness tends to be.

The same is true for the culture at large. One can identify a vast array of distinctive subcultural groupings. Indeed, the example of the high school is much like the study of one star in a given solar system. When one looks at the array of subcultural groupings now in existence, it is more like looking at all the stars in all the galaxies on a clear summer night. The array is amazing.

The phenomena of overlap and interchange apply equally in the larger culture. Some persons in some small groupings overlap and successfully participate in another subcultural grouping. Other persons participate for a period of time in one subcultural grouping and then successfully make the transition to becoming a participant in another subcultural grouping. Nonetheless, there is considerable sociocultural exclusiveness between these subcultural groupings.

SUBCULTURAL CHURCHES

The third consequence related to the first two is that we have developed an interesting array of subcultural churches. In an analysis of mill towns a number of years ago, researchers identified the workers' church, the foremen's church, and the owners' church. In our time, there is a much greater array of subcultural churches that live out the enormous proliferation of groupings.

When you look carefully, you see that there is no such thing as a "large church." A large church is a collection of smaller groups, or congregations, or subcultural groupings, that have just enough in common to share the same set of facilities and the same pastoral staff. When you analyze the significant relational groupings in a church, you will discover distinctive subcultural groupings with distinctive goals and value systems; distinctive customs, habits, and traditions; distinctive language and communications networks; distinctive leadership and decision-making processes; distinctive sacred places of meeting; and a distinctive vision of the future.

ENORMOUS DIVERSITY IN LOCAL CHURCHES

As the culture has become more heterogeneous, we see a fourth consequence in the enormous diversity of local churches. Our pastors have greater difficulty in this current time than in the time gone by when they move from one church to another. One reason is that when a pastor moved from Grover's Corners to another town, the culture was relatively homogeneous—there was some parallel commonality with where he had moved to. It may not have been George and Emily next door, but it was Bill and Sue.

As pastors move now from one church to another, there may be little commonality at all. Indeed, the high probability is that in our time a pastor is moving from one collection of socioeconomic, cultural, vocational, and theological groupings to an entirely different collection of subcultural groupings. Sometimes it is like moving from rural North Dakota to Los Angeles; sometimes it feels like moving from northern Indiana to South America.

THE INDIVIDUAL AND COMMUNITY

We need to recognize the consequences that stem from the culture's search for community and the trend toward cultural heterogeneity. The proliferation of groupings, the developing exclusiveness, the subcultural churches, and the wide diversity of local churches—all of these developments on the mission field mean that many of the ways we have been used to doing ministry do not work in this setting, in this time. When pastors move to new churches, it is important for them to learn to *look* at their new churches realistically and prepare to minister in fresh new ways. The old ways may no longer work as they move to a new setting. (Indeed, the old ways may not have been working at the old setting!)

The resource for dealing with this emerging trend of cultural heterogeneity is the dynamic of individuality and community. The way forward in our time, theologically and biblically, is to understand that the individual discovers his or her own identity in community. And the community discovers its identity in individuals. To stress individuality over against community (or vice versa) is to stress only one side of the dynamic. The art is to keep in dynamic tension the relationship of individuality and community.

It is decisively important that we work wisely at the issue of the relationship of individual and community. On the one hand, some propose an individualistic entrepreneurship. On the other hand, some cling to the organization ("go along to get along") and suppress their own individuality in favor of the corporate entity. A compromise between the two will not help. It is important that both resources be powerfully and equally present at any given moment in our pilgrimage.

Individuality is discovered in community. We know *who we are* in relation to the community in which we have found home. And we must point beyond an understanding of the community that is simply a collection of individuals. There is something wholistic and covenantal about who we are as a body that is more than simply the sum of the parts.

Some philosophical systems invite individuals to collapse their identity into the identity of the whole. The way beyond that is not to insist on an individualistic form of individualism. Some people focus only on individuality as over against community, while others focus on community as over against individuality. The way forward is not by occupying a middle ground. One must keep both significantly present. Individuality is found in community. Community is led forward by people's new discovery of individuality in the midst of roots, place, belonging, and sharing and caring.

It thus becomes decisive for the missionary pastor, in a relational way, to construct new communities of reconciliation, wholeness, caring, and justice. Note that the pastor can proceed in an informal, relational way, not in an organizational, institutional way. There are already too many groupings like that.

Reconciliation: The grouping helps persons deal with the alienation and estrangement, bitterness and grief in their lives.

Wholeness: The grouping helps persons with the fragmentation, compartmentalization, psychological disorientation, and societal dislocation that have impacted their lives.

Caring: People "look" at one another; they care, in genuine, deep-felt, covenantal ways.

Justice: The grouping helps to address the injustices and prejudices with which people struggle.

These new communities are *not* committees. They are "families." The new communities "live together" in all spheres of life—family, educational, vocational, political, civic and community, recreational, and religious. They do not retreat from the world. They are not simply a "religious family." They live in the world, as best one can. They are not overcome by the world. Missionary pastors and missionary leaders help to construct these new communities. This missional task is decisive.

9. The Search for Meaning

CENTRAL LEADERSHIP TASK: MEANING

The missionary pastor's third task, in an intentional way, is to create a new theological direction and specific, shared purposes as to:

1. what our specific missions in the world are
2. what our central convictions are
3. who we are

The task is to help people discover some sense of Why?, What is the meaning?, What is the purpose of life?

As Best One Can

The search for meaning is the search for value and significance, purpose and understanding in everyday, ordinary life in the light of the gospel. The search for meaning has to do with making sense of life today, *as best one can.*

It is not possible to develop a comprehensive and detailed meaning structure for all of life. To be sure, philosophers and theologians have made valiant efforts in this direction. Some of their constructs and systems have stood—for a time. It is not altogether clear, however, that an encompassing, detailed, and conclusive meaning for all of life would, in fact, be helpful.

What most people long for, yearn for, hope for is enough meaning to sustain one for today in this life's pilgrimage. And that understanding of meaning is not static or neat, tidy, and orderly. That understanding of meaning is dynamic and interactive.

To be sure, some persons—for whom life has been extraordinarily chaotic, abrupt, tragic, and apocalyptic—seek to develop very definitive, fixed views about life. Their search for detailed certainty is their way of assuring themselves that something is

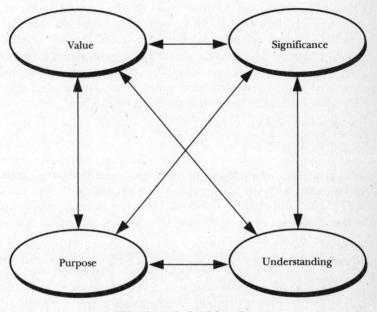

The Search for Meaning

definitive, sure, and certain amid the chaos that they have been and are experiencing.

But for most people, the search for meaning is "on the way." It is a search to discover just enough meaning, as best one can, to sustain one for this present moment.

VALUE AND SIGNIFICANCE

This search for meaning is a search for value and significance. People do not want their lives to be empty and worthless. People struggle for some glimmer of value and significance for their own lives. Finally, people want their lives to count. In the end, people do not want to go to the grave feeling that their life has been utterly useless—they want to have the sense that they have made some contribution.

What scares most of us about death is dying. What further scares us is that, in the end, our lives might not have counted for anything—might have had no value or significance.

Many of us work very hard to avoid death, even as we know it is inevitable. It does help us to know that our time on this earth has counted—with friends and family, job and church, community and country. The ditches we have dug, the papers we have graded, the clothes we have washed, the children we have reared, the work we have accomplished in simple everyday life—somehow our life has had some value and significance.

PURPOSE AND UNDERSTANDING

The search for meaning is the search for purpose and understanding. We do want life to have some sense of value and significance. Likewise, we want life to have some sense of purpose and understanding. We do not want life to be pointless or always obscure, vague, and chaotic. We look for some insight, some intuition that helps us to have a sense of understanding and a sense of purpose about our lives.

Ordinary, everyday people ponder the meaning of life. It is not simply philosophers and theologians, not just professors and preachers who do so, although they may use more sophisticated words to express their thinking. Without some understanding of life, one lives in despair and darkness. Futility and death become one's only companions. People long for, yearn for some glimmer of purpose and understanding in this life's pilgrimage.

From ditchdiggers to doctors, from waiters and waitresses to engineers and scientists, from manufacturing representatives and flight attendants to fathers and mothers, children, and youth— all are experiencing a longing to understand. People in all walks of life theologize about this time on earth. And mostly, people construct some modest—almost fleeting—sense of purpose and understanding that helps them to make sense of everyday, ordinary life.

EVERYDAY, ORDINARY LIFE

Note that it is a search for meaning and purpose in *everyday, ordinary life*. People are not looking for meaning and purpose in an idealized, romanticized understanding of life. What we need help on is discovering meaning and purpose in everyday, ordinary life in the light of the gospel.

For some few, life is a matter of great achievements. But for most, life is a matter of eking out a daily existence, clutching and clinging as best one can to some fragment of understanding and purpose, much like the drowning man clings desparately to a piece of driftwood to keep him afloat for the moment. And for many, that fragile piece of driftwood delivers sufficient purpose and understanding for that moment. What gets most of us through the tough times, as well as through everyday, ordinary life, is not some comprehensively complete system of beliefs but some simple phrase or modest insight that is like a lantern lighting our path, that helps us on our way.

In the Light of the Gospel

Most of us need help discovering this modest, fragile sense of meaning and purpose in everyday, ordinary life in the light of the gospel. There are a range of philosophies that have sought to explain life. When I add "in the light of the gospel," I am heading us toward theological, rather than philosophical, directions. Our sense of direction is found in the light of the gospel, not somewhere else.

It is not found in some philosophical system. It is found in the ever-unfolding leading of God, as God goes before us and leads us toward the future that God has both promised and prepared for our lives. The future toward which God leads us is a future in everyday, ordinary life, not a romanticized, idealized understanding of life.

We are a wilderness people; we are not a people of paved roads and polished palaces. It was not pleasant in the desert as the people of Israel wandered through. God does not guarantee us a future of pleasantness. God leads us toward a future in mission. There will be tragic times, as well as sinful, unpleasant, incidental, celebrative, and hope fulfilled times.

THE TREND TOWARD THEOLOGICAL PLURALISM

The search for meaning and purpose in everyday, ordinary life is living itself out in our time in the trend toward theological pluralism. Alternative understandings of the meaning and purpose of everyday, ordinary life have moved to the fore as older understandings related to agrarian and industrial cultures have made less sense in a technological, intergalactic civilization.

Theological pluralism is the process whereby alternative understandings of the meaning and purpose of everyday, ordinary life have escalated from several to many and from many to multitudinous, from one solar system of meanings to a multiplicity of galaxies of meanings.

We are, in our time, an intergalactic civilization. Our children see the world through the eyes of persons who understand an expansive range of galaxies. Those of us who are older look at the world as the earth. Our children look at the world as the universe. When our children look at the universe, they see a vast array of galaxies.

I am well aware that Copernicus helped people to see that the earth was not the center of the universe. And ancient astronomers, well before Copernicus, have understood the vastness of the universe. But even so, when we have used the word *world,* what comes to mind is this planet and perhaps the sun, moon, this solar system, and, more vaguely, the stars. For our children, recent discoveries in space, as well as *Star Trek* and *Star Wars,* have helped expand their imaginations to a multiplicity of galaxies that is virtually limitless—not simply Mars or Pluto. The new perception of *world* is intergalactic. And the range of meanings has become an intergalactic pluralism.

This trend toward theological pluralism has had an important influence on the local church. To be sure, the Christian church has always had a significant degree of theological pluralism, and appropriately so, including:

1. a strong (though not necessarily complete) consensus on the central issues and questions to be discussed
2. significant divergence of opinion over the solutions, but generally within a reasonable range of parameters
3. a creative dialogue on the life and work of the church.

But much of this century has seen the emergence of a theological pluralization, wherein there is little (if any) prevailing consensus on even the central issues and questions to be discussed. This pluralization has rapidly occurred because of:

1. the breakdown of earlier understandings in giving value and significance, purpose and understanding to life.
2. the vastness of the emerging view of the universe—exponentially more extensive than ever before in the history of humankind

Precisely because of this theological pluralization, the religious structures no longer provide the integrative frame of reference for society in modern technological cultures.

As a result, modern society in America constructed an alternative meaning structure of a "civil religion" to perform the integrative function. This civil religion formed a national understanding (for some) that gave meaning and purpose to everyday, ordinary life. For a time, the "integrative vacuum" created by the emergence of theological pluralization was filled by the development of this civil religion. But this so-called civil religion, as a national consensus, has collapsed.

THE CONSEQUENCES

The search for meaning and purpose in everyday, ordinary life and the related emerging trend of theological pluralism have yielded four principal consequences.

COLLAPSE OF LOCAL CONSENSUS

First, local consensus has collapsed. By "collapse," I mean that most of the understandings that made sense of everyday, ordinary life in agrarian and industrial civilizations have suddenly lost their force, have become ineffectual. Any theological effort to shore up those older understandings *will not work*.

Furthermore, I want to emphasize that this collapse is the collapse of a *local* consensus. Our plight is more precarious than the collapse of a national consensus. To be sure, there was an effort to discover a civil religion that would constitute the option of a national consensus beyond the options of a prior time. But that effort toward a civil religion did not hold sway in many elements of this country. Indeed, its contribution was precarious and fragile. But if that national civil religion were the only meaning construct that had collapsed, that would have placed us in a somewhat less serious predicament.

What has collapsed is any *local* consensus as to the meaning and purpose of everyday, ordinary life. By local, I mean *your* town. Gone is any "local consensus" on the meaning and purpose of everyday, ordinary life in most communities.

Pastors no longer go to a town in which there is local consensus. It is no longer like Grover's Corners, Our Town. Not even Grover's Corners can run from what is happening in our galaxy and the galaxies beyond. In the remotest corners of the planet it is no longer possible to live in a simple, homogeneous culture where there is a shared theological consensus.

Some people have said, "Even though there is no longer a national consensus, at least in our community, in our town, we have a consensus as to the meaning and purpose of everyday, ordinary life. We have a sense of goals and values that we hold in common. We have a common shared vision of the future." Today, that local consensus has collapsed.

And that is an excellent thing to have happened. The earlier theological understandings cannot make sense of everyday, ordinary life in the light of the gospel *in our time*. Any effort to take a theological understanding that helped in a past time and bring it over to this time is doing a patchwork job that finally will not work. It is like patching an old tire that is already well worn with many patches, when what is needed is a new vehicle.

Every age generates the theological understanding that helps make sense of that age and time. It will not help to continue to wrestle with the issues of an agrarian or industrial civilization. Significantly, we want to wrestle with the issues in a technological, intergalactic civilization. New issues will invite new theological workings.

TENDENCY TO POLARIZATION

The second consequence of the emerging trend of theological pluralism is that the trend toward theological pluralism became, in many circles, a battleground of theological polarization.

In theological pluralism, there is some modest consensus as to the central issues and questions. The debate centers on the appropriate, alternative answers. Even in the heat of the debate, there is a fabric of cohesiveness present, provided by agreement on the parameters of the central issues and questions. But when even that shred of cohesiveness collapses, many persons head to the "land of theological polarization" for refuge. That is, they seize on one set of issues and related answers and rigidly, inflexibly, and stubbornly cling to that specific understanding as the only reliable and certain understanding available.

This tendency to theological polarization is understandable. People have a foundational search for meaning. The more uncertain the times, the less clear any local consensus, the more complex and confusing life seems to be, and the vaster and broader the range of options, the more rigid and fixed some people become in insisting that their precise view is the only view that will make sense of everyday, ordinary life.

DRIVE TOWARD CONFORMITY

The third consequence is that this tendency to polarization frequently becomes a drive toward conformity. The person or persons who have agreed on a rigid, inflexible view of life now insist that all persons in the grouping view life exactly the same way. Conformity comes to mean agreement not simply on the central issues and questions but on the specific "right answers."

And some persons, threatened by alienation from the grouping, conform. Some do so in their desperation to have some meaning and purpose in life. Even as they innately sense that the view is inadequate for the times, some cling to the conformity because it is all they can see for the moment.

But this drive toward conformity is insidious and defeats creativity. It prevents persons from exercising their own creativity, imagination, and resources to discover new meanings for the present time.

The drive toward conformity is shameful. It pits person against person—all in the name of religion. Some pastors have been known to "lay on their own view pretty thick."

Finally, the drive toward conformity is silly. It is foolishness. Even those who shout the loudest innately sense that their narrow, rigid perspective will not last, that it is like a carefully built snowman that will eventually melt away on a very warm day.

DISCOVERY OF NEW MEANINGS

Fortunately, it is precisely the silliness of the drive toward conformity that makes transparent the foolishness of any narrow, rigid perspective. This revelation frequently becomes the occasion for the discovery of new meanings for the present time.

To be sure, there is sometimes the tendency for a "new meaning" to be universalized, that is, to declare that this newfound understanding is applicable for all time. No, it is helpful for *this* time.

Theology is always done both over against some other understanding persistent at the time and in relation to the current search for meaning and purpose. The discoveries of this theologizing have value *for now*. Any effort to absolutize and universalize a specific perspective must be resisted.

Frankly, the art is to encourage persons to think, wrestle, and puzzle—constructively and creatively—as to what new meaning is becoming helpful to them. The more persons are actively and creatively wrestling with both the issues and possible alternatives, the more likely that some new constructive meanings will be discovered—for this time.

It thus becomes decisive for the missionary pastor to participate intentionally in creating a new theological direction. Note that the word is *direction,* not *solution.* What is needed is a way forward, not a tidy, narrow solution. The missionary pastor helps persons to discover the central meaning and value issues *for this time.* And it is precisely the missionary pastor who advances the discussion as to the meaning and value alternatives that would be helpful.

Note further that it is the missionary pastor who helps the local church to discover:

1. what our specific mission tasks in the world are
2. what our central convictions about everyday, ordinary life are, in the light of the gospel
3. who we *now* are, on a mission field

This is the proper order. Theology is never done in a vacuum. We do not think through deductively who we are, then our convictions, and then our mission.

We *discover* our theology as we engage in specific mission tasks in the world. The theologians most helpful to the theological task are missionary pastors, who discover their theology in the heat of the battle. The discovery of new meanings can best be advanced as missionary pastors and missionary leaders move forward in mission.

10. The Search for Hope

CENTRAL LEADERSHIP TASK: MISSION

The missionary pastor's fourth task, in a missional way, is to launch and lead intentional missional groupings to meet specific, concrete human hurts and hopes—both societal and individual—in the world.

MEMORY AND HOPE

Where are we headed? What kind of future are we building? The fourth foundational search in this life's pilgrimage is the search for hope. Hope is stronger than memory. Memory is strong. Hope is stronger. People live on hope, not on memory. Take away a person's memories, and they become anxious. Take away a person's hopes, and they become terrified.

When people cannot see the realization of *some* of their hopes in the present or immediate future, they postpone their hopes to the distant future. People search for hope more than they do for memory.

Four dynamics contribute to the behavior of any person or any grouping. They are the dynamics of:

- memory
- change
- conflict
- hope

Any present moment in the life of an individual, a grouping, an institution, or a local church can be understood as these four dynamics impinge upon and live themselves out in that present moment. A full discussion of these four dynamics, especially of hope, may be found in *Twelve Keys to an Effective Church: The Leaders' Guide*, pp. 107–21.

Present and Immediate Future

If people cannot see *some* of their hopes for a reasonably stable and reliable future being realized in the present or immediate future, they will postpone their hopes down the road to the distant future. And if they cannot foresee some of their hopes being realized in the distant future, they will postpone their hopes down the road to the "next life" future. The art of being a missionary pastor in our time is to help persons who have postponed their hopes to the next-life future discover the realization of some of their hopes in the present and in the immediate and distant future.

I remember Mrs. Lott. She said to me as we were standing on the porch of her church, "Kennon, I make every decision I make on the basis of whether it will help me to be a part of God's kingdom or not." This is not a past-based orientation to behavior. This is a future-based orientation to behavior. She is living in the present and looking forward to the future.

In quiet, desperate ways, or in ways that are painful and nostalgic or abrupt and eruptive, people search for some sense of hope in this life's pilgrimage. To be sure, some search for hope in the fleeting flimsies of this world. Some search for hope in religion. Religion *is* the last fortress of the cynic. Beyond that, there is only emptiness, loneliness, and death. The search for hope is a desperate search.

Stable and Reliable Future

What we search for is a sense of hope that is stable and reliable, not fleeting and fragile.

People do not expect their future to be *always* stable and reliable. Most people want an "almost" reliable, stable future—that is, now and then having flexible stability and reliability. All sorts of events change, modify, and reshape the future. People know this reality.

People also know the old philosophical dialogue between Heraclitus and Parmenides: "Nothing is constant; everything changes," and the response, "Yes, but the constancy is change itself." People want just enough of a sense of stability and reliability that they can get through today, the coming week, the coming month, and maybe the coming year.

In this life's pilgrimage, people's search for hope is a yearning and longing for *some* of their hopes to be fulfilled. People are realistic about their hopes. Oh, people occasionally romanticize the fulfillment of *all* their hopes. But most people have had enough of their hopes dashed, destroyed, and betrayed to be realistic about their hopes.

Most people have just enough gentle cynicism to be realistic. Be at peace about cynicism. Cynicism and hope are good friends. Cynicism helps hope to be realistic. Cynicism without hope becomes despair. People yearn for the fulfillment of *some* of their hopes.

Two things are true about God's kingdom:

1. The kingdom is now here, now there.
2. The kingdom is not yet in its fullness.

The kingdom is now here, now there, in every event of reconciliation, wholeness, caring, and justice. There, the kingdom happens. And the kingdom is not yet in its fullness.

When people focus on the "not-yet" nature of the kingdom, they tend to focus their hopes only on the other side of the river. Those people who focus on the this-worldly understanding of the kingdom, that it is now here, now there, tend not to anticipate the kingdom in its fullness. It is "both/and," not either/or. The kingdom is indeed now here, now there, in the present, in the immediate future, and in the distant future. And the kingdom is not yet in its fullness. We live in hope—the kingdom has come and also is coming in its fullness.

The missionary pastor helps people envision the realization of some (not all) of their deepest longings, yearnings, and hopes in the present and the immediate future. The task is not so much a matter of dragging people into the present out of a past to which they are clinging and clutching. The task is more to help them discover some sense of a stable and reliable future.

THE TREND TOWARD SOCIETAL SPECIALIZATION

Societal specialization is the emerging trend of our time that reflects a profound search for hope. Societal specialization is the process whereby the culture increases the range of options available to persons for their future.

SPHERES OF THE CULTURE

Societal specialization has increased and is increasing, even more rapidly, the range of resources available to persons in the following spheres of the culture:

1. family
2. educational
3. vocational and economic
4. political
5. civic and community
6. recreational
7. religious

And the ground swell that drives societal specialization is the foundational search for hope. The search for a yet more stable and reliable future fuels the trend of societal specialization.

There is a sense in which a culture (or society) sometimes seems as though it has a life of its own. That is, the society cannot be described as simply a collection of the subcultural groupings. The whole has a dynamic that is distinct from the parts. At times, it seems as though the culture, by its societal specialization, is seeking to provide a place wherein all people can live out their best gifts.

One should not be naive about this. There is considerable disenfranchisement in most cultures. There are the haves and the many, many have-nots. There are petty distinctions, and there are powerful caste systems. But sometimes it seems as if the soul of the culture works to tear down such barriers as it tries to provide more possibilities for all people.

EDUCATION: AN EXAMPLE

In some cultures, there was a time when the few children who were educated were educated within the family. Then came a time when many children went to a one-room schoolhouse and maybe completed fifth grade. Consider the vast array of educational resources that the culture has generated now: preschool, kindergarten, elementary and intermediate school, middle school, high school, college, vocational schools, technological schools, graduate schools, postgraduate schools, and continuing education.

What is at stake? The culture is specializing itself in order to deliver more options for the futures of the people in the culture. What drives the creation of such a vast array of educational resources is a search for hope, a search for a reasonably stable and reliable future.

To be sure, considerable numbers of persons do not have full access to all of these resources. Some of these resources are spread unevenly in different regions of the country. And even then, there is an unevenness of opportunity yet to be corrected. At the same time, the educational sphere of the culture has been increasingly specialized with an array of possibilities far greater than what was available a hundred years ago, or even forty years ago.

The same is true in the economic sphere of the culture. A hundred years ago the list of the vocations in this country was much shorter and simpler than the volumes of occupational code classifications for all of the vocations that are currently being practiced in this country. The same could be said for each sphere of the culture. Each has expanded and become increasingly specialized.

THE VALUE: AN ACCELERATION OF POSSIBILITIES

In the years to come, there will be an enormous expansion of the possibilities whereby people can maximize their own best gifts and competencies. This is the principle value of the trend toward societal specialization. The present available possibilities are beyond the wildest imaginings of our great-grandparents. What will be available in the future will expand exponentially.

The hook is that there has developed a gap between those who can afford the necessary educational training and those who cannot. And a further consideration could be raised as to whether the basic educational system is providing the necessary foundational skills and competencies so that persons are in a position to move on to do advanced training for the possibilities available.

The biblical principle is that there is a diversity of gifts. Each person has been given distinctive gifts and competencies. The church and the culture are called upon to "open wide the doors" so that all persons can develop their competencies to the fullest.

The biblical principle should *not* be used as an excuse for a widening of the chasm. With a benign passiveness, some have almost come to the position of saying, "Well, some are given greater competencies than others—the others will have to do the best they can." People are gifted with *distinctive* competencies, not greater or lesser. The art is to help people discover and maximize what they do best.

The acceleration of possibilities, therefore, has the value of providing more options for persons, in all spheres of the culture. As people exercise the options that best live out their gifts and competencies, they are then able to feel a sense of fulfillment of some of their deepest yearnings, longings, and hopes. They are able to create a reasonably stable and reliable future.

THE CONSEQUENCES

COMPARTMENTALIZATION AND ALIENATION

The first consequence of societal specialization is the compartmentalization of the culture into separate, distinct spheres and the subsequent alienation of each sphere from the other spheres. The various spheres of the society—family, educational, economic, political, social, recreational, and religious—become cut off from one another.

In a much earlier time, the following diagram might have illustrated the relationship of the several spheres of a society:

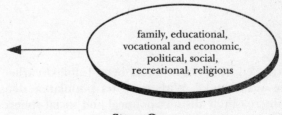

family, educational,
vocational and economic,
political, social,
recreational, religious

Stage One

That is, on the frontier, the family unit, geographically separated by days from the nearest other families, tended to fulfill all spheres of the society.

As time passed and the population density increased, a more distinctive set of relationships emerged in terms of societal spheres.

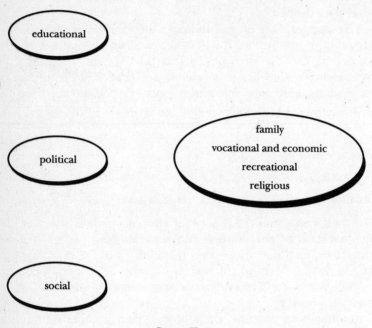

Stage Two

Whereas the educational task had been fulfilled earlier at home, now there was a school. With a greater population density, there emerged increasingly distinct political and social spheres.

As the trend of societal specialization continued, the various spheres of the society became further and further separated.

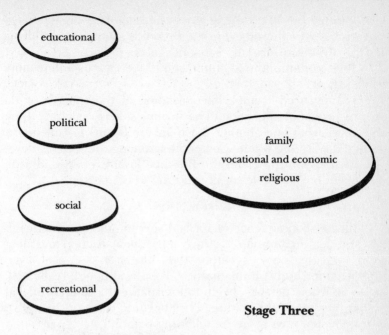

Stage Three

Ultimately, society reached a fourth stage.

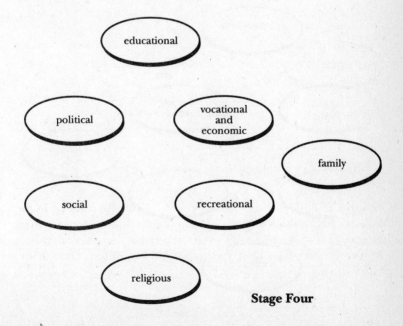

Stage Four

What started out like a single planet in Stage One became more like a solar system (Stage Two) and then a galaxy (Stage Three) and finally seven virtually separate galaxies (Stage Four), with very little communication, interaction, overlap, or interchange among them.

This "advanced" compartmentalization of the spheres of the culture results in alienation. The various spheres begin to function apart from one another. Each sphere begins to function as though it were the whole. Competition among the spheres develops, each seeking to claim the full-time loyalty, energy, and development of the whole society and the whole person.

FRAGMENTATION AND DEHUMANIZATION

The further consequence of societal specialization is fragmentation and dehumanization. As the compartmentalization and alienation increase, persons within the culture experience severe fragmentation and dehumanization. People, although really seeking to be whole persons, begin to internalize the compartmentalization they see in the culture. They begin to think of themselves in fragmented ways as in the following diagram.

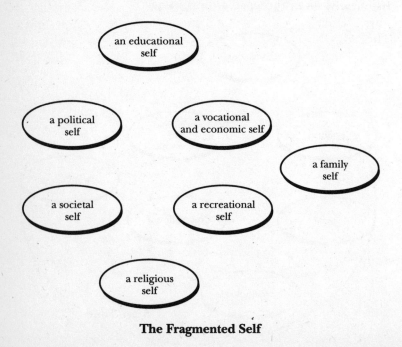

The Fragmented Self

The more fully a person internalizes the culture's compartmentalization and fragmentation, the more fully the person experiences alienation within the self and dehumanization of the self.

The foundational search for individuality is a search to be a "whole person." The search for community is a search to belong as a whole person in a whole community. Experiencing fragmentation, however, the person feels less human. To be human is to be whole. To be compartmentalized and fragmentalized is to experience dehumanization.

THE ISOLATION OF THE CHURCH

The third consequence of societal specialization is the isolation of the church from the rest of the culture. **The church becomes the ghetto where God lives.** As the various spheres of the culture become separate entities, each becomes preoccupied with its own direction and future, its own growth and development, and its own resources and needs. Hence, the ghettoization of the culture moves forward.

The religious sphere is left to fend for itself. Some are delighted with this development. They have always wanted to "protect" the church from the contamination of the world. They have always wanted to create a "miniculture" *inside* the religious sphere. Their view of the best arrangement would be the following:

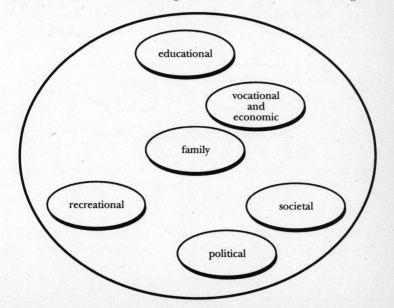

The Isolated Religious Sphere

That is, virtually all of life would be lived *inside* the safety and security of the church. No, God calls the church to be *in the center* of people's lives, not *to be the center* of their lives.

Others, sensing quite clearly the ghettoization of the church, take yet another tact. They recognize the compartmentalization and fragmentation, the alienation and dehumanization. Their proposal is not to withdraw from the world into the religious sphere but to declare that the religious sphere is the most important—"the highest" of the spheres. Their view of the best arrangement would be as follows:

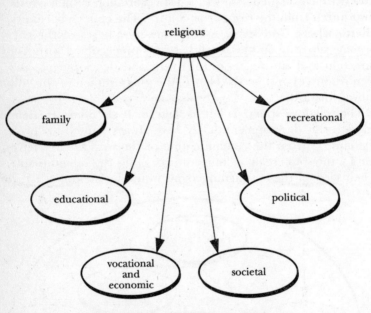

The Hierarchical Religious Sphere

Neither of the above proposals constitutes an adequate solution. The first denies the world. The text does not say, "For God so loved the church." Rather, it declares, "For God so loved the world."

The second proposal denies the church. When the church is "master," it is no longer the church. The church is called to be servant, not master. The church is called to mission, not mastery. It should be *in* the world, not *above* the world. The church is called, not to be an end in itself, but to help persons to discover fulfillment in their search for individuality, community, meaning, and hope. Jesus said, "I am come that you might have life, and have it more abundantly."

The central leadership task for the missionary pastor is to help persons to discover some sense of hope—some sense of a stable and reliable future. This is *not* best done by drawing people into "a ghetto where God lives." In that case, the church would be creating its own compartmentalization-alienation and fragmentation-dehumanization. God calls us not to live apart from the world but to live in the world.

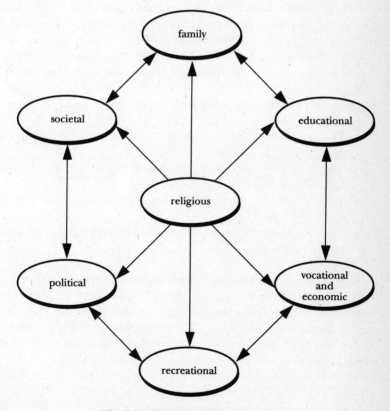

The Wholistic Religious Sphere

The task is best done as missionary pastors launch and lead intentional missional groupings that bridge the various spheres of the culture. The art is to identify a specific human hurt and hope and deliver concrete, effective help in all spheres of the culture. One thus attacks the human hurt in a wholistic way, not a compartmentalized way.

In the process, the missionary pastor helps to build bridges in all spheres of the culture. The task is not easy. Nor is it always pleasant. But one must take seriously the societal specialization that has happened already and will increasingly happen. It is no longer feasible to be a professional minister in the safety and security of a religious ghetto. We are called, in this time, to be missionary pastors.

The four foundational searches are expressed in distinctive, particular ways within each cultural and historical setting. For example, these four found a different, distinctive expression in the churched culture of the 1940s and 1950s, as compared with the ways they found expression within the depression culture of the 1930s, or in the agrarian culture of the early part of this century.

Consider the following emerging trends in our current culture:

- The search for individuality can be seen in the trend toward the dislocation of power.
- The search for community is being expressed in the trend toward cultural heterogeneity.
- The search for meaning is apparent in the trend toward theological pluralism.
- The search for hope is evidenced in the trend toward societal specialization.

We can count on these four emerging trends having an increasingly decisive impact in the culture and on the church, and being important to developing the foundations for a new understanding of the nature of leadership. This new understanding of leadership is best lived out by missionary pastors who focus on the four central leadership tasks important on this mission field.

PART FOUR.
THE HEART OF THE MATTER

11. Leadership Values

THE REAL ISSUE

Missionary pastors, as leaders, focus on the central leadership tasks important on this mission field:

1. helping persons rediscover power in their own lives and destinies
2. constructing new communities of reconciliation, wholeness, caring, and justice—in the name of Christ
3. creating a new theological direction and specific, shared purposes
4. launching and leading intentional missional teams to meet specific, concrete human hurts and hopes—both societal and individual—in the world.

The ways in which these four central leadership tasks live themselves out will vary widely, depending on:

- the missionary pastor and his or her specific competencies
- the specific mission field on which each missionary pastor serves
- the resources and competencies present in the mission outpost team serving on that mission field

The creativity and imagination, the compassion and courage, the discoveries and directions of each missionary pastor and mission team will create the best way forward on each specific mission field.

The way forward is grace and compassion, trusting missionary pastors to discover how these four central leadership tasks are achieved by them on their specific mission field. The fatal mistake would be to have someone suggest that these four central leadership tasks should be lived out in one prescribed way.

Some persons may be tempted to start drawing up lists that would require each central leadership task to be done in a certain way. Then we would be headed to legalism and law.

The issue is *not* whether missionary pastors can figure out how to do these central leadership tasks. They can—and they are doing so. Missionary pastors—many have already emerged and many, many more are emerging—have the competencies to figure out the specific how-tos.

The *real* issue is:

- What can pastors do to grow forward their leadership competencies as missionary pastors?

The need for our time is missionary pastors, not professional ministers. Missionary pastors can grow themselves forward by cultivating *new understandings* and *new practices* in:

1. leadership values
2. leadership environment
3. constructive perspective
4. evaluation process
5. leadership structures
6. missional structures
7. church development

Likewise, local churches can grow forward their own new understandings, practices, and behavior patterns in these areas. Denominational leaders and denominations as a whole can advance their understanding, behavior patterns, values, and objectives in these areas. Working together, much progress will be achieved.

A word of counsel. Begin where you are. Begin with what you can achieve. *Focus on whichever of the seven areas you can best grow forward now.*

These areas are best grown forward among the grass roots, not from the top down. Do not wait on your denomination. You would put yourself in a passive, reactive stance. Put yourself in a proactive, constructive stance. Discover three to five persons who have common longings with you and complementary competencies. Grow and develop together.

LEADERSHIP IS LEARNED, NOT TAUGHT

A LEARNED COMPETENCY

Leaders learn to be leaders. People are not born leaders. Leadership is not a matter of genes or heredity, size or stature. Leaders are not manufactured, the product of some neat and nifty methodology. Leaders do not "pull themselves up by their own boot straps," as though the stuff of leadership was innately within them.

People learn to be leaders. Leadership is learned. Leadership cannot be taught. The opportunity and possibilities are *within* the person who seeks to develop his or her own leadership competencies. Mentors help. Teachers and resource persons will contribute greatly.

But all of the efforts to "teach" leadership come to naught, not because there are not excellent teachers involved, but because the focus is on what the teacher is teaching the person, rather than on what the person is proactively learning. You are the person who can learn leadership. You are the person who can best grow forward your leadership competencies as a missionary pastor.

DISTINCTIVE EXPRESSIONS

People express their leadership competencies in distinctive ways. Some have the myth that the only "real" expression of leadership is that of the hard-driving, forever-charging, quick-decision commander. It is not helpful to stereotype the nature of leadership into any one single narrow expression of leadership.

There are at least four distinctive ways in which missionary pastors express their leadership competencies:

- a leading-caring manner
- a supportive-giving spirit
- an analytical-diagnostic way
- a relational-motivational spirit

Each of these ways is a distinctive expression of leadership competencies.

LEADERS AND THE GROUPING

There is a sense in which leadership is a gift from the grouping to the leader. In an intriguing, dynamic way, three things are true:

1. Leadership is the art of helping the grouping to discover fulfillment in life's foundational searches.
2. Leaders learn to be leaders.
3. Leadership is a gift of the grouping.

Missionary pastors learn to be leaders in a grouping. There is no such thing as a leader without a grouping, just as there is no choral director without a choir or quarterback without a team or concertmaster without an orchestra. Leaders are not leaders in a vacuum. There is a dynamic relationship between a leader and a grouping.

The grouping senses the leader can help the grouping toward the discovery of fulfillment in its foundational searches. The grouping "confers" upon the leader the gift of leadership, sometimes unexpectedly. The leader claims, nurtures, and develops his or her leadership competencies in the context of the grouping. The leader and grouping grow forward together in mutual ways.

LEADERSHIP VALUES

GROUPINGS AND LEADERSHIP VALUES

All groupings develop a set of values as to what constitutes the nature of leadership. Whether it is a local church, an annual conference, a denomination, or any other organization, all groupings select, develop, and reinforce a specific set of leadership values.

As we discussed earlier, any grouping, in order to be a grouping, develops:

- a goals and values system
- a set of customs, habits, and traditions
- a language and communications network
- a leadership values set and decision-making process
- sacred places of meeting
- a common, shared vision of the future

All of these resources enable a grouping to develop the following positive values:

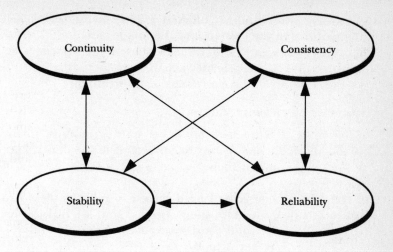

Thus, the grouping survives and thrives; it has sufficient "glue" and cohesiveness to continue as a grouping.

It is imperative that a grouping develop and reinforce a specific set of leadership values. If an organization does not *consistently* do so, the results look like this:

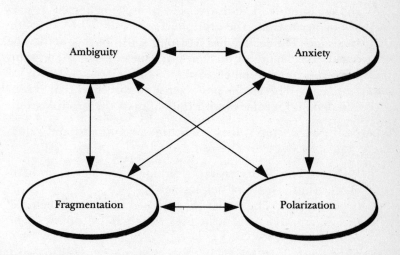

The lack of a consistently reinforced leadership values set will eventually threaten the existence of the organization.

It is precisely this leadership values set describing what a leader "looks like"—that is, how a leader behaves *as leader*—that contributes to the certainty and cohesiveness of the grouping.

Two Sets of Leadership Values

Over the years, I have discovered that most groupings finally adopt and reinforce one of two major sets of leadership values. Again and again, one of these two sets is persistently present in a given grouping.

For the sake of simplicity, I have chosen to refer to these two distinctive sets of leadership values as set A and set B. In order to maintain continuity and consistency, each organization develops and reinforces either A or B.

Each has a specific set of values as to what leadership "looks like." Each values a certain set of behavior patterns as to what constitutes a leader. In leadership values set A, the leader is:

1. *Proactive:* The leader has an anticipatory, forward-moving spirit of action. The leader is not simply active in a busy way.
2. *Relational:* The leader has a genuine sense of compassion and community. The leader sees himself or herself as part of, not apart from, the grouping.
3. *Missional:* The leader has a strong sense of mission in the world. That sense of mission gives meaning to the leader's work and the grouping's work.
4. *Intentional:* The leader has a sense of direction that is self-initiated and resonates with the hopes of the grouping.

Whereas in leadership values set B, the assumptions and values are:

1. *Reactive:* The leader reacts to situations that arise and frequently has a sense of helplessness.
2. *Organizational:* The leader is concerned for the well-being of the organization—its structures, committees, policies, and procedures.
3. *Institutional:* The leader has a very strong sense of concern for the survival of the institution.

4. *Passive:* The leader is primarily responsive and does what is needful, as occasions arise.

I am indebted to the following sources for helping me come to this understanding:

- research, interviews, and studies with many local churches, adjudicatory groupings, and organizations
- experience as a pastor, professor, and consultant
- research and insight from McGregor and from Waterman and Peters

The research of both Bob Waterman and Tom Peters is more recently known and available. I commend to you their emphasis on people, service, and quality.

It will be helpful to note the earlier contribution of Douglas McGregor in *The Human Side of Enterprise* (New York: McGraw-Hill, 1960). McGregor's research led him to conclude that all organizations make one of two sets of assumptions about human nature and human behavior and that underlying each organization's policies and procedures is its commitment to what McGregor calls Theory X or Theory Y.

Theory X makes the following assumptions about human nature and human behavior:

1. The average human being has an inherent dislike of work and will avoid it if he can.
2. Most people must be coerced, controlled, directed, threatened with punishment to get them to put forth adequate effort toward the achievement of organizational objectives.
3. The average human being prefers to be directed, wishes to avoid responsibility, has relatively little ambition, wants security above all (pp. 33–35).

Theory Y makes the following assumptions:

1. The expenditure of physical and mental effort in work is as natural as play or rest.
2. Man will exercise self-direction and self-control in the service of objectives to which he is committed.
3. Commitment to objectives is a function of the rewards associated with their achievement.

4. The average human being learns, under proper conditions, not only to accept but to seek responsibility.
5. The capacity to exercise a relatively high degree of imagination, ingenuity, and creativity in the solution of organizational problems is widely, not narrowly, distributed in the population.
6. Under the conditions of modern industrial life, the intellectual potentialities of the average human being are only partially utilized (pp. 45–49).

I find his work helpful as a way of understanding that organizations do, in fact, make certain assumptions about human nature and human behavior. Local churches and denominations certainly do.

Think of recruiting volunteers in local churches. Now read again the assumptions of a Theory X organization. You will have just read the set of assumptions upon which many local churches attempt to recruit volunteers.

Think of giving financially to the work and mission of the church. When you read the Theory X assumptions again, you will be reading the set of assumptions upon which many stewardship and finance campaigns are run.

Think of the personnel policies some churches have. Read again Theory X. You will have just read the set of assumptions upon which many personnel policies are based.

More often than not, a given local church, in order to have continuity, consistency, and cohesiveness, will do its recruiting, try to raise its money, and develop its personnel policies on the basis of the same set of assumptions about human nature and human behavior.

I see a definite correlation between my leadership values set A and McGregor's Theory Y. Likewise, there is a correlation between my set B and McGregor's Theory X. McGregor's work early on intrigued me. I began to research more fully, therefore, the values of leadership that groupings tend to select, develop, and reinforce. In a focused way, I was interested in discovering the set of values each grouping had in terms of what a leader looks like—that is, the values set as to how a leader behaves *as leader*. With considerable frequency, I discovered that leadership values sets A and B were present, one values set in one grouping, the other values set in another grouping.

LEADERSHIP VALUES SET A

People learn leadership best in a grouping or organization with leadership values set A, not set B. Note that individual leaders may behave sometimes in an A pattern of leadership, and sometimes in a B pattern of leadership. Leaders, as individual persons, will vary their behavior. But an organization, in order to maintain continuity, consistency, and cohesiveness, must continually reinforce and reward a consistent set of values as to the nature of leadership.

You can visualize this contrast best on a spectrum.

A	B
Proactive	Reactive
Relational	Organizational
Intentional	Passive
Missional	Institutional

It is important to distinguish between the ways in which *individuals* behave and the way the *organization* reinforces and rewards its understanding of the nature of leadership.

All organizations choose to be either at the A point on the spectrum or at the B point. It is important that the organization has clarity as to the values of leadership it endorses, develops, and reinforces. Only in this way can the organization have a sense of continuity, consistency, and cohesiveness.

Someone may be tempted to propose a middle ground—call it C—as a compromise understanding located somewhere in the middle of the spectrum. Such a proposal would miss the point. Individual leaders will be both proactive and reactive, relational and organizational, and so forth. But the organization, *as a whole*, cannot give "mixed messages" as to the nature and values of leadership. The organization cannot provide consistency, continuity, and cohesiveness if it is based upon some compromised amalgamation.

IMMEDIATE IMPLICATIONS

Groupings that have adopted leadership values set A have these characteristics:

1. *Proactive:* A strong sense of self-directed, self-initiated action, with power and authority, exists in the grouping.
2. *Relational:* There is a genuine spirit of compassion in the grouping.
3. *Missional:* A solid sense exists of common, shared meanings as to the purpose of life.
4. *Intentional:* There is a high level of creativity and hope.

Whereas, in groupings that have adopted leadership values set B, the qualities are:

1. *Reactive:* There is considerable passive-aggressive behavior in the grouping.
2. *Institutional:* The amount of subliminal resentment toward the organization is strong.
3. *Organizational:* Low-grade hostility is persistently present.
4. *Passive:* There is a pattern of displaced anger and despair.

In B groupings, the motto of leadership is, Go along to get along. Sometimes the motto is simply, Don't rock the boat.

RESULTING IMPLICATIONS

There are two important, resulting implications. First, on a mission field, it is decisive that together we nurture forward leadership values set A. This set of values as to the nature of leadership will be *most helpful* to you as you develop your competencies as a missionary pastor. This values set will be most helpful to the functioning of your mission team.

In a churched culture, a local church could "get along with" a focus on set B. With persons seeking out churches on their own initiative, professional ministers and local churches could fall back on values set B. No more.

Second, on a mission field, persons are drawn primarily to groupings that live out of leadership values set A. This set of values resonates best with their own foundational life searches. One way of illustrating this correlation is as follows:

Leadership values set A	Foundational life searches	Leadership values set B
Proactive ⟷	Individuality	Reactive
Relational ⟷	Community	Organizational
Missional ⟷	Meaning	Institutional
Intentional ⟷	Hope	Passive

A fuller way of illustrating this correlation, taking seriously the emerging trends of the culture, is in the following sequence of diagrams.

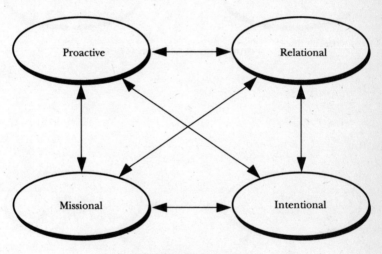

Leadership Values: Set A

People are helped best with their foundational life searches, in relation to the emerging trends in the culture, by a grouping that has selected and that reinforces and rewards leadership values set A. Thus, both unchurched persons and churched persons are drawn primarily to local churches with set A. Precisely in these

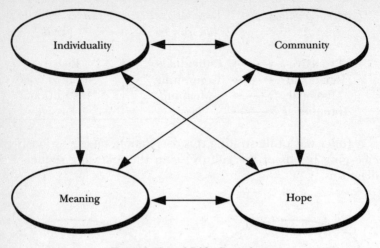

Foundational Life Searches

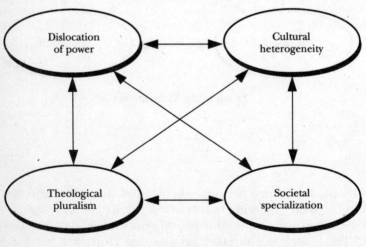

Emerging Trends

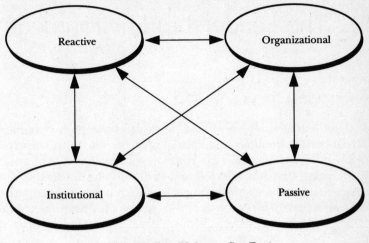

Leadership Values: Set B

mission teams persons learn best the nature of leadership important for these times.

As a missionary pastor, help your mission team to nurture leadership values set A.

12. The Leadership Environment

GROWTH AND DEVELOPMENT

People learn leadership best in a leadership environment wherein certain qualities are actively present. The most constructive grouping in which you can develop your leadership capacities is a grouping that has selected and is developing leadership values set A and that is providing a leadership environment that encourages leadership growth and development. Both contribute strongly to helping persons advance their leadership competencies.

The best environment for leadership development includes these features:

- objectives
- authority
- decision making
- continuity
- competency
- compassion
- local development

When only one or two of these qualities are present in a local church, that constitutes a *poor* environment for leadership development. When three or four qualities are present, that is a *medium* environment. When five to seven qualities are present, that constitutes an *excellent* environment.

In a sense, these qualities are the soil in which persons nurture forward their leadership competencies. The "richer" the soil, the more likely that grouping is to cultivate excellent leaders.

For a moment, think of three groupings or organizations (a local church, a denomination, or any other grouping). You will find it both intriguing and fun to assess which of these "environmental" qualities is richly present in each of the three.

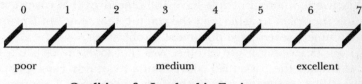

Qualities of a Leadership Environment

OBJECTIVES

People learn leadership best in a leadership environment of objectives, not activities. In an environment of objectives, people learn a sense of intentionality and direction. In an environment of activities, people learn busyness and fragmentation.

It is not the case that the more activities a person has, the better the leader he or she becomes. The more activities people have, the tireder and more confused they become.

On a mission field, we will have our fair share of despair, depression, and despondency. Some people seek to cope by engaging in a flurry of activities. Some persons sense the decline of their church and imagine that a busier and more plentiful set of activities will stem the tide.

The more activities an organization has, the fewer leaders the grouping will produce. The faster the merry-go-round, the fewer the leaders. What will help is to grow a new understanding of leadership that focuses more on objectives and accomplishments, and less on activities and busyness.

In the busyness of activities, people learn to focus on quick closure, immediate satisfaction, and short-term results. They lose sight of what is important and focus on what is urgent. They develop a poor pattern of leadership behavior.

The development of a few key, major objectives helps the person to learn a leadership behavior pattern that is:

- intentional
- directional

- anticipatory
- forward-moving

I am not, therefore advocating a narrow, strict "management by objectives," wherein people have 168 objectives that cover everything they plan to achieve in the coming year. Nor am I proposing a ninety-seven-page document of objectives.

I am describing a use of objectives that looks more like a fast break down the basketball court than a neat, tidy game plan for everything you plan to do in the coming year. Yes, I am encouraging you to give up the three walls of newsprint or butcher paper on which you have listed everything you almost thought about doing in the coming year.

Develop two to four key, major objectives that are important to your missionary work. These will help you to grow forward your leadership competencies. Elsewhere in the book, I discuss the criteria for an excellent key objective and the ways in which these two to four key, major objectives can help you to evaluate your leadership growth and development. The important point here is that people learn to be leaders best in a leadership environment of objectives.

As a missionary pastor, develop your key, major objectives. Help your local church to develop its key, major objectives for mission.

AUTHORITY

People learn leadership best in an environment wherein there is a high delegation of authority, not responsibilities. People do *not* learn leadership in an environment of responsibilities. They learn passive behavior there, not leadership.

Two principles will help. First, the greater the range of authority, the more likely the level of leadership competencies is to grow. The more fully persons are given authority, the more likely they are to develop their leadership competencies.

A person who has been given a range of authority of 8 is more likely to expand their leadership competencies to an 8, rather than a 3. A person whose authority range has been limited to a 3 is more likely to develop their competencies only to the level of a 3.

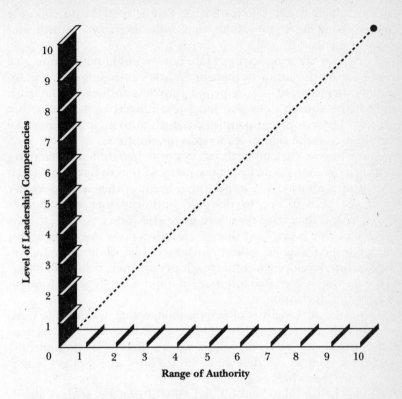

People develop their competencies in direct relation to the authority that has been delegated to them, not the responsibilities they have been asked to take. In any organization, the higher the delegation of authority, the higher the level of competencies *and* the more leaders the organization helps to nurture forward.

Second, the higher the level of competencies, the more critical the range of authority. A person whose range of competencies is an 8 but who is given a range of authority of a 3 will be lost by the organization. It is decisively crucial to provide persons with an authority range that, at a bare minimum, is commensurate with their current competencies.

The church is particularly good at *not* doing that. One of the pivotal reasons the church loses competent leaders daily is because it is perfectly willing to give them a multiplicity of responsibilities but virtually no authority. People tend *not* to continue participating in organizations that stifle their own growth and development.

I can hear someone saying, "Oh, but we would not want to give someone more authority than he or she can handle." Is the solution, therefore, to be sure people have less authority? The truth is that the church does not delegate authority well. Would that its mistake were giving people too much authority. That mistake would err on the side of leadership development.

But while we remember the several who had difficulty handling authority, we too easily forget the many who were not given a rich range of authority. We forget them because they are no longer with us. Our failure to delegate authority was stifling their growth, and they have therefore gone elsewhere.

One of the "worst best things" churches do is to give people a list of responsibilities without authority. The whole approach to leadership development is to "teach people their responsibilities." That is the regrettable premise of most church workshops in leadership development.

Consider the long lists of responsibilities that are given to leaders of local churches in the "fading denominations." In meticulous detail, every conceivable responsibility is thoughtfully included. And as the denomination declines, the lists get longer and more overwhelming.

It may be useful to back off and ask—after many years of handing out responsibility lists to local church leaders, with a continuing denominational decline—why is this procedure of leadership development not helping? It is not helping because it does not deliver authority.

Authority yields action. Responsibilities yield complacency. Authority grows leaders. Responsibilities grow passive behavior. Finally, one has to decide. To be sure, there are trade-offs both ways. One can be generous with authority and know:

1. Such an environment will nurture leaders.
2. Such an environment will run the risk that some may not handle well the authority delegated to them.

Or one can focus primarily on responsibilities and know:

1. Such an environment will nurture passive behavior.
2. In such an environment, there will be very little risk that someone might not handle authority well.

The point is that **more authority and fewer responsibilities help persons grow forward their leadership; less authority and more responsibilities help persons develop passive behavior.** High authority is better than high pressure. The sin of the church is that it cajoles and pressures persons into accepting responsibilities but then does not delegate sufficient authority.

We would do a better job of leadership development if we:

1. Help people to discover the two to four key, major objectives for the coming year that match their specific competencies.
2. Give them ample authority in leadership, decision making, and budget to achieve their objectives.

To do them one further favor, we would hide from them any long list of responsibilities. Some things will not get done, but more persons will develop themselves as excellent leaders.

As a missionary pastor, help your local church claim and develop its sharing of authority. Delegate authority well. The more power you give away, the more power you create—in people's lives and destinies.

DECISION MAKING

People learn leadership best in an environment where decision making is participatory and straightforward. They learn leadership worst where the decision-making environment is top-down and drawn out.

In a local church, four "levels" of decisions need to be made:

As: the specific central characteristics that a local church is planning to expand or add in the coming three years. These are the 20 percenters that deliver 80 percent of the results.

Bs: the supportive key objectives that help to expand or add a specific central characteristic. These are key objectives you plan to achieve this year.

The key prinicple for a participatory decision-making environment is this: The more people who participate in the A decisions and the fewer people who participate in the D decisions, the better the decision-making environment. Conversely, the fewer people who participate in the A decisions, and the more who participate in the D decisions, the poorer the decision-making environment.

Cs: the midrange decisions that come to your core council on a month-to-month basis.

Ds: the week-to-week decisions that help your local church move forward in incidental ways. Whether to have blue or yellow name tags at next Wednesday's covered-dish supper would be a D decision.

In a healthy decision-making environment as many persons as possible are invited to participate in the A decisions, and decreasing numbers of persons focus on B, C, and D decisions. An unhealthy participatory decision-making environment would be the reverse:

Level of decision	Participatory and healthy	Top-Down and unhealthy
A	Long-range planning committee and congregation	A few influential persons
B	Board, Council	Finance Committee
C	Task forces and work areas	Board, Council
D	Individual persons	Congregation

In many local churches, there has been an effort at "consensus decision making." But the hook has been that the focus of those decisions has been on the Cs and Ds, with the As and Bs being reserved to a top-down group. In fact, the consensus process has been used as a "front" to hide a top-down approach.

Most people in fact do not want to participate in the C and D decisions. They are happy for those to be decided by whomever. But most people do want to have some say in the 20 percenters—the A-level decisions—that affect the direction and future of the local church. When they feel blocked from the As, they develop passive behavior.

The best diagram of a participatory decision-making process would be two intersecting pyramids: one for the decisions (solid line) and one for the range of persons important to participate (dotted line).

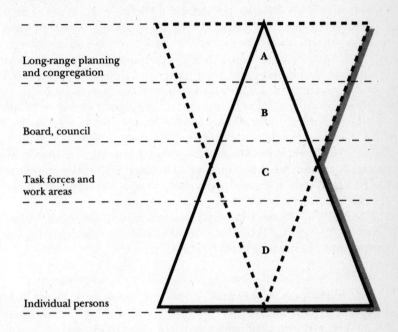

Long-range planning
and congregation

A

B

Board, council

C

Task forces and
work areas

D

Individual persons

Note that comparatively few decisions would be at the A level. In the course of a year the bulk of the decisions in an organization are Ds. The Ds are best delegated to individual persons. The more Ds handled by a board or council, the higher the level of passive behavior in a local church. The more persons who participate in the As, the higher the level of leadership development.

The key principle for a straightforward decision-making environment is this: The shorter the time frame, the better the decision-making environment. If it takes three months to make a thirty-dollar decision, we are doing damage and harm to the leadership-development environment.

One of the dilemmas in the local church is a propensity for indecision and analysis paralysis. We analyze some decisions up one side; then we analyze them down another side. We hash it and rehash it and then hash it over again. We worry some decisions to death. Committee meeting after committee meeting is consumed with this. And we seem to do this more with Cs and Ds. It is as if the smaller the decision, the more time it will take.

Three reasons contribute. The first is *avoidance*. The more time we spend on Cs and Ds, the more the grouping can avoid wrestling with the A decisions. Some groupings, particularly those that have developed a behavior pattern of dependency, use their preoccupation with Cs and Ds as an avoidance technique.

The second is a *lack of practice in the delegation of authority*. Frankly, the best thing to do when someone brings up a D-level decision is immediately to delegate that decision to whomever would make a wise decision. What usually happens, however, is a twenty-minute discussion in the grouping. The fact is that the more frequently Ds are delegated, the more frequently individuals will decide them—even before they bring them up.

Delegate all Ds and most Cs, particularly if you want to be a missionary pastor. When a D-level decision is delegated to an individual, these things will happen:

1. The person will likely make an excellent, solid decision.
2. Or the person will make a poor decision—and learn from his or her mistake.
3. The grouping will save twenty or more minutes.
4. The grouping will focus on the As and Bs.
5. The leadership-development environment will be protected and enriched.

The goal is not to see how many decisions the grouping can make. The art is how many decisions can be proactively delegated. It takes practice.

The third reason for spending too much time on lesser decisions is *a quest for "certainty."* Frankly, it is easier to be certain about C and D decisions. On a D, one can achieve a 90 percent level of certainty that blue name tags will be better than yellow ones next Wednesday night. On a C, one can achieve an 80 percent level of certainty that red choir robes will work out better than white ones. But whether to advance on a given missional objective—an A—one may achieve only a 70 percent level of certainty. Hence we stick to the Cs and Ds because the level of certainty is higher.

The hook is that the longer we avoid the As, the less certain is our future as a local church, and more importantly, the fewer leaders we are likely to develop. Thus, in a spirit of grace, not legalism, let me suggest these general rules of thumb:

- If it is an A, take 1 to 3 months to decide.
- If it is a B, take 1 to 3 weeks to decide.
- If it is a C, take 1 to 3 days to decide.
- If it is a D, take 1 minute to 1 hour to decide.

In facing any decision, then the grouping must ask:

1. What level of decision is this—A, B, C, or D?
2. What is the shortest time frame we can use to achieve a helpful decision?

Think of it as more like a fast break down the basketball court than like a carefully constructed chess match. (Even in chess matches, though, there are time limits.) Part of what you are doing is achieving a decision. Also part of what you are doing is developing leaders. People learn leadership best in a participatory, straightforward decision-making environment.

As a missionary pastor, nurture a participatory, straightforward, decision-making pattern in your own decisions and in your local church.

CONTINUITY

People learn leadership best in an environment of continuity, not discontinuity. Leadership—particularly the character and quality of leadership important on a mission field—is learned over a period of time. Three sources of continuity are helpful to leadership development.

First, there is the continuity that is delivered by having two to four long-range objectives. In most settings of mission, it is possible to develop two to four key objectives that look one year to three years ahead, or on occasion, five years. One does not need more than two to four such objectives. More is not better. Having two to four that are long range is important to one's leadership development.

To be sure, on a mission field, many of our objectives will be short term. They focus on today, this week, this month. The dynamic of a mission field, with its chaos and uncertainty, makes short-range objectives most important. It is precisely because of this chaos and uncertainty that it becomes extremely important to have two to four objectives that are long range.

In a more settled time, such as the churched culture of the late 1940s and 1950s, a principal source of continuity was delivered by the relative stability of the times. No more. These are pilgrimage times. These are wilderness times. The continuity is in the direction in which we are headed, not the settled place we have left behind.

A second source of continuity is in the team. We benefit in our leadership development in being part of a competent, compassionate team. The richness of learning and sharing, struggle and discovery, creativity and caring that such a team delivers is decisive. It is important for one to be a part of such a team for more than one to three years.

One of the problems on the current scene is the "ancient custom" of pastors moving every three to four years. It is regrettable. One could get away with that practice in a churched culture, where there was considerable continuity in the setting and in the local church. The more turbulent the times, the more turnover in the community and in the local church, the more important it is to have the pastoral continuity of a missionary pastor.

Moreover, as one lives and works with the people in a community over a period of time, one's leadership competencies grow and develop—for two reasons: First, the shepherding reason. It takes three to four years of living with a people to develop the shepherding relationships of mutual trust, respect, integrity, credibility, and confidence to emerge as a trusted leader.

Second, the learning reason. The longer one stays, the more mistakes one makes—and the greater the possibility of learning from one's mistakes. The leadership curve accelerates because the learning curve accelerates.

It was said of one pastor that he had been in the ministry for twenty years. Someone wisely pointed out that he had really been in the ministry for only four years. He had just done it in five different places. Some people do turn the barrel of sermons over every four years and simply recapitulate again what they have done before. As a result, they seldom develop their leadership competencies fully.

The third source of continuity is in the post itself. Part of the continuity comes from the two to four long-range objectives. Part of it comes from living and working with a congregation over the long haul. And part of it comes from growing and developing long-term one's understanding of the post in a given setting.

Remember the rotation principle that was in vogue thirty to forty years ago? The idea back then was that a person could be in a given leadership post for only three years and then had to rotate off. The rotation principle was implemented:

- so people would not get "burned out"
- so more people would have a turn
- to avoid having people build their own "empires"
- so there would be "fresh ideas" in the post

And the principle worked very well in the churched culture of the times because there were reasonable numbers of persons available for the posts and because these were primarily churched persons whose backgrounds in "church work" enabled them to "hit the ground running."

The rotation principle works less well on a mission field. With new Christians, the "start up" learning time in any leadership post is considerable. That is as it should be with persons new to the faith. The hook is that just about the time they are coming into their own, they are rotated off. It takes a first year to begin to get on board. It takes a second year to build the team that will help. It takes a third year to begin to deliver on the key objectives for the post. And then one is rotated off, just as one is getting going. It leaves an unfulfilling, unsatisfied sense in the person.

The better way forward—particularly if you want to develop solid leaders—is to leave them alone to do good work and to grow as leaders as long as the following five criteria hold:

1. They are accomplishing significant objectives (doing good work).
2. They are matched with their best competencies.
3. They are "growing in the work" (their leadership competencies are advancing).

4. People are satisfied with their results.
5. They work vigorously to add new people in new leadership posts.

Someone may ask whether this would prevent new people from coming on board. It makes no sense, however, to do to new people what we have been doing to current people—rotating them off before they come into their own. This is just repeating the same mistake twice. The art is to help new persons to new posts where they can develop their own leadership competencies.

But someone will still say, "Everyone should have a chance at the key posts:" Finance chair, Pastor Parish chair, trustee. Remember, though, that these are *not* the key posts on a mission field. The key posts—the real power posts, if you will—relate to the central characteristics of:

1. specific, concrete missional objectives
2. pastoral and lay visitation in the community
3. corporate, dynamic worship
4. significant relational groupings

There is considerable opportunity for new persons to develop strong leadership competencies in relation to any one of these central characteristics.

Someone may suggest that a continuity principle rather than a rotation principle runs the risk of empire building. Maybe so. But you run the risk of turning people over too frequently and therefore of having fewer leaders emerging. What helps in our time is developing an increasing range of genuinely competent leaders. And they need the continuity of a given post to develop their leadership competencies.

As for empires in a local church, they have usually been built in a leadership vacuum. Because there were not enough leaders around, one person was able to build his or her own empire. The greater the number of competent leaders, the less likely that is to continue. Would you rather build leaders or bust empires? Yes, you could invest your time in busting the empire. Sometimes that does make sense. What really helps is increasing the range of competent leaders.

To be sure, it may make sense to continue a rotation principle with a few leadership posts (e.g., chair of the administrative board, chair of the trustees). I would not disfavor that. But we need to develop a stronger principle of continuity and less of a principle of rotation. This principle of continuity is decisive for leadership development on a mission field.

As a missionary pastor, stay long enough on a specific mission field that your work benefits from substantial continuity. Develop leadership practices and sources of continuity in your local church.

COMPETENCY

People learn leadership best in an environment of competency, not willingness. When the team of persons with which one is working is competent, then one can most fully develop one's leadership abilities. It is not necessary that all of the team be extraordinarily and outstandingly competent. Such teams rarely occur. Rather, most effective mission teams have a reasonable range of complementary competencies present.

One mistake pastors make is to look for someone who is willing, not someone who will do it well. **The art is to look for someone who will do it well, not someone who is willing.** Sometimes pastors convince themselves that there is a shortage of leaders in their church, which then becomes their *excuse* for recruiting someone who is willing to do some leadership post rather than someone who would do it well. That simply makes it more difficult to recruit competent leaders.

When reasonably competent leaders see a pastor begin to bring on board "someone who is willing rather than someone who will do it well," those who are competent drift yet more fully into the background. They become harder to find and more reluctant to come on board. For each "willing" person you recruit, you may lose three competent leaders who will recede into the background.

Persons who are genuinely competent thrive on working with a team of persons who are comparably competent. They have already had their fair share of experiences of having had "to carry a team of willing persons." They have already learned that such a team appreciates their competencies but also becomes dependent on and resents their competencies.

It would be better to leave a post vacant than it would be to fill it with a "willing" person. No, somebody does not need to do that job if they are only going to do it in a mediocre way. It is unfair to them, however willing they may be, to put them into a post that does not match with their competencies. And wishful, wistful thinking on your part that it "might work" is simply temptation trying to lead you astray.

To go for quick closure—to fill a post with someone who is willing but who likely will not do it well—has severe consequences:

1. It does damage and harm to the persons who are willing. They would grow best in a post that more fully matches their own competencies.
2. It hurts the team. The team now has to "carry" a person. That slows the team down more than if the post were left empty.
3. It severely damages your ability and the team's ability to attract reasonably competent leaders. Indeed, the minute you fill the first open post with a "willing worker," in that minute you have taught competent leaders that you are less interested in competencies and more interested in "willingness."
4. You will have damaged seriously your own abilities to develop your own leadership competencies. You will advance your leadership competencies best, they will thrive and flourish most fully, with a team of competent leaders.

Yes, for purposes of leadership development it is better to have somewhat smaller teams of genuinely competent leaders than to have a larger team of primarily "willing" persons.

What I have just said should *not* become someone's excuse for elitism. That would simply be another way of creating a caste system. I am unalterably opposed to caste systems, anywhere. Rather, what I have said should be the occasion for wisdom.

The art is to help each person become part of some team—mostly, a small, working team—wherein their own competencies contribute to the team in comparable and complementary ways, and wherein their own competencies can grow and flourish. The art is to help them discover where their gifts can best be shared.

That takes the wisdom of looking long-term to grow and develop the leadership competencies of the whole team, rather than looking short-term to "fill a slot." You teach people your own level of competencies and the level of competencies to which you are willing to grow by whether you recruit to fill slots or whether you match persons to places that will expand their leadership competencies.

An intriguing thought: Some few pastors may go for the short-term, quick-closure "solution" of a willing person because of their own tendencies toward codependency. Innately they know the "willing person" is not finally a solution; it is a quick fix. And they may be content with that, because they now have yet another person on the team who will develop a pattern of dependency on them.

One does *not* become a leader by developing a larger number of dependent persons. One leads by developing a larger number of leaders. Your own leadership competencies grow best as you help others to advance their leadership competencies. **Leaders grow leaders. Leaders who grow leaders become leaders—yet more fully.** Leadership is best learned in this environment of competencies.

As a missionary pastor, grow forward your competencies. Help all people in your congregation to develop their competencies. Advance the principle, "Well, not willing."

COMPASSION

People learn leadership best in an environment of compassion, not legalism. Note that an environment of compassion counts on people to live life to their best. Compassion does not coddle or settle for second best. Compassion is strong and vigorous. Yet it is patient and kind. It plays for the long haul, not the short term. And its sense of kindness is to help persons grow forward their best competencies.

What some people call kindness is cruelty. Their passive understanding of being kind contributes to a person's becoming passive and dependent. A proactive sense of kindness may sometimes be tough, sometimes calls a spade a spade. It is a strong, vigorous, honest kindness of constructive encouragement. It is a leadership values set A form of kindness and compassion. **Leaders grow best in a coaching, not a correcting, environment.**

An environment of rules and regulations, legalism and laws best develops passive, dependent persons. Leadership values set B thrives on the development of policies and procedures, requirements and standards, penalties and punishment. The result is passive, organizational, institutional, reactive—persons who are primarily dependent.

The illusion would be to think that groupings with leadership values set B are cruel, mean, and unkind. Quite the contrary. Groupings who have opted for set B generally think of themselves as considerate, helpful, and kind. They develop their rules and regulations, policies and procedures out of the misguided intention of wanting to be helpful—of wanting to be fair, equitable, and kind. The premise is that when people know the rules and regulations, they are less likely to make mistakes. Yes, and they are less likely to be creative as well.

You see, on the one hand, you can opt to help people avoid mistakes. On the other hand, you can opt to help people be creative. Both cannot have equal priority. Creativity *includes* making mistakes. One option or the other will always be dominant. The more policies and procedures and the more rules and regulations, the more the environment becomes one that nurtures passive, dependent persons.

In allegedly gentle and kind ways, local churches with leadership values set B work to develop policies and procedures to "help everyone understand how we function." The premise is, "We want to be sure everyone fits in, knows what is expected, and will make fewer mistakes." The implicit goal—and result—is passive, dependent congregations.

Most local churches have enough policies and procedures to last them through the next three millennia. This is particularly true of set B local churches, where policies are created on the exception rather than the general rule. Some event happens that is not pleasing to some. That one event causes the formation of a new policy— Policy Number 127. The likelihood of that event happening a number of times in the coming decade is remote. But it happened once or twice. Therefore, we need a policy to be sure it never happens again.

Study the wedding policies of some churches. It is a wonder some couples ever get married. The focus, regrettably, is not on the growth and development of their marriage relationship but rather on what they can do and cannot do (mostly the latter) in the sanctuary. Couples are given a booklet but not on the foundations for an excellent marriage.

The booklet the church gives them is on the policies related to the use of the sanctuary. The tone is, *"No* candles may be placed anywhere except at points A and B in the chancel." The tone is not even, "Feel free to place candles wherever makes best sense to you and the minister (or our church wedding director)." The wedding policies—all well intended—are "nay-saying" in context and spirit.

Study the building-use policies of local churches, particularly "set B" local churches. The policies are a long list of dos and don'ts (mostly don'ts). Indeed, one way of understanding the list is to know that each item on the list has a history of one or two times when that happened. "If it happens once or twice, we had better develop a policy."

The art is to develop persons, not policies. The longer the list of policies, however, the less likely that is to happen. In fact, whenever you discover a church with a long list of building policies, mostly you know that it has opted for leadership values set B. The message is, "New people, we welcome you—but please don't move the furniture."

Study the personnel policies of some churches. They cover every conceivable possibility, mostly in the following spirit: "If you don't do such and such, then you won't receive such and such." (Consider the alternative, "When you do such and such, count on receiving such and such.") The best personnel policies are written *with* the persons who plan to follow them. The worst personnel policies are written only by the committee that plans to enforce them.

Some local church policies are more extensive than the Koran. When you consider the wedding policies, building-use policies, and personnel policies of some churches, you can see that the scribes and pharisees are still busily at work. It is an irony that some of these self-same set B churches (and denominations) are gravely concerned about the oppressed and the rules and regulations that stifle them.

I am not against some policies and procedures, as long as they are open and constructive. It is helpful and valuable to have a *few*—the fewer the better. Too many policies creates a spirit of legalism and law, an environment of suffocation and claustrophobia. People grow their leadership best in an environment of compassion and good will.

Clearly, people do not develop their leadership in environments of abuse and anger. Hostility and hatred are shallow soil in which to develop leaders. Likewise, leaders do not develop well in the soil of legalism and law. Rules create regulators. Compassion creates leaders. Their best development occurs in the rich, full soil of compassion.

As a missionary pastor, nurture your compassion; temper your legalism. Help your local church be an environment of strong compassion. Resist legalism.

Local Development

People learn leadership best in an environment of local development, not one of centralized development. Local development creates leaders. Centralization creates bureaucrats. An emphasis on centralization creates an environment in the grass roots where people feel someone is always "looking over their shoulder." And generally someone is. Centralization creates caution, not creativity.

In an organization, whether a local church or a denomination, an emphasis on centralization usually develops when the grouping is fearful for their future. A preoccupation to do the right things—and to make *no* mistakes—sets in. And who would know what to do best? The central headquarters, naturally. Centralization produces fewer leaders. Centralization creates constrictions, not constructive action.

When a local church is in trouble, the tendency is for the minister and a few key leaders to decide they "know what must be done." Furthermore, they tend to decide that some centralized committee must now make most of the decisions. The irony is that it will be this minister and these key leaders who are most critical of a fading denomination, as it heads toward doing the same thing—prescribing that specific programs and organizational structures must exist in every local church.

When a local church or a denomination emphasizes centralization, the lead statements from "the main office" are:

- "Here is what you need to do."
- "Here is what you have not yet done."
- "Please report your results soon."

Whether it be the minister's office in the local church or the centralized office of the denomination, the message is the same. Centralization creates control. Control creates complacency.

When a local church or a denomination emphasizes local development, the lead statements from "the main office" are:

- "How are things going?"
- "Any way I can help?"
- "Thanks for your good work."

Whether it be a missionary pastor or the denominational mission leader, the message is the same. Local development grows leaders.

We have confused connectedness and centralization. Connectedness is not centralization. Connectedness is congregations in mutual mission, which does not have to eventuate in centralization. Connectedness can be achieved by a maximum of mutual networking and a minimum of "top-down headquarters." Indeed, in true connectedness the people at the headquarters are always very clear that they are working for the local congregations, not the other way around. The focus is on helping the local congregations to succeed in mission. In a centralized environment, it is the reverse. The local congregations have the task of helping make sure that the central headquarters succeeds. The primary emphasis will always be on one or the other.

In our time, the best emphasis is on local development, and the focus of that development is best on the mission field. The mistake of centralization is to focus on the denomination and whether it can survive. The focus of local development is on the mission field and how we can help persons with their lives and destinies.

There will come a day when missionary pastors are appointed to serve a mission field, not a local church. Missionary pastors will be called by local churches to serve a specific mission field, not solely a local church. One day denominational mission team leaders will say to their missionary pastors, "From today forward, you are appointed to this mission field and this local church." When the appointments are read, the name of the specific mission field will be read, not simply the name of the "sponsoring" local church.

In those denominations that call their pastors, the calling committee will be very clear that the pastor is being called to serve a specific mission field, not solely a local church. When the announcement is made to the congregation, the newspapers, and the denomination, the announcement will be very clear. "We are calling X [name of pastor] to serve as our missionary pastor in Y [name of community]. Our local church gives thanks to God that we can sponsor X's work and mission."

There will come a day when many, many local churches will be willing to pay to have a pastor appointed (or called) to their mission field, not solely to their local church. Indeed, many key leaders in local churches already see the wisdom of this development. Mostly pastors who are more comfortable as professional ministers raise objections.

Will there be some abuses when we begin this practice? Yes. Are there abuses now? Yes. The issue is to choose which set of abuses you are willing to live with. The most common abuse now is that persons on the specific, local mission field are neglected. The excuse given is, "I'm too busy tending to the congregation." Many professional ministers are indeed too busy—tending to the organization and institution, not the congregation.

When we begin the new practice, there will be "new abuses." Some would worry that the congregation would then be neglected. It is hard to see how some congregations could be neglected any more than they are now. In point of fact, what will get neglected—hopefully so—is the organization and institution. We have already spent more years and energy on these than is reasonable.

I certainly recognize that, in the new practice, a missionary pastor will serve the mission field and the congregation and will invest less time and energy in the organization and institution of the local church. And some things now being done will get left undone. Be at peace. Those things have not been helping that much anyway.

Local churches have a long, long tradition of sponsoring missionaries. And those missionaries have been sent all across the planet. *Much more* needs to be done to sponsor an increasing number of missionaries around the earth.

In the new practice, local churches will discover that they have been and increasingly are "sponsoring" their pastor as their missionary pastor on this specific mission field. Many, many local church leaders already understand that this direction for local development makes sense.

Someone will say, "But won't people say that they pay their pastor to tend to the congregation?" Yes, and the person who has made that comment to me has generally been a pastor, not a layperson. To be sure, some laypersons could be found who would say the same. But many, many key leaders already see the wisdom. In their own work and business, they have had to do exactly the same in recent years.

There are trade-offs in every system. Since it is not reasonably possible to do all three with equal strength, which two are the best two to focus on?

A: unchurched persons and groupings on the local mission field
B: persons and groupings in the congregation
C: the organizational and institutional structures of the local church

Professional ministers choose B and C. Missionary pastors choose A and B.

A denomination that chooses B and C will want to train pleasant funeral directors who will wait patiently until the dying patient has succumbed; they will then preside, with solemn dignity and grave decorum, over a thoughtful funeral. A denomination that chooses A and B will best focus on the local development of excellent missionary pastors and mission team leaders.

One further word will help. Local development focuses on leadership, people, and productivity—in mission. Centralization has always focused on property, possessions, and preservation. In local churches and denominations that focus on centralization, the board of trustees emerges as an important, powerful group. They are the trustees of the property and possessions. Their task is to preserve them. Their focus is on the eleventh and twelfth of the twelve central characteristics.

In an environment of local development, the important, powerful grouping that emerges is *the trustees of the mission,* not the property. Their focus is on the first and the second of the twelve characteristics.

In many local churches, however, the trustees of the property are viewed as the persons with power. An environment of centralization contributes to this. The "central headquarters" can, at least, *hold* the property. And that very act regrettably communicates a "value signal" to the congregation.

In fact, we are called to be stewards (trustees) of the gospel more than of the property. God has entrusted us with a compelling mission. The real value is in the mission. The real power is with the trustees of the mission.

God has called us to a strong mission. Leadership development is crucial to the cause. Leadership is best learned in a grouping that has selected leadership values set A and that provides a leadership development environment of objectives, authority, decision making, continuity, competency, compassion, and local mission development.

As a missionary pastor, nurture whichever of these you can best advance in the coming years. Do not wait on your denomination to do this for you. That would be passive, dependent behavior. Nothing of major consequence is blocking you. I can think of no specific injunctions that would prevent you.

Begin today. In your family life, head toward leadership values set A. Develop the fertile soil of a leadership development environment within your family. Stand over against those things that would do harm to the leadership environment you are developing.

Help persons in your local church to apply these leadership development principles within their own families and in their work and business. Next, choose a mission team important in your pilgrimage and mission. Grow these leadership development practices with them. Help your local church advance this understanding of and these practices of leadership development in its work and mission.

Begin today. As a missionary pastor, advance your leadership development in strong, constructive ways.

13. A Constructive Perspective

THE PURPOSE OF EVALUATION

The purpose of evaluation is *not* simply evaluation. The central purpose of evaluation, in any vocation, is to grow forward the capacity for self-evaluation.

THE PRO

There are important, distinctive competencies central to any given vocation, whether it be medicine, ditchdigging, music, secretarial work, golf, law, or custodial work or being a missionary pastor. Each has its distinctive competencies. But what differentiates the pro in any of these vocations is the capacity to discern what one is doing well, to recognize what one is doing poorly, and to initiate constructive action toward improvement.

The pro's capacity for self-evaluation has helped him or her to emerge as a pro—a master of the craft. It is not simply that the pro has developed a certain range of competencies important to the particular vocation. The pro has developed the capacity for self-evaluation.

THE MENTOR

This capacity for self-evaluation is learned. People are not born with it. People learn to develop their capacity for self-evaluation from observing a trusted colleague or mentor who has developed his or her own capacity for self-evaluation. *People lead in direct relation to the way they experience being led.*

In relationships with mentors, growing pros are able to learn from persons who:

1. are intensely interested in advancing their own competencies, gifts, and strengths
2. are continually self-evaluating the level of their own work

3. invite and share rigorous feedback and consultation in improving their abilities
4. are examples of how life is best lived

This is *not* to suggest that mentors are saints. Mentors, too, have feet of clay. But it is the qualities of intensity, self-evaluation, consultation, and example that contribute to fulfilling the role of mentor.

Thus, in the relationship between the growing pro and the mentor, evaluation does *not* take place by being autocratic, top-down, removed, and remote. Rather, the emerging pro discovers the mentor as one who is intensely self-critical *and* who invites and shares ongoing consultation (suggestions, ideas, criticism) from and with the growing pro and others.

In association with the mentor, the growing pro discovers that evaluation takes on the character of self-evaluation, not evaluation of and by others. The mentor, in fact, spends more time in self-evaluation than in evaluating others. Refreshingly, the growing pro is surprised to discover in the mentor the intensity of a rigorous self-evaluation and the genuine openness to consultation. In that discovery, the growing pro is on the way to developing the capacity for self-evaluation.

THE ASPECTS OF EVALUATION

Evaluation consists of two aspects: self-evaluation and consultation. The pro is the pro because he or she understands that evaluation includes both aspects. Pros did not become pros because they knew how to do a specific vocation in an outstanding way. Indeed, it is really the other way around. Pros learned how to do that vocation well because they developed their capacity for self-evaluation and consultation.

In a real sense, these two aspects of evaluation are related to the foundational life searches for individuality and community. The pro has discovered enough of the sense of his or her own individuality to have the integrity for self-evaluation. And the pro has discovered enough of a sense of roots, place, and belonging to seek out the wisdom and consultation of persons in the community.

Self-evaluation is rigorous and thoughtful, honest and intense, specific and constructive. Honest self-evaluation is not sentimental or platitudinous. It is not ego inflation, not "what a good boy am I." Thoughtful self-evaluation is not an exercise in self-flagellation, self-deprecation, defeatism, or ego deflation. Self-evaluation is a realistic assessment of one's own current competencies.

Consultation is advisory and helpful, collegial and constructive. Some are surprised to discover that a pro seeks out consultation. They may have thought that being a pro means one no longer seeks the counsel of others.

But it is precisely the pro, as he or she becomes more competent, who seeks out the wisdom and consultation of others. Now the pro is not looking for narrow advice, legalisms, or laws. Nor is the pro simply looking for a pat on the back.

Pros are looking for sound, sensible critique, collegially shared. Pros are genuinely open to sharing their own best wisdom and suggestions. They are looking for a thoughtful assessment of their strengths and weaknesses and for excellent suggestions for advancement and improvement. Pros are looking for *coaching* and are most open to excellent coaching, mentoring, and consultation.

WHAT EVALUATION IS NOT

EVALUATION AND MORALE

Morale among ministers is low. Adjudicatory leaders tell me this again and again. District superintendents, presbytery officers, and mission directors all speak of how *low* the morale is among their ministers. They have shared with me their deep concern about the low morale in their districts.

Again and again, these leaders have made valiant efforts to lift the morale. District letters, phone calls, reports, meetings, cheering, chiding, scolding, supporting, lamenting—all have been tried. The morale stays low.

Several factors are contributing to the low morale, particularly among the fading denominations:

1. This is a mission field. The old ways that used to work in a churched culture no longer bring the desired results.
2. Ministers continue to receive training to be professional ministers. The training does not prepare them for the work that is needed.

3. The middle class is shrinking. Those denominations who "placed their bets" for growth there are fading.

4. *The current evaluation process creates low morale.*

Perhaps other factors are also contributing to low morale among ministers. Certainly these four reasons, in and of themselves, create low morale well enough.

It would be easy enough to focus only on the first three factors, on developing strategies and objectives to overcome them. That might be a temptation—indeed, one might become preoccupied there. But that would be a mistake. The implications of the fourth factor need to be addressed. Indeed, it is precisely the evaluation process that missionary pastors have the strongest and most direct influence to change today, by the way they practice evaluation this year.

There is a direct correlation between the evaluation process used by a denomination and the morale of its ministers. **The more hierarchical the orientation of the evaluation process, the lower the morale among the ministers.** The lower the morale among the ministers, the more likely a denomination is to be fading and dying.

This sets up a vicious cycle. The more fading the denomination, the more the denomination creates an even more hierarchical, top-down evaluation process. The more hierarchical the evaluation process, the lower the morale; thus, the more fading the denomination. And so it goes.

TOP-DOWN EVALUATION

A hierarchical, top-down evaluation process is marked by several characteristics. First, and most obvious, the evaluation process comes from someone at the top. The group or committee designing the evaluation process may be a national board or agency or an annual conference board of professional ministry or a denominational task force. Wherever its specific locus, it works from a hierarchical perspective.

Hardly ever does the committee *actively* seek the consultive participation of the grass roots—the ministers, the persons who will be evaluated. Hardly ever are the grass roots asked, in discerning ways, to contribute their best wisdom and judgment on what evaluation process would be most valuable and helpful to them.

Rather, the top-down committee designs the evaluation steps, the rules and procedures, the instructions and the forms. Down to the last detail, the evaluation process originates from the top.

Second, a top-down evaluation process has an abundance of instructions and forms. The committees designing the evaluation process tend to create detailed instructions to be followed and complex forms to be filled out. There is a tendency to want to cover every conceivable possibility.

They develop instructions and forms to cover the exception, rather than the general rule. Nothing is left to chance; they are reluctant to count on the creativity and competencies of the pastor and local church personnel committee. Every base must be covered. Moreover, the top-down committee develops an affection for, ownership of, and a vested interest in the instructions and forms, policies, and procedures it has created.

The instructions and forms produced by the committees designing the evaluation process are many and various. A typical personnel committee packet of materials often looks like a three-ring notebook designed to hold a 50-page manual, now stuffed 129 pages full. The documents in the manual usually include:

1. a long theological discourse on the appropriateness of evaluation (usually with no mention of a theological foundation for self-initiated growth and development)
2. detailed instructions, filled with minutiae and injunctions (with very few, if any, open-ended, invitational suggestions)
3. complex, regimented forms for everybody to fill out and send in to headquarters, which may or may not contribute to the pastor's local growth and development.

Third, the top-down process calls for some committee to evaluate the pastor. Depending on the denomination, it may be called the personnel committee, the pastor-parish relations committee, or whatever. Usually, this committee is expected to conduct an annual evaluation, though it may meet more frequently than once a year. And the direct or indirect outcome of the evaluation is customarily focused on whether it makes sense for the pastor to stay or leave and on the pastoral salary for the coming year.

Fourth, the top-down evaluation approach asks the committee to evaluate the strengths and weaknesses of the pastor's competencies against a long, comprehensive list of competencies. (I have never seen a short list in a top-down evaluation process.)

The competency list may detail ten, fifteen, or thirty areas of competencies. The personnel committee is asked to indicate the pastor's rating on a scale of 1 to 10 for each competency on the list. The personnel committee is then asked to summarize its findings and to share them with the pastor and the adjudicatory leader.

PROBLEMS

Three problems are readily apparent with a top-down evaluation process. The first problem is quickly evident. The standard against which the pastor is judged is the "model minister"—the successful professional minister of the churched culture of the 1940s and 1950s. This is the image that the personnel committee has been trained to have in their collective mind's eye.

The list of competencies in the evaluation form is usually a list of professional minister competencies. Study the list closely. The weight of the competencies is toward activities *inside* the local church. Regrettably, pastors are heavily influenced by the list. They conclude that the list is the norm for what is means to be an effective pastor. They pattern their behavior accordingly. The personnel committee and the denomination reinforce these conclusions.

The result: The evaluation process creates pastors who try to improve competencies that used to work well in a long-ago, churched culture. Key principle: **The way people are evaluated shapes who they become.**

The second problem is evaluating the pastor over against an ideal. Now, most of the personnel committee instructions include a disclaimer that that is not the intent. Some evaluation guidelines even go on to state that the list of competencies simply represents a composite of the range of competencies found among large groupings of ministers.

It is quite clear nonetheless that the personnel committee is asked to evaluate their pastor on *all* the competencies on the list each year. But no one person is competent in every area. God has given each of us different gifts. If God had wanted to create perfect pastors, likely God could have done so. It is the sharing in diversity that creates mission and community.

Rather than using all the competencies on the list, a better way would be to evaluate the pastor only on those particular competencies that directly relate to the church's major objectives during that year. Thus, the personnel committee could:

1. review which particular central characteristics their church has been expanding and adding this year
2. recall the major objectives that their pastor was planning to accomplish, in support of what the church is expanding and adding
3. underline only those competencies on the comprehensive evaluation list that *directly* relate to the major objectives of the pastor
4. evaluate the pastor's work specifically in relation to those key objectives for the year

Pick the competencies that apply to this year's objectives. Evaluate the pastor only on those this year. Avoid the unnecessary negative reinforcement that comes from pointing to weaknesses that do not apply to this year's work.

Furthermore, personnel committees could think in terms of "last year," "this year," and "the coming year." Committees could encourage the growth and development of pastors by evaluating their performance, not against some static, comprehensive list, but rather in terms of how their levels of specific competencies this year compare with their levels of those specific competencies last year and what they could look toward developing in the coming year. Evaluate them in relation to themselves, not some static ideal. This would be a more constructive, helpful approach to pastoral evaluation.

THE MAJOR PROBLEM

Having shared the above suggestions, I note that there is yet a third, major problem with any top-down evaluation process, namely, that there is simply no constructive purpose. The committee is asked to do an evaluation of the pastor's work. This objective sounds innocent enough, reasonable enough. Regrettably, the personnel committee sets out to do precisely that.

The committee is asked to do an evaluation of the pastor's work. As a result, the key constructive step in any evaluation process is missing. Indeed, the whole focus of a constructive process has been missed. Thus, in a top-down evaluation, generally, the steps are as follows:

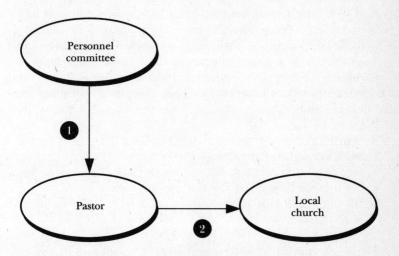

1. The personnel committee does an evaluation of the pastor's work.
2. The pastor does an evaluation of the church.
3. There is agreement, as best one can, on whether or not it makes sense for the pastor to stay or leave.
4. The personnel committee decides the pastoral salary for the coming year.

To be sure, top-down evaluation approaches sometimes include a provision for the pastor to do an evaluation of his or her work. But at no point is the pastor invited to *initiate* the evaluation process by producing a personal self-evaluation for feedback and coaching from the committee. Rather, the pastor's self-evaluation, what little there may, tends to be defensive or passive, not proactive. Indeed, when the personnel committee gathers, the focus of the discussion is on the committee's evaluation of the pastor, not on the pastor's sharing a personal self-evaluation for the committee's consultation.

Each year personnel committees gather to do what the denomination has asked them to do. It is not fair to blame personnel committees for the predicament. They are trying to do, as best they can, the task that headquarters has assigned to them.

And so the personnel committee gathers, awkwardly and bashfully, to evaluate the pastor. Put aside any memories of the exceptionally harsh, vindictive gathering, with sides being chosen and rumors flying. The grapevine remembers those gatherings too well. Mostly, personnel committee meetings are awkward and bashful, tentative and uncertain. The committee members generally:

1. share some of the things they like about the pastor's work
2. mention some of the things they dislike
3. decide whether it makes sense for the pastor to stay or leave
4. set the pastoral salary for the coming year
5. fill out the forms from headquarters as best they can and mail them in

There is a qualitative difference between a meeting of the pastor-parish relations committee to do an evaluation of the pastor's work and a consultive evaluation in which the pastor initiates, as the first step, the sharing of a personal self-evaluation for the purpose of obtaining feedback and coaching from the committee.

In a top-down evaluation process, the primary responsibility for the evaluation is with the committee. In a consultive evaluation process, the primary responsibility for the evaluation is with the pastor.

In a top-down process, the weight of the committee's discussion is on what they think of the pastor's work. In a consultive evaluation, the weight of the discussion is on the pastor's evaluation of his or her own strengths and weaknesses of the work, counting on the committee to share its best, excellent consultation.

Top-down evaluation processes are customarily designed by top-down committees who are accustomed to hierarchical methodologies. Hence, the focus regrettably is on the committee's evaluation of the pastor. The pastor is seen as their employee, and they are playing the role of the boss. Some interesting results occur as a consequence of that fatal mistake.

Top-Down Results

The results are fascinating. Indeed, they are amazing to behold. The top-down evaluation process successfully creates:

1. passive-aggressive behavior
2. low-grade hostility
3. subliminal resentment
4. eruptive forms of anger

Other than these four results, a top-down process does not accomplish a single thing. (On reflection, the top-down process does also produce reactive, passive, organizational, institutional pastors.)

Key principle: **The evaluation process of an organization develops the nature of leadership in the organization. To change the nature of leadership, one must change the evaluation process.**

All one has to do is "listen well" in a gathering of pastors. There will be conversation about the weather, family, hobbies, and work. There will be conversation about the denomination, the bureaucracy, the powerlessness, the frustrations, and the sense of lostness. The morale is low.

Denominational leaders frequently ask me, "Help us with the morale among our ministers. It has never been worse." Many denominational leaders are deeply aware of this predicament.

Grassroots pastors and grassroots denominational leaders are in the best position to overcome this problem as they:

1. grow forward the twelve central characteristics in local churches
2. advance the motivational resources that contribute to action, implementation, and momentum
3. develop the dynamics of memory, change, conflict, and hope
4. construct a new understanding of the nature of leadership
5. *create a consultive, not top-down, evaluation process.*

In some of the fading denominations, professional ministry boards and agencies have worked diligently and with good intentions to make the current, top-down evaluation process more so-phisticated. But if the initial premise is wrong, then to make the system more sophisticated is to make matters worse. When one is headed in the wrong direction, to do so in a more sophisticated "vehicle" simply allows one to go the wrong direction quicker and faster.

I am amazed at the charity and goodwill of pastors. They sense that the top-down process reinforces passive-aggressive behavior, advances a sense of low-grade hostility, deepens subliminal resentment, and increases the likelihood of eruptive forms of anger. It is a wonder pastors handle the results as well as they do.

If the top-down evaluation process really helped to coach pastors in their own leadership growth and development, denominational leaders would not be talking about low morale. They would be rejoicing with their colleagues over their growth and development.

As a matter of fact, however, the more sophisticated the top-down evaluation process becomes, the more defense mechanisms pastors understandably create to protect themselves from the yearly exercise of an hierarchical top-down evaluation.

If the top-down evaluation process really helped, bureaucratic leaders in the fading denominations would be pointing to a turn-around in morale and membership. Even on a mission field, some bureaucratic leaders would think that way. But as a matter of fact, the more sophisticated the top-down evaluation process has become, the more the fading denominations have continued to decline.

I am not suggesting an exact, one-to-one correlation here. Earlier, I did note that there *is* a direct correlation between top-down evaluations and low morale. Here, I am suggesting that I would think a long, long, long time before continuing to follow the same top-down evaluation process, making it more sophisticated and complex. The problem is not that it is not yet sophisticated enough. The problem is that *it is hierarchical.*

Some fading denominations have been declining for twenty years or more. Over the same time frame, they have been "improving" their top-down evaluation process. It is appropriate to ask the question, "What can we do differently that might help?"

One thing we can do differently is to abandon the use of a top-down evaluation process.

TOP-DOWN AFFINITIES

Before moving on, we must ask what draws denominational leaders to create a top-down evaluation process? The results—in passive-aggressive behavior, low-grade hostility, subliminal resentment, and eruptive forms of anger—are self-evident. Why would people continue to perpetuate any top-down evaluation process?

One reason is that some of them work out of a philosophy of hierarchicalism. For all the language of collegiality, the deeply rooted perspective is that of a caste system. We will see variations, depending on the individual. But persons with a hierarchical philosophy of life tend to create top-down evaluation systems. The top-down system reinforces "who is in charge."

A second reason is that for many persons that is the same way they have experienced being evaluated. Remember: **People evaluate in direct relation to the ways they experience being evaluated.** It may have created passive behavior, hostility, resentment and anger in them, but it is the primary way they have experienced evaluation.

A third reason is that some people think the personnel committee's evaluation of the pastor in a top-down process is for the best. "It cannot, surely, be all that harmful. Heaven's sake, pastors need help." For some persons, their good intentions cause them to support to a top-down process.

A fourth reason, now and then present, is that some few persons harbor a passive anger "that ministers are not producing better." A top-down evaluation process will help to "whip the troops into shape." Fortunately, I have not found this reason to be present frequently, yet it crops up often enough to deserve mention.

A fifth reason, also infrequently present, is that a top-down process gives grumbling personnel committees something to do so that they "stay off the back" of the adjudicatory leader. One of the frequent laments adjudicatory leaders hear is, "Guess what our pastor has done (or not done) now? Why can't you help us to get a competent pastor?" A top-down evaluation process satisfies the distress or anger of the local committee and keeps the adjudicatory leader's phone from ringing. The committee takes its "dis-ease" out on the pastor.

To be sure, the first three are more pervasive reasons as to why some persons have an affinity for creating top-down evaluation processes. The fourth and fifth reasons, while certainly contributing, are lesser influences.

It is interesting to note that top-down evaluation processes are created, for the most part, by a group of persons who never plan to experience the evaluation approach they help to create. Whether it is a denominational task force, regional committee, or annual conference board of professional ministry, the abiding question usually is, "What type of evaluation process can *we* design for *them* to use?" Hardly ever is the design committee's perspective, "What type of evaluation process can be constructive for me?"

The golden rule is a most helpful motto for any committee planning to construct an evaluation process: Do unto others as you would have done unto you. That is, create an evaluation process that is genuinely mutual and supportive, evaluative and consultive, and not hierarchical, authoritarian, or top-down.

14. The Evaluation Process

THE NATURE OF SELF-EVALUATION

The missionary pastor has the capacity to initiate a consultive evaluation. In a consultive approach to evaluation, it is decisive that self-evaluation be the first step because the first step in any evaluation sets up the quality and direction of the whole process.

Some may suggest that a top-down process is "best" for those persons right out of seminary but that a consultive evaluation process might work with persons who have been in the ministry for twenty years or more. No. It is vital that the beginning minister *learn early* how to do a consultive evaluation of his or her work. Note well: The process of evaluation trains the next generation of leaders. It is decisive that the pastor begin as soon as possible to develop a proactive, intentional, relational, and missional understanding of evaluation and leadership.

I know of no denomination that prohibits pastors from developing a consultive evaluation. To be sure, many denominations point pastors toward a top-down procedure, but there is no current prohibition on a consultive evaluation. Thus, you are free to do so. Begin. This year.

Key Objectives

The first step is your own self-evaluation. There are six components to your self-evaluation. First, set forth the two to four key, major objectives you hoped to accomplish during the year just ending. It will be most helpful to you for these objectives to meet the following criteria:

1. written down
2. having a strong sense of your ownership
3. specific and measurable
4. reflecting realistic time horizons

5. concrete and achievable
6. complementary and mutually reinforcing

It may take you two or three years of practice to build your ability to develop solid, key objectives. Usually, in the first year of doing a consultive evaluation, you will discover that your two to four objectives were a bit fuzzy and generalized. That is fine. Count on advancing your competency to set key, major objectives in the early years of consultive evaluation, not the first year.

Note that your concern is to set forth two to four major objectives, not eight to ten. Mostly, you will want only two to four "20 percenters." Key principle: Twenty percent of the things a person does yields 80 percent of the results; 80 percent of the things a person does yields 20 percent of the results. In your evaluation, focus on the 20 percenters. And be sure that there are no more than two to four. Now you are working smarter, not harder.

RESULTS

The second component of your own self-evaluation is to state the results you have accomplished on each of these key objectives. Be as specific and as accurate as you can. Do not underplay or overstate the results.

Some pastors, shy about their work, have a tendency to play down what they have accomplished. That may be a reaction against having known someone who was "always tooting his own horn." Thus, the pastor wants to avoid seeming to be a braggard.

Some pastors underplay the results because they are still struggling with low self-esteem. Be at peace. Why should you think less well of yourself than God does? God's grace is amazing, and what God is doing in mission through you is decisive for the kingdom.

Pastors who are tempted to overstate the results of their work are few and far between, but they do exist. Their sense of one-upmanship is extraordinary. Whatever anyone else has done, they have done it better. By their account, they have far surpassed this year's key objectives. It makes one wonder whether they set their objectives too low.

Sometimes what drives these pastors is a fear of failure. Sometimes it is a compulsiveness toward perfectionism or an obsession with success. Whatever the reasons, the outcome is to overplay the accomplishments for the year.

It is important to state the results for the year realistically and accurately. The pastor who underplays the results and the pastor who overstates the results are both simply still learning how to develop their capacity for self-evaluation.

STRENGTHS AND WEAKNESSES

The third component of your own self-evaluation is to assess the strengths and weaknesses of your results. This aspect will be difficult if you were not clear enough on the two to four major objectives you planned to accomplish for the year.

This assessment will also be difficult if you have underplayed or overstated the results of your work. It is important to be clear on your two to four major objectives and accurate in stating the results of your work. Then you will be in the strongest position to assess the *principal* strengths and weaknesses of your results. Consider thoughtfully and prayerfully what you can discern in your results. Do not make long lists of every strength and weakness of which you can conceive—do not be a bean counter. State the principal strengths and weaknesses succinctly, with wisdom and judgment.

INSIGHTS AND DISCOVERIES

The fourth component of your own self-evaluation is to consider what you have learned as you have been working on each major objective. Ask yourself:

1. What would I do differently?
2. What creative idea have I discovered?
3. What new insight has come to me?

Sometimes our best lesson comes as an excellent mistake; sometimes, as a solid success. The art is to learn.

We can learn much from those around us. We can learn much from a self-evaluation of our own work. Some say, "Life is a great teacher"—it is, but only when we let it be.

If we allow ourselves to be concerned with whether we are failing, we may miss what we can learn. If we are so preoccupied with success, we may lose sight of what we can learn. What new ideas have come to you? What lessons have you learned?

SPECIFIC COMPETENCIES

The fifth component of your own self-evaluation is to assess your growth and development in relation to your growth objectives for the year. At the beginning of each year there are two important decisions that will help you, as a missionary pastor, to direct your intentional growth:

1. Choose two to four key, major objectives that you plan to accomplish during the year.
2. Select the one or two specific competencies you plan to develop in yourself during the year.

Often pastors choose yearly objectives and then have some vague idea of getting some "continuing education." They plan to take some seminar on this or that, but without enhancing and developing any specific competency. Focus well on improving specific competencies, not on generalized goals or objectives.

The best way forward is to develop specific competencies that *are directly related* to one or more of your key, major objectives for the coming year. Even better, create a threefold interface between:

1. the "expands" and "adds" among the central characteristics on which your church is focusing for the year
2. your own two to four major objectives
3. your own one or two specific competencies that you are advancing

Be certain to select *specific* competencies, not general competencies. It would be too general to say something like, "I want to be a better pastor." It is still too general to say, "I want to be a better preacher."

If, for example, you want to be a better preacher, state which one or two specific competencies related to preaching you want to develop. Here are some possibilities:

1. exegesis of specific Old Testament texts or books
2. exegesis of specific New Testament texts or books

3. sermon research and resources
4. sermon construction
5. sermon delivery
6. theological development in preaching
7. Advent preaching, Lenten preaching, etc.

Or if, for example, you want to improve your competency in visitation, state with which specific grouping you will focus your self-development. Here are some possible groups that would serve as a focus for developing visitation skills:

1. first-time visitors
2. newcomers to the community
3. relational unchurched
4. constituent unchurched
5. neighborhood unchurched
6. community unchurched
7. service agency unchurched
8. regular worshipers
9. hospitals, nursing homes
10. emergencies
11. members
12. inactive members

Each distinct grouping calls for certain specific visitation competencies, not just generalized ones.

You are probably already specifically competent in your visitation with one or more of these groupings. So, given your church's objectives and your own two to four key objectives, select a specific visitation grouping with which you plan to develop your visitation competencies.

The spirit of this fifth component in self-evaluation is always to put yourself in a proactive "growing and developing" stance, not a passive and reactive stance. **You are the best person to assure that your life will count.**

You are the best person to advance your own competencies as a missionary pastor. In this fifth component, you assess what you have achieved toward your own growth objectives for the year just ending.

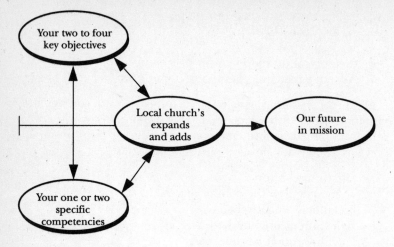

AREAS FOR CONSULTATION

The sixth component of your own self-evaluation is to identify the three principal areas on which you would appreciate consultation from your consultive team. Help them to know the key areas wherein you would benefit from their consultation.

That is, get your consultive team working for you. Be specific about what help you count on from them. See them as one of your best resources for developing your competencies as a missionary pastor.

It is important to remember that persons on your consultive team will have had their own fair share of experiences with a top-down evaluation process. As you clearly identify the areas in which you want their consultation, you will help them to shift the perspective from top-down evaluation to a consultive evaluation. As your consultive team sees your *genuine* interest in their consultation, some of their own best wisdom and judgment is more likely to emerge.

THE COMING YEAR

The seventh component of self-evaluation is to look to the coming year and select the two to four key, major objectives important for the year ahead; and the one or two specific competencies that would be valuable to grow and develop during the year ahead. It is important that you look ahead and make these choices. Do not sit back passively, counting on your consultive team to tell you the key objectives and growth objectives for the coming year.

As a missionary pastor, bring your own best wisdom, judgment, vision, common sense, and prayer to bear, so that you choose your own best direction forward. Put yourself in a proactive stance toward the coming year.

THE STEPS IN CONSULTIVE EVALUATION

SELF-EVALUATION

The decisive first step is your own best self-evaluation. We have just discussed the six components of your self-evaluation. These further observations will help you with this first step.

First, as you learn to evaluate your 20 percenters, you will be in a wiser position to evaluate your 80 percenters. It would be a mistake to try to do a self-evaluation of all your work. This is one reason that people may have difficulty early on—they try to evaluate too much. Take it thoughtfully and gradually.

Keep in mind that you are trying to develop your capacity for self-evaluation. That is the goal, not trying to evaluate all of your work.

Second, give yourself *just enough* time to develop your own self-evaluation, but not too much time. Three months would be too long. Too much time creates analysis paralysis. Three days would be too brief. Too little time creates "reflection shortfall." Three weeks would be about right to mull over your own self-evaluation. You will know best the time frame helpful to you.

Give yourself just enough time that you can relax, search, pray, and puzzle through your own best self-evaluation of your work. Draw on your best wisdom, judgment, vision, common sense, and prayer.

Third, do your self-evaluation somewhere away from your office. Your office is filled with its fair share of unfinished projects. Perhaps you would choose a setting that, by its very nature, reminds you of one of your key, major objectives. Perhaps your best setting is a retreat environment where you can reflect and pray. You will know best.

Fourth, use a simple, straightforward self-evaluation worksheet, such as the example in the appendix, on which to state your self-evaluation. Use key phrases, short sentences, and an outline format, not a narrative format. You are not writing a term paper, a conference report, or a sermon manuscript. You are wanting to create the essence of a best self-evaluation. Keep the details simple so you can focus on your best thinking.

CONSULTATION

The second step—the consultation step—is the one in which pastors share their best self-evaluation with a consultive team. Note three important points.

First, the pastor *shares*—not tells. The session with the consultive team is not the time to lecture or preach. It is not a didactic session in which the pastor "educates" the consultive team. It is not a session in which the pastor defensively justifies past work. It is not a hierarchical setting in which the pastor, in a top-down way, informs the consultive team of his or her self-evaluation.

Nor is the session one in which the consultive team reads the pastor's self-evaluation, then immediately reacts. The pastor "walks them through" the evaluation. Usually, each member of the consultive team has a copy of the pastor's self-evaluation. Copies are usually distributed in advance so some thought and study can be given before the consultation session.

When the consultive team gathers, it is important that the pastor walk the team through the self-evaluation, sharing

- background and rationale
- implications and feelings
- new insights since completing the self-evaluation

These comments should be thoughtful and open, not apologetic, strident, or defensive. Generally, the pastor can guide the team through his or her self-evaluation in thirty minutes (certainly, no more than forty-five).

The purpose of consultation is coaching, not correcting. The spirit of the consultation session is therefore one of mutuality and sharing, deep thought and good humor. The spirit is one of advancing, growing, building, and developing, not one of conserving, holding, protecting, or preserving. The spirit is collegial and community, not top-down and authoritarian.

Second, the pastor shares his or her *best* self-evaluation. This is not something hurriedly thrown together the night before, tentative and hastily done. Nor does the pastor count on the consultive team to do all the evaluating.

It is important for you, as a missionary pastor, to develop your capacity for self-evaluation. Thus, what you share with the consultive team is a best effort—it may be a third or fourth draft, but certainly not a first or second draft. The reason for doing several drafts is not to improve the grammar, punctuation, and spelling. Rather, it is to improve the thinking and reflection, the substance and conclusions, in your self-evaluation.

Third, the pastor shares his or her best self-evaluation *with a consultive team*. This is not an evaluation committee. The orientation of the group's purpose is coaching, not correcting. The focus is toward growing and developing, not dictating.

Frequently, your consultive team will be three to five persons whose wisdom and judgment you respect and trust. One or more of these persons may be drawn from your local church pastor-parish relations or personnel committee.

It will help to place on your consultive team persons who will help you to expand your competencies. Try not to fall victim to "the hip pocket" syndrome, where pastors carefully pick the people they "have in their hip pocket," people whose loyalty they can count on. Loyalty may not necessarily produce wise consultation or excellent missionary pastors.

You will want on the consultive team persons of integrity and credibility with whom you have a mutual trust, respect, and confidence. You will not be helped by a group whose adulation and personal loyalty gets in the way of sharing wise consultation.

Wise consultation is more than one side giving advice and the other side listening. Advice often tends to be a series of tired, tidy slogans. Wise consultation draws out your own best thinking and prods you to expand your horizons of thought. Wise consultation is searching, puzzling, mutual, and collaborative.

As for the amount of time for this second step, think in terms of thirty to forty-five minutes. This time factor will help your consultive team focus on the principal areas that would be most helpful to you. Remember: Planning expands to fill the time available. Likewise, evaluation expands to fill the time available. Therefore, limit the time. You and your consultive team will stay focused on the 20 percenters.

MUTUAL AGREEMENT

The third step invites mutual agreement between you and your consultive committee as together you:

- identify the results of the past year's two to four key objectives
- evaluate the strengths and weaknesses of those results
- share your insights and discoveries
- acknowledge the specific competencies that you have grown and developed during the year

This does not mean there is unanimity, nor does it mean that a vote is taken on each item and the majority rules. It does mean that you and your consultive team discover together, seeking to reach a mutually held feeling of agreement. From time to time, this may result in your agreement to disagree.

The consultation session will be lively, with good humor and deep thought. There is wisdom in diversity as that diversity has a central focus, namely, discovering reasonable mutual agreement on the above four factors.

Allow thirty to forty-five minutes for this step. In fact, the consultation schedule for the four steps might look something like the following:

Topic	Time Invested
1. Sharing of self-evaluation	30–45
2. Consultive team's sharing	30–45
Brief break	
3. Pastor and team developing areas of mutual agreement	30–45
4. Consensus on the coming year	30–45

You will want to design a schedule that will be most helpful to you. I would encourage you *not* to take a break after each step. It will take too long, you will get bogged down in details, and it will end up being more frustrating than helpful.

Sometimes it will help you to do steps 1 and 2 in one session (say, 8:30–9:30 on a Saturday morning), have a thirty-minute break, and then do steps 3 and 4 from 10:00 to 11:00. Consultive sessions tend to be more creative and helpful in the morning time, when people are freshest and at their best.

Avoid having a consultive evaluation on a Monday evening. People would have just started their work week, and they would come to the meeting already tired.

If you want to meet in the evening, try to conclude by 9:00 P.M. While conflict may create creativity, after nine o'clock it creates feuding and fussing. You are not trying to prove who is "right." As a missionary pastor and consultive team, you are trying to coach one another.

THE COMING YEAR

The fourth step focuses on where you are headed, not where you have been. There will have been solid successes and excellent mistakes this past year. You have discovered much. But what has been, has been. The key question now is, What kind of future—in mission—are you building for the year to come?

The mutual agreement of step 3 will put you and your consultive team in the best position to discuss:

- the three principal areas for consultation you have identified
- the two to four key objectives you see as important for your work in the year to come
- the one or two specific competencies you are looking forward to developing in the coming year

Likely, this step in the consultation session will be an investment of thirty to forty-five minutes.

All four steps comprise a whole. This fourth step is the most decisive. You may have missed something important on your self-evaluation. Your consultive team's sharing may not have been as creatively helpful as you had hoped. The areas of mutual agree-

ment may be tenuous. Yet in this fourth step, you and your consultive team can still come "into your own together" as you put
well in place the year to come.

All four steps are important, but do not invest so much energy
in steps 1–3 that you quickly brush by step 4. This fourth step
lays the groundwork for both your productive mission and solid
leadership growth in the year ahead and helps you to develop an
even more helpful consultive evaluation a year from now and, in
the year to come, you may benefit from sharing with your consultive team several times across the year.

A Concluding Word

The spirit of consultive evaluation is coaching, not correcting.
**Under threat, people wither. With encouragement, people
achieve.** With correcting, people try to avoid mistakes. With
coaching, people try to create.

Consultive evaluation is best done in a team spirit. See your
consultive group as a team. Avoid an attitude of "me versus them"
that would result in negativism and isolationism. As best you can,
live out the dynamic of the individual-in-community with your
consultive team.

Consultive evaluation, as a process, frees the personnel committee to focus its best wisdom on:

long range, future staffing
personnel searches, hiring, and termination
equitable, reasonable personnel policies
congregational and pastoral communication
salary and housing recommendations
personnel budget development
pastoral continuance recommendations
liaison with the denomination

As pastor, you will want to participate actively with your personnel comittee in the accomplishment of these matters.

But, it is difficult for a personnel committee—with all of these
responsibilities—to also serve as a consultive evaluation team. It
is usually too large a group and it has too many "mixed" responsibilities. Certainly, your consultive team is related, in whatever
way makes constructive sense, to your personnel committee. One

or two persons may be on both. And, at the same time, the value and importance of consultive evaluation is best advanced by you and your consultive team as your share, pray, and grow together.

To be sure, there are both advantages and difficulties with consultive evaluation. Those persons who have an affinity for a top-down approach will immediately see the difficulties.

One objection might be, "We do not have laity who can do a consultive evaluation process. It would take too much training." Some of these same persons currently lament that we do not have laity who can do the current top-down evaluation process—in spite of all the personnel-committee training various denominations have tried over the years.

Another objection might be that pastors could abuse the openness of consultive evaluation. Life is a matter of trade-offs. I would rather run the risk of that abuse than to continue to abuse pastors with a top-down approach. I would rather have an open system wherein pastors can grow and develop their leadership competencies than continue to use a system that provokes passive-aggressive behavior, low-grade hostility, subliminal resentment, and eruptive forms of anger. *I would rather grow the person than the pain.*

Furthermore, I would rather have the church model what responsible consultive evaluation looks like than see it mirror the top-down processes of the culture. Heaven knows the number of people in the culture who suffer under top-down evaluations every day. Their sense of powerlessness is increased. Their sense of despair is deepened.

Indeed, as persons in your local church participate on your consultive committee, you will be helping them to discover a way in which they can develop consultive evaluation in their own work and vocation. Persons in your congregation will discover this consultive evaluation approach on the grapevine and in conversation with you. You will help them.

Consultive evaluation helps persons to reclaim some sense of constructive power, some sense of growth, some sense of hope that their lives might count. Consultive evaluation is at the very heart of a new understanding of the nature of leadership. The top-down evaluation process does grievous harm to pastors and personnel committees. The top-down evaluation process currently in use is training a next generation of pastors who will be yet more dysfunctional on the mission field.

As a missionary pastor, consider these three objectives. First, *begin this year to do your own consultive evaluation.* If your denomination insists on a top-down evaluation, do both. Think of a pier out over the ocean. Sometimes one of the pilings becomes weakened and decayed because of the waves, salt, and weather. Then we set the new piling right beside the old one. As the decayed one weakens further, the new piling takes up the load.

By not moving to advance and improve your own evaluation process, you only lend your power to the current top-down practice. The top-down evaluation system has to feed on your "power" to stay alive. It has no inherent worth in itself.

Do not wait on your denomination to do this for you. That would be passive, dependent behavior. That only models passive dependent behavior for your people. Give them more help than that.

Do not launch a study committee in your annual conference to "revise the evaluation process." Change happens as enough people behave as though the change had already happened.

Second, *help your family (particularly your kids) develop their own capacity for self-evaluation.* You will be sharing with them a great gift for this life's pilgrimage.

Third, *in a missional way, share the principles of consultive evaluation with some grouping or organization in your community that would appreciate and benefit from learning.* Help them adapt the principles to their organization. Serve as consultant more than crusader. Perhaps, one or two persons on your consultive team would have fun doing this with you. To be sure, this objective may be one you consider in a year or two. As you share the principles of consultive evaluation, you will develop your own understanding of them even more fully.

Both the areas of leadership development and of consultive evaluation will help you to grow forward a new understanding of the nature of leadership and of the central leadership tasks of missionary pastors.

15. Leadership Structures

Missionary pastors are best helped to grow forward their mission when the leadership and missional structure of their local church facilitates rather than hinders this mission work. Some organizational structures facilitate and help. Some hinder and block.

As a missionary pastor, you will know best how to proceed in your local church as you consider:

- the criteria for structures for mission
- the principles of organization
- the qualities of missional structures

Think through which of these three you can begin implementing this year.

CRITERIA FOR STRUCTURES FOR MISSION

RELATIVE

Structures are relative, not absolute. All organizational structures have an interim status. They are for the moment, the day, the season. All structures are temporary, intermittent, provisionary. Each structure has its day in the sun and then is no more.

All structures rise and fall, come and go. We have seen this with the organizational structures of the Greek city-states, the structures of the Roman Empire, the papal empire of the medieval period, and the rising nation-states of Europe. We have seen this with the structures of an agrarian society in the past century and with the structures that came into being with the Industrial Revolution. We have seen this with all sorts of structures in our time.

All structures are the invention of humankind. This includes the structures of the church. God has ordained the mission, not the structures. Across the centuries, God's mission has moved forward with now this structure and now that structure. Persons in the church have been most creative in inventing a structure that matches the mission of that time.

In all spheres of life, we discover and seize upon one particular way of ordering and structuring our work and life. One way works for a time. Then it becomes dysfunctional. A new structure is invented to take its place. No structure is absolute.

DYNAMIC AND FLEXIBLE

Structures are dynamic and flexible, not static and rigid. The principle of structural relativity does not mean that one structure is as good as another. That would reflect a comparative, static understanding of structural relativity. Rather, the relativity has to do with the dynamic and flexible character of structures.

Structures are dynamic, not historified; they are not fixated in relation to a point of history. At their best, structures grow and develop. They are not ossified and petrified. Frequently, however, the mistake of the church has been to historify and universalize one structure for all time. In a given historical setting, one partic-ular structure has been successful. The denomination, in its fear-ful concern about fading and declining, has then tried to make that organizational structure mandatory everywhere. But one structure, successful in one place, cannot be historified. No one structure can be universally applied.

No particular structure can be universalized in an absolute way as mandatory for all local churches. Instead, each structural con-figuration must be assessed on its own merits. Critical to that assessment is the extent to which the particular structure facili-tates a dynamic, flexible patterning of relationships among the mission team and a sense of hopeful direction for the mission.

We need an eschatological understanding of the relative nature of structures. The "being" is in mission and hope, not structures and organization. Structures should be living, breathing, moving, changing, developing. An eschatology of structures is more help-ful than an ontological understanding of static structures.

We sometimes hear it said, "But we've always done it this way." Occasionally, that may be a thinly veiled way of using an alleged claim of historical precedent to have that person's own way. But more often than not, the person is simply confirming the learned behavior pattern of organizational structure that is current in the grouping. Their statement can be most helpful. It teaches you the current "organizational habits" of the grouping. Furthermore, it alerts you to the potential rise of anxiety level as the grouping attempts to make the transition to a more helpful structure for mission.

Organizational structures are intriguing entities. It is interesting how quickly groupings sanctify a particular structure and universalize the need for it. In one denomination a new organizational structure was invented in 1968 that they called the "Council of Ministries." In the twenty-plus years since then, it is intriguing to note the number of persons who are prepared to do battle and insist that every local church *must* have a council of ministries.

Now, God's mission has moved forward on this planet for almost two thousand years without ever knowing what a council of ministries looked like. But the message some people now give is that you cannot have an effective local church without such a council.

The irony here is that the structural concept of a council of ministries came into being in the mid-1960s in order to provide coordination of the busy programs and activities of churched-culture local churches. The initial purpose was to provide coordination and cooperation for the local church's programs and activities planning, primarily on an annual basis.

The further irony is that it came into being just about the time that the decline in church culture was becoming evident. The structural "solution" was being sanctified for a "problem" that was becoming extinct. The "programs and activities" ways of being the church was already becoming increasingly dysfunctional.

Local

Structures are local, not hierarchical. In our time, it is decisive that church structures stand in opposition to the emerging trend of dislocation of power. That means more than just speaking out against the trend. More fully, it means creating church structures that maximize both the power of the local participants and their fullest human potentials. Thus, a streamlined organizational structure and a proactive, solidly participatory and consultive decision-making process become paramount.

Individuals and groupings have the genuine capacity to function and flourish in a dynamic, flexible, structural environment. Indeed, given the rigid inflexible structures of much of contemporary society, it becomes crucial that the church's future structures demonstrate clear ways in which persons can rediscover power in their own lives and destinies.

These future structures for mission need to emerge and evolve out of local centers of actual life, rather than being superimposed by a remote, hierarchical system. "Grassroots" adjudicatory leaders are the most effective in our time. Historically, all the initial Christian communities were autonomous. There was considerable connectedness—that is, networking, linkage, and common work. As time passed, there developed an increasingly hierarchical centralization of church structures. The more closed, centralized, and hierarchical the structure, the harder it is for local churches to fulfill the eschatological nature of their life and mission together.

Connectedness, not centralization, is decisive to our mission. The barest minimum of power should be dislocated from local levels of authority and leadership to regional, national, and international church structures. The hierarchical tendency to dislocate local power to these other levels reflects the culture's influence on the church. The hierarchical principle, pervasive in the culture, has likewise simply become pervasive in the church.

In one denomination, there was an excellent policy in place—namely, a local church could organize itself in whatever ways made best sense to its board, its pastor, and its regional adjudicatory officer. It made good sense. But then that denomination withdrew that possibility. Oh, they did allow for a couple of organizational options. But the general message was clear: "Those at the top know best how local churches should organize themselves."

Frankly, the spirit and tenor of things has been that the people at the top know best how local churches should be organized. The spirit has not been to discover new, creative structures that will advance the church's mission. It is not accidental that many people are drawn to congregations where the structures emerge in local ways more than hierarchical ways. In our time, people wrestle greatly with the trend of dislocation of power.

CONNECTEDNESS

Structures for mission are connected, not centralized. "Local" does not mean isolationist. We do not live in a vacuum. It is not possible for Grover's Corners to exist somehow apart from the world. Local "hands-on" mission most frequently leads to world mission. Indeed, God calls us to be in mission across the planet, not simply in our own backyard.

And here is an insight that has grown out of many interviews and consultations: When people discover their longings and competencies to share concrete, effective help with a specific local human hurt or hope, that sensitizes them in powerful ways for world missions.

Note this word of caution: The statement, "We should take care of our own before we take care of others," is *not* a plea favoring local mission. The comment really means, "We should take care of those who are already inside this local church." Persons who say we should take care of our own are rarely involved in any hands-on way in local missions. The phrase is mostly used in a self-centered way.

Those persons who contribute money to their local church (some of which goes to support national and world missions) tend to use their financial contributions as their excuse not to become involved in hands-on local or world mission. They rationalize by saying, "Oh, yes, we are in mission. We give money to the following causes. . . ." Financial support for missions does not relieve a congregation from its responsibility to give personal support for mission(s) and mission teams.

The mission field of our time will require more than money. We will need the effort of an extraordinary abundance of missionary pastors and missionary teams, locally and across the planet. A strong connectedness is important for these missionary pastors and mission teams.

MISSIONAL

Structures are missional, not institutional. One should not even need to say that—it seems self-evident. But yet so many organizational structures are primarily devoted to the institution.

We do not have to look too hard or too far to find situations where:

1. The majority of the local church's committees are structured to focus on matters inside the local church.
2. The majority of volunteers recruited by the local church are asked to do work inside the local church.
3. The nominating committee spends the majority of its time filling organization positions focusing inside the local church.
4. The best leaders are asked to serve in posts focusing inside the local church, primarily in relation to the functional, organizational, institutional characteristics.
5. The majority of the committees invest most of their meeting time discussing inside-the-church issues.

These are five classic symptoms of an *institutional* organizational structure.

By contrast, remember the mission spirit that was popular some years ago: "Our local church is committed to giving 50 percent of our budget to missions and 50 percent to local church operations; for every dollar we spend on ourselves, we plan to send a dollar abroad for missions." To be sure, this excellent sentiment was influenced by the efforts of the Marshall Plan following World War II. At the same time, the spirit of the point is most important.

On the mission field of our time, the organizational structure for a "mission outpost" would look like the following:

1. The majority of the local church's committees are structured to focus on matters outside the local church, that is, in the world.
2. The majority of volunteers recruited by the local church are asked to do work outside the local church.
3. The nominating committee spends the majority of its time filling missional positions focusing outside the local church.
4. The best leaders are asked to serve in posts focusing in mission outside the local church.
5. The majority of the committees invest most of their meeting time deciding mission strategies for their work in the world.

These are the five classic symptoms of a *missional* organizational structure.

It finally boils down to a matter of priorities. In a missional organizational structure, a careful analysis of its priorities for allocating its leadership would likely result in this breakdown:

- Outside in the world: 70 percent
- Inside the church: 30 percent

Whereas in an institutional organizational structure, an analysis of its priorities for allocating its leadership resources would likely result in the following breakdown:

- Outside in the world: 30 percent
- Inside the church: 70 percent

There will come a day when local churches are asked, at the time of their annual meeting, to report to their denomination the following:

1. What is the number of volunteers recruited by the church who are doing active mission work outside the local church?
2. What is the number of volunteers recruited by the church who are doing active work inside the local church?

These questions will confirm the value of nurturing forward organizational structures that are increasingly missional.

Missionary pastors help to grow structures that are relative, dynamic and flexible, local, connectional, and missional. Moreover, such structures help missionary pastors to grow themselves forward.

It is not a matter that you wait for the structures to change before you change. It is not an either/or. It is a both/and. As *you* nurture forward your competencies as a missionary pastor, also nurture forward the leadership structure that will help. Likewise, as the structure advances more fully toward a relative, dynamic, local, connectional, missional structure, that change will help you develop even more as a missionary pastor.

PRINCIPLES OF ORGANIZATION

JUST ENOUGH

Several principles of organization will help you in the development of a local church organization and missional structure.

These principles, in reciprocal manner, help persons to grow themselves forward as missionary pastors and mission team leaders.

Key principle: **Have just enough people on just enough committees to achieve wise decisions and accomplish significant results.** Note clearly that the goal is not fewer people on fewer committees. The goal is wise decisions and significant results.

On a mission field, the terrain is tougher and the stakes are higher than in a churched culture. Wise decisions and significant results become ever more decisive. The more complex the organizational structure and the more energy put into the maintenance of the institutional organizational structure, the less energy available for wise decisions and significant results. Conversely, the less complex the organizational structure and the less energy put into the maintenance of the missional organizational structure, the more energy available for wise decisions and significant results.

Simplicity, not complexity, is the principle on a mission field. The organizational structure is simple and lean, not complex and cumbersome. Missionary pastors and mission team leaders take a "vow of poverty" in relation to committees. Encourage a poverty of committees and a plenty of mission. An economy of committees is decisive on a mission field.

Too much energy, time, and leadership resources have been invested in perpetuating a complex organizational structure of committees that once worked reasonably well in a churched culture and was, in fact, a reflection of that culture's preponderant institutional organizational systems. Some almost had the premise that the more committees a church has, the more successful a church is.

The more committees, however, the less mission. The fewer committees, the more mission. This is particularly true when a local church begins focusing on creating more mission teams and fewer committees. The distinctions are as follows:

Mission team	*Committee*
1. is gathered by a leader	1. is appointed by a nominating committee

2. has common longings and complementary competencies	2. represents various areas
3. delivers concrete, effective help	3. contributes recommendations, suggestions, and some work
4. focuses on specific human hurts and hopes	4. focuses on various issues
5. bases its action in the world	5. bases its coordination in the church
6. has a relational, community life, and a flexible organizational structure	6. has a functional life, with some community, and a prescribed organizational structure
7. "lives" together in the world	7. has regular meetings

A mission team looks more like a M*A*S*H unit at the front lines. A committee looks more like a study group in a library.

It is a myth that every cause needs a committee. Many persons with many causes have convinced the national leadership of various denominations that their causes need to be replicated by a committee in each local church. Given a plethora of causes and resultant committees, the organizational chart of a local church looks more like the committee structure of some government agency or a map of the galaxies.

Quite simply, **a cause needs a leader, not a committee.** Search out the leader for that cause in your local community. As a missionary pastor, discover the leader or leaders whose longings and competencies are a match for that cause. Nominate one of those persons to the post. Give them the opportunity to advance the cause and build their own team in whatever way makes best sense to them. Do not give them a committee. As leader, they will know best whether to gather a mission team, a task force, a network, two committees, or whatever.

A leader can gather a committee. A committee cannot gather a leader. The best way to kill a cause is to give it to a committee. A cause needs a leader.

We need more mission teams and fewer committees. Ironically, while the risks are greater on a mission team, more persons come alive on a mission team. While the risks are fewer on a committee, fewer persons come alive in the regularly stated meetings of a committee.

A local church will certainly want to have *some* committees. Committees do helpful, useful work. I am not proposing that committees be eliminated, only that there are too many committees. We need fewer committees and more mission teams. To achieve this, we will want to pare back the institutional organizational structure of committees to a bare-bones minimum. Many local churches have a few mission teams, but they tend to have more committees. It needs to be the other way around.

There will come a day when a denomination will have an annual report form that asks each local church:

1. List each mission team in your local church.
2. List the names of the leaders and members of the team.
3. Identify the specific human hurt and hope with which each is in mission.
4. State the concrete, effective help that they have delivered this past year.
5. State, as specifically as possible, the results that have occurred in people's lives and destinies.

For the present, the annual report form mostly asks the local church to list the committees, the names of the committee leaders and members, and something about the work they are doing.

In a sense, I have an "old-fashioned" understanding of the church. I have a first-century understanding, not a churched-culture understanding. In the first century, a majority of the congregation was involved in the mission, and some were involved in committees. Or consider it this way: On any pioneering mission field on the planet today, what we would do is develop an abundance of mission teams and just a few committees. It is time to do that on this mission field.

OWNERSHIP

People who participate in any three of these four—mission, visitation, worship, grouping—will have high ownership for their church, whether they ever serve on a committee or not. That is, someone who participates in three of the first four central characteristics is a person who has discovered and is sharing help, hope, and home. They are living out and fulfilling their foundational life searches of individuality, community, meaning, and hope. For them, it is not a matter of mere ownership, it is *home*.

The old myth was, The more people on more committees, the higher the ownership for the local church. The truth was, the more people on more committees, the more meetings that were held and the less mission that was achieved.

As a missionary pastor, it is important to keep your organizational committee structure simple enough that it can be explained to new members in ten minutes. If it takes an hour to explain it, the organizational structure is too complex.

Remember that most new members join a church longing for and looking for help, hope, and home. The first and second central characteristics (specific, concrete missional objectives, and

The Central Characteristics of Successful Churches

Relational Characteristics	Functional Characteristics
Help — 1. Specific, Concrete Missional Objectives 1 2 3 4 5 6 7 8 9 10	7. Several Competent Programs and Activities 1 2 3 4 5 6 7 8 9 10
2. Pastoral/Lay Visitation in Community 1 2 3 4 5 6 7 8 9 10	8. Open Accessibility 1 2 3 4 5 6 7 8 9 10
Hope — 3. Corporate, Dynamic Worship 1 2 3 4 5 6 7 8 9 10	9. High Visibility 1 2 3 4 5 6 7 8 9 10
Home — 4. Significant Relational Groups 1 2 3 4 5 6 7 8 9 10	10. Adequate Parking 1 2 3 4 5 6 7 8 9 10
5. Strong Leadership Resources 1 2 3 4 5 6 7 8 9 10	11. Adequate Space and Facilities 1 2 3 4 5 6 7 8 9 10
6. Solid, Participatory Decision Making 1 2 3 4 5 6 7 8 9 10	12. Solid Financial Resources 1 2 3 4 5 6 7 8 9 10

pastoral and lay visitation in the community) deliver a sense of help. The third central characteristic (worship that is corporate and dynamic) delivers a sense of hope. The fourth central characteristic (significant relational groupings) delivers a sense of roots, place, belonging—home. New members search for community, not committee.

The best new-member orientations help persons to discover a sense of direction as they seek fulfillment in their foundational life searches. New members discover that sense of help, hope, and home as they discover their own sense of mission, shepherding, worship and prayer, and belonging.

The orientation would focus on the ways the church plans to resource them in these areas and the ways the church is resourcing the mission field in these areas. In the midst of this perhaps, a very brief time would be given to describing the simplified committee structure the church has recently implemented. The focus would be more on "missionship" than ownership.

As a missionary pastor, discourage the use of a new-member orientation to "recruit" the new member. A typical new-member orientation includes a range of persons spending "a few minutes each" telling something about the work of their committee. A "list of opportunities" is then handed out. (Notice that virtually every item on the list is for a job inside the church.) The effort is to recruit the new member to fill some vacant slot in which "we need help."

The best purpose for a new-member orientation is to help the person to think through his or her role as a resource, using questions such as the following:

1. Which of the foundational life searches is most important to you now?
2. Which specific human hurts and hopes do you have longings to help?
3. What are your specific gifts and competencies?
4. Where does your own sense of discovery, fulfillment, and mission lead you?

The focus is on our helping, resourcing, and sending out the new member, rather than on recruiting them to help us. If a "list of opportunities" is shared, the majority of the list will focus on the emerging mission teams who are serving in the world. There will be a much smaller list of the committee opportunities inside the church.

We are "resourcing" the new member. They are not resourcing us. Remember that they are frequently *new* to the faith. It is a mission field now. It is we who are helping them. It is not they who are going to help us.

This is not so much a matter of words. This is a matter of spirit and theology. It is a theology of service, not a theology of survival. Our task is serving the new members, not getting them to help us with our survival. *As persons experience serving, they serve. But as persons experience survival, they struggle to survive.*

As a missionary pastor, share the same serving spirit with current members. In our time, persons will have a stronger sense of ownership as they participate in three of the first four central characteristics.

The sixth central characteristic—a solid, participatory decision-making process and a streamlined organizational structure—has to do with the "committees" of the local church. I wish I had a nickel for every time I have heard someone say, "Put so-and-so on a committee; that will help get them active again." Nothing in the Bible says, "Be ye therefore on a committee, for blessed will be your reward in heaven." The twelve characteristics are listed in their order of importance. When we encourage persons to discover ownership by means of a committee, we are pointing them to the sixth central characteristic. When you help a person to discover how they can share in three of the first four, there you have a person who has ownership—*for the mission.*

LEADERS

Key principle: Match the organizational structure to the leaders. Do not try to squeeze your leaders into the slots of a prescribed organizational structure. Match the plays with the players.

There are three helpful steps:

1. Consider your leadership resources.
2. Decide your key objectives.
3. Design a minimal organizational structure.

The first step is to look closely at the leadership resources you currently have. Not the ones you wish you had, not the ones you think you should have—look at the leaders you have.

Think through the strengths, gifts, and competencies that are genuinely present among the leaders and grass roots of your congregation. Look at the leadership resources in the community. Look at the leadership resources present on your mission field.

You may not find an abundance of leaders. On a mission field, there is usually a shortage of personnel for the mission at hand. The point is not abundance. The point is to look for the resources that are in fact there.

The second step is to decide your key objectives. Think through where you are headed as a local church. What kind of future are you building:

- for the lives and destinies of families on your mission field?
- for the character and quality of life in the community?
- for the advancement of peace and justice in the world?
- for the mission and strength of your local church?

Think through the strategies for mission that are important for the future.

Study the twelve central characteristics of effective churches. Claim your current strengths. Decide which current strengths you plan to expand. Decide which new strengths you plan to add. Now, decide the key, major objectives that are important for the future.

The third step is to design just enough of an organizational structure. That is, create a minimal organizational structure that matches with your leaders and congregation and that helps, not hinders, them to accomplish their key objectives. Form follows function. Structure follows strategy. Organization follows objectives.

When local churches fit their leadership resources into a denomination's prescribed organizational structure and then think through their goals, they put the cart before the horse. To make matters even worse, that prescribed structure is usually too complex and cumbersome on a mission field.

The best sequence for structure development is as follows:

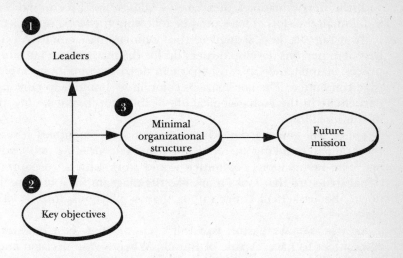

The worst sequence for structure development is the following:

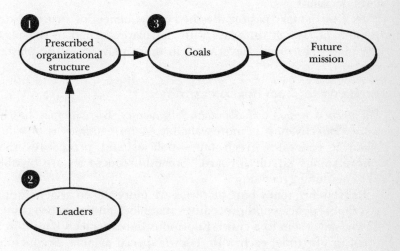

There is an important implication for nominations committees in local churches. No longer would a nominations committee start with the denomination's prescribed organizational form and try to fill in all the slots. That would be following the worst sequence.

By using the best sequence, the nominations committee can best help persons develop ownership for the mission and not simply for maintenance. It can help them discover community more than committee. The nominations committee should help persons participate in the eschatological life of the church, not simply its institutional life.

There will come a day when nominations committees invest their time in thanking current leaders and encouraging new leaders. The nominations committee would work with an organizational structure that looks more like the diagram for a fast break down the basketball court rather than a playbook full of 197 plays.

As a missionary pastor, you will come to know best how few committees to have. A rule of thumb: When a wise decision and significant results can be achieved by an individual, do not give the project to a committee. This is especially true of C- and D-level decisions.

As a missionary pastor, use the best sequence for structure development. Match the plays with the players. Send in the plays the players can run. Never send in more plays than the players can run.

EFFECTIVENESS AND BUREAUCRACY

Effectiveness is more valuable than bureaucracy. Bureaucracy has its value. Effectiveness is more valuable. A bureaucracy is of value when it generates green tape—policies and procedures that "move things rapidly forward." Some bureaucracies are capable of generating green tape.

Regrettably, many bureaucracies are more skilled at generating red tape—policies and procedures that block and stop, bog things down, slow them to a crawl. Enormous bureaucracies have developed in our time, each with its own special agenda. Frequently, that agenda includes the bureaucracy spending considerable energy in justifying its own existence and increasing its size.

The trend toward bureaucracy is the trend toward oblivion. As valiantly as individuals in a bureaucracy struggle to deliver green tape, the red tape seems to grow at a more rapid pace. It is precisely these nameless, faceless, ponderous bureaucracies of cumbersome policies and procedures, as slow moving as a glacier, that contribute to people's experiencing a pervasive sense of powerlessness in their lives and destinies.

To a large extent, denominational bureaucracies are simply a cultural reflection of the bureaucratic character of our present society. Their organizational structure, their policies and procedures, their interface (and lack thereof) with the grass roots, their agendas and concerns—all are remarkably comparable to many of the bureaucracies of the culture. Some green tape is produced. Much red tape is delivered.

Many, many individuals who serve on national church boards and agencies are extraordinarily competent. It is precisely because of their competencies that they have been asked to serve in a national capacity. To be sure, as with any large bureaucracy, some persons are less competent than others in their respective posts.

Even the most competent persons in the boards and agencies lament the snail's pace and red tape. The dilemma has less to do with individuals and more to do with "the nature of the beast." To be sure, some boards and agencies have developed "more successful" bureaucracies than others.

On the whole, the bureaucracy of a denomination seeks to do good work and frequently does. The dilemma may be this: the bureaucracies of most mainline denominations grew up in a culture marked by two characteristics:

1. It was a churched culture.
2. It was a bureaucratic culture.

There was a confidence in the culture that the bureaucracies of culture could successfully tackle the major problems in the society. There were excellent illustrations of this in some of the government bureaucracies of that time. The recent "best efforts" of some of these governmental bureaucracies have been less effective than before.

This may signal that the organizational methodology of bureaucracy, which worked well in an earlier time, is less able to be effective in the chaos and emerging trends of this culture and these times.

The dilemma may be that the organizational structure of a denominational bureaucracy is facing a similar plight. Church bureaucracies may have been more "at home" in the culture in which they grew up. Their work may have been more helpful in a churched culture wherein bureaucratic organizational structures flourished. Their help may be more limited on a mission field. The critical need, however, is effectiveness, not bureaucracy.

A mission field calls for improvisation and creativity. A bureaucracy produces grand strategies and great programs. A mission field calls for planning sessions that last one to three days. A bureaucracy has the ability to have planning sessions consume three to five days. A mission field calls for missionary pastors and mission team leaders. A bureaucracy is more comfortable with professional ministers and laity.

The issue is ultimately one of effectiveness versus ineffectiveness. Some people say, "Thank God, we are not a business," as their way of escaping a responsibility for effectiveness in mission. They try to excuse sloppy work, incompetent planning, misspent energies, and inept, mediocre results with the comment, "I am glad we are not a business." They are using the metaphor of business as an excuse for their own ineptness and ineffectiveness.

The organizational principle of effectiveness does encourage the concomitant values of excellent mistakes and creativity. There is a direct correlation between the value of excellent mistakes and the level of creativity in an organization. This correlation does not condone a pattern of inept, incompetent, mediocre work. Rather, it encourages the value of creativity. Quite simply, **the more positive the recognition for excellent mistakes, the higher the level of creativity in the grouping.**

People's creativity is advanced when the organization encourages improvisation, initiative, spontaneity, and new ideas. In many organizations it would help to give an annual award for the best mistake of the year.

People hide their creativity when the organization delivers negative reinforcement for an excellent mistake. Blame creates blockages. People become frozen, tense, and tight. People seek to please rather than produce.

The organizational principle of effectiveness values strong creativity and excellent mistakes. Effectiveness encourages productivity, not pleasing passivism. The organizational principle of

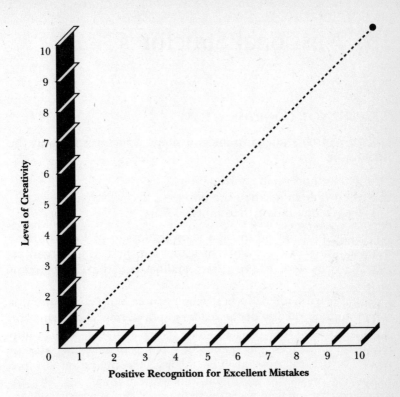

effectiveness works over against any effort by the church to excuse mediocre effort.

God calls us to effective mission. The Scriptures are quite clear. There is and will be an accounting for the effectiveness of our mission. To use business as "the fall guy" does not release us from an accounting with God for the effectiveness of our work. We are accountable for new ideas, excellent mistakes, strong creativity, and for our effectiveness. A central principle of organization is to create structures that are effective in mission.

As a missionary pastor, help your local church to develop a simple structure that follows the basic principles of organization. This is a first-century time. This is a twenty-first century time. This is a mission time.

16. Missional Structures

ACTION, NOT COORDINATION

Local church leadership and missional structures live out the qualities of:

- action more than coordination
- the whole more than the parts
- long range rather than quick closure

Missionary pastors and mission team leaders grow forward their understanding of the nature of leadership best in an organizational environment where these qualities are the predominant norms.

People learn leadership best when action, not coordination, is a predominant quality of the leadership and missional structure. A preoccupation with coordination creates managers and administrators, not leaders. The quality of action is dynamically present in a structure for mission. The quality of cooperation is more pervasively present in an organization for survival.

An emphasis on action results in accomplishments and achievements. An emphasis on coordination results in complacency. Now, I am not against coordination. I do *not* favor a lack of coordination. I am against coordination as a predominant quality in local church structures.

The choice is not *either* action *or* coordination. The choice is which one will receive the predominant emphasis. Do not have a preference for 70 percent coordination and 30 percent action. Have a preference for 70 percent action and 30 percent coordination.

This is easier said than done. Think how many times you have heard the statement, "We'd better be sure this is well coordinated." Or, "That sounds like a good idea; let's take it to the committee for coordination." Read the minutes of local church and denominational committee meetings. Count the times coordination is the focus. Indeed, the plea of coordination is frequently used to slow down action.

Some who work in a bureaucracy are not bureaucrats. Some are pioneers. To be sure, many who work in a bureaucracy are, in fact, bureaucrats. To be a bureaucrat is to have a particular mentality and perspective, not a particular post or position.

By and large, bureaucrats have a conserving, holding, protecting, and preserving mentality, with a focus on coordination. By contrast, pioneers have a growing, developing, advancing, and building perspective, with a focus on action.

Some bureaucrats have an addiction to meetings and coordination much like some persons have an addiction to alcohol. One of the reasons bureaucrats call so many meetings is because of their addiction to that environment. The meeting is, for them, a narcotic fix. Amid the rules and regulations that they manufacture, the red tape and paper trails that they create, it is the meetings that they call that deliver to them a sense of relationships, purpose, power, and community.

Indeed, one reason bureaucrats convene a three-day meeting to accomplish what could be achieved in one day is this primordial addiction to meetings. Furthermore, they know when the meeting is over, they will reluctantly have to go back to manufacturing rules and regulations, creating red tape, and following paper trails. Dimly, they sense the purposelessness in those activities.

We can no longer afford the luxury of the leisurely quality of coordination in a churched culture, which is where this quality was developed and emphasized. It goes hand-in-hand with a bureaucratic culture. The quality of action is central to a mission field.

When one examines closely the two qualities of action versus coordination and the distinctive ways they influence an understanding of the nature of leadership and the related values, objectives, and behavior patterns, one discovers the following intriguing correlation:

action	vs.	coordination
decentralization	vs.	centralization
productivity	vs.	power

An emphasis on action includes concomitant emphases on decentralization and productivity. An emphasis on coordination includes concomitant emphases on centralization and power.

Action, decentralization, and productivity are companions in the adventure toward achievement in mission. Coordination, centralization, and power are cousins in the effort to survive.

Sometimes coordination is the slave of centralization, not its cousin. People interested in productivity head toward action and decentralization. But people interested in power head toward coordination and centralization. The quest for power gathers the bedfellows of coordination and centralization. They are the "shills," the "fronts," in the quest for power.

Persons are sometimes drawn to power. Underneath, in compulsive, desperate ways, they are living out their foundational life searches. For them, the solution is power. Hence, they develop an organizational structure that is designed in their best interests, not in the interests of the organization and its mission.

More often than not, they are committed to the policy of centralization. The alleged purpose of centralization is to coordinate efforts and to cut costs. The statement is made, "If we are to survive, this must be done."

In fact, centralization also cuts morale, initiative, creativity, and productivity. Centralization may save some money on the front end. Its costs, in the long run, are substantial.

Leaders of centralization frequently support the quality of coordination. Why? Because coordination is in the best interests of those leaders who are committed to a policy of centralization. Coordination is encouraged by those persons who are already on top of a centralized organization.

By contrast, action, decentralization, and productivity are grass-roots qualities that mission teams, short-term task forces, and a wide range of grass-roots coalitions support as central to the organization. The quality of action is in the best interests of the grass roots.

The important point to note is that the quality of coordination is not simply an accidental value that has a "boy scout," "clean as a spring rain" character. Coordination is a quality that serves the best interests of the leaders of a centralized organizational structure. The "quality" of coordination is the way to control, to see that not too much happens.

A commitment to decentralization and a corollary commitment to "frontline" action, accomplishment, and achievement are dynamic commitments for proactive grass-roots leadership. They stand over against centralization and coordination as ineffective qualities for contemporary organizational structures. Someone once said, "In a centralized system, we were top-heavy in management. We were keeping beautiful track of what we were not doing." **People interested in productivity are drawn to action-oriented, decentralized groupings.**

You may wisely ask, "As we head toward action, decentralization, and productivity, will the people at the top be willing to give up power?" That is a very wise, thoughtful question. People who have a desperate, addictive need for power have great difficulty giving up their addiction. And even persons at the top who have power but are not addicted to it sometimes find it more comfortable to keep all of their power rather than give up some of it.

And that is the key. Decentralization does not mean that persons at the top are giving up all their power. Oh, to addictive power individuals, giving up just a little power does feel like they are giving all of it up. All of that power is precious and comforting and delivers the necessary "narcotic power fix" to sustain an addictive pattern of behavior.

The reality is that decentralization invites a strong focus on local sources of power. There would still be appropriate sources of power at the denominational level.

Persons at the top, however, have already been giving up power. As a denomination continues toward stable and declining, the power and influence of the denomination heads toward fading and eroding. The more a denomination declines, the more power is lost by people at the top. It is a wiser course to give up some power—constructively, through decentralization—rather than to continue to give up power destructively and by default. The issue is not whether people at the top are going to give up some of their power. The issue is which way are they going to do it.

Persons committed to centralization are committed to coordination. Without the quality of coordination, it is not possible to achieve centralization.

When a denomination gets into trouble (becomes stable and declining) the leaders of that denomination make the incorrect assumption that the solution is better coordination of an overall denominational effort. Persons who participate in centralization tend to conclude that coordination is the solution to a stable and declining phenomenon. As a matter of fact, that denomination became as strong as it is because of the decentralized grass-roots action and the productivity of local churches. Look at the stages:

1. Originally, the denomination grew because of the decentralized action and productivity of grass-roots local churches.
2. The denomination became strong enough and bureaucratic enough that some persons introduced the concepts of coordination and centralization.
3. The denomination allowed itself to be influenced by the organizational methodology of bureaucracy—and had the resources to build one.
4. The denomination, for a wide range of reasons, became stable and declining.
5. Top-down leaders reemphasized the importance of coordination and centralization.
6. The denomination continued to decline.
7. More denominational meetings were held.

We have been through these stages enough times to have learned.
The strongest future grows out of an emphasis on action, decentralization, and productivity. The best way forward is with:

- the *local action* of missionary pastors, mission team leaders, and grass-roots missionary congregations
- the *decentralized action* of denominational leaders, who see themselves increasingly as "grassroots" missionary leaders

In an important development, some denominational leaders—whether district superintendents, mission directors, presbytery officers, bishops, or area ministers—are increasingly investing their major leadership, energy, and time with their specific mission field. These grass-roots denominational leaders are making decisive contributions.

They see themselves more as a mission leader of their mission field and less as a denominational leader of the church-at-large. They see themselves delivering decentralized action rather than centralized coordination. They invest much more time advancing specific local churches and much less time attending denominational meetings. This is a trend whose time has come.

To be sure, there is a dynamic between local and centralized sources of power. In our system of government, we have developed a carefully constructed balance of power between three branches of government. We created that balance because there was an extraordinary reaction against the autocratic power found in England and Europe. Thus, the people who founded this country crafted a carefully constructed fragmentation of power.

No one branch of the government received too much power, because there was a healthy intuition to distrust centralized power. That distrust grew out of the reaction against autocratic power. Today we see that healthy intuition of distrust growing out of the foundational search for individuality and the unwillingness to grant an external force too much power over one's life and destiny.

There is a negative reaction toward power, particularly centralized power. As the trend toward dislocation of power has focused itself increasingly at international levels, we are seeing a reaction against that trend and toward local power and autonomy.

In the long run, the way forward is not to live in a state of reaction toward centralized power. The way forward is to construct healthy, dynamic, decentralized structures for action and productivity.

For the present and immediate future, it is decisive to cultivate these decentralized, local sources of power. The understanding of the nature of leadership important on a mission field makes this emphasis the compelling direction forward. The trend toward dislocation of power makes this imperative. The organizational methodology of a centralized bureaucracy has seen its day. The time for coordination is over. The time for action has come.

THE WHOLE, NOT THE PARTS

People learn leadership best when the whole, not the parts, is a predominant quality of the organizational and missional structure. There are two basic ways to construct an organizational structure:

- focus on the whole
- focus on the parts

Some organizational structures are primarily constructed, developed, and implemented by a structuring of the whole. Some organizational structures have been constructed by a structuring of the parts. The latter approach was fairly prevalent in the churched culture, wherein the organizational methodology of bureaucracy was widely employed.

Each approach has a distinctive organizing principle. The starting point of the first approach is the whole. The starting point of the second approach is the parts. In organizational structure design, where one begins is where one ends up.

The originating premise of each approach has these concomitant results:

Whole	Part
1. wholistic	segmentalist
2. integrative	compartmental
3. dynamic	departmentalized

The beginning point shapes the results. (Currently the preferred spelling of the first result is *holistic*. That spelling is reminiscent of holy and therefore skews what is at stake. To me, the spelling *wholistic* more straightforwardly indicates the point—namely, a focus on the whole.)

Each approach can be analyzed by an examination of:

1. its basic perspective
2. the way each is structured
3. the way each works in actual practice

Indeed, these three categories—perspective, structure, and practice—are helpful in the study of any organizational system.

Perspective. Each approach looks at the world in distinctive ways. The first approach has as its primary perception a view of the whole. The second approach builds on a perception of the parts. The first is wholistic; the second segmentalist.

In a certain sense, one could say both are true. Yet perception is reality to the person with that perception. The originating perception results in organizational structures that are constructed distinctively and that function distinctively in actual practice.

Each approach would acknowledge that there is a relationship between the whole and the parts. The first approach would have a secondary perception of the parts. The second approach would certainly confirm the value of the whole. But the originating perception heads each approach down a distinctive path.

Structure. Each approach is structured distinctively. With the first approach, the core organizational structure is composed of persons who represent the whole. With the second approach, the core structure is composed of persons who represent the parts.

In the first approach, persons "get to" the core structure because of:

- their capacity to see the whole
- their competency to give leadership to the whole

They have an integrative perspective and competency of leadership.

In the second approach, persons "get to" the core structure because of:

- their capacity to see a given part
- their competency to give leadership to a specific part

They have a compartmental perspective and competency of leadership.

Practice. Each approach functions distinctively. In the first approach, the core organizational group focuses on the central issues that have impact on:

- the mission of the whole
- the well-being of the whole

The focus is on the dynamic and developmental strategies that will advance the whole.

The meetings of the core group focus on the central, common issues. Persons "around the table" actively contribute their wisdom and competencies to the development of wholistic strategies.

The work of the core group has a wholistic character. The persons function as a team in a flexible, dynamic way. Turf issues are minimal. All share the turf of the whole, rather than each being preoccupied with his or her own turf.

In the second approach, the core structure focuses on the issues that have impact on:

- the mission of each department
- the well-being of each department

The focus is on the departmental strategies that will advance each department. The assumption is that the well-being of each compartment provides for the well-being of the whole.

The meetings of the core structure focus on the plans of each department. The chair usually asks that each department's report be brief. Persons "around the table" listen attentively to what each department is doing and, from time to time, ask questions and contribute excellent suggestions.

The work of the core structure has a departmentalized character. The persons function as the chairs of specific departments. Turf issues arise from time to time. The core structure spends some of its work in clarifying these turf issues and in "interpreting" who is responsible for what.

A simplified analogy will help. Once, long ago, local churches had a core group whose focus was the whole. Since most local churches in that time were small and since the terrain was a mission field, people "got to" the core group because of their wisdom and capacity to see the whole. Since chaos was the terrain and mission the central objective, the core group functioned as a flexible, dynamic mission team.

Times got better. A churched culture emerged. Busy programs and activities were developed. Many causes arose. Bureaucratic structures became the organizational methodology of the time.

Someone suggested; "Wouldn't it be wonderful if each person on the core group became the representative of a specific program area?" The thought had been that the whole will continue to be looked after, and we can now give even greater attention to each program area, to each part. Actually, at that point the whole began to die.

A focus on the parts does not automatically help the whole. In recent times, a number of denominations have lived out this analogy. The intentions were good. The results were not.

As long as it was a thriving churched culture, the whole could "survive" while the core structure focused on fine-tuning the parts. But when the whole comes into jeopardy, a core structure that has been built to focus on the parts is less helpful.

The whole is greater than the sum of the parts. The second approach tends to assume that the sum of the parts is equal to the whole. But attention to the parts—even all of the parts—does not necessarily advance the whole *as whole*. The whole deserves and must have nurturing and development. This is especially true on a mission field, where the whole, more than the parts, is "under attack."

That is, in a churched culture, the "enterprise" of the Christian faith is supported and encouraged and seldom ever questioned. On a mission field, the very essence of the enterprise is questioned, attacked, and ignored. The time for the whole has come. The day of the parts is over.

On a mission field, any core structure built on the second approach, wherein people "get to" the core only as representatives of the various parts, will find itself in a dilemma. This systemic, structural, organizational dilemma is best called the *tree-forest flaw*. People cannot see the forest because of their preoccupation with the trees.

Each person gets to the council bringing the tree of which they are in charge. Each person counts on the council to provide coordination and cooperation so that each tree around the table will get "its fair share of water" on an annual basis. But suppose you ask that council, "What major priority to advance the whole are you, as a team, growing forward in the coming three years?" Usually, the response is a blank look or a puzzled silence.

That council cannot see the forest because of the trees. They have been so busy ensuring that each part gets its fair share of water each year. They have two difficulties:

1. seeing the whole
2. looking more than one year ahead

The test is very simple. Read the minutes of most councils for October of a given year. Then read the minutes for October two years earlier. The names will have changed. The discussion will be the same.

The council that looks at the whole, not the parts, is a council that decides on one to four long-range priorities that will advance the whole. For example, a given council might decide that a priority is mission with families with preschool children. (Note: There will be single-parent, double-parent, and blended families. All are blessed in the eyes of God.)

The council with a wholistic priority for mission with preschool families takes steps such as the following:

- Missions develops a mission team that delivers concrete, effective help to a specific human hurt or hope among preschool families in the community.
- Evangelism focuses its best visitation with newcomer and unchurched preschool families.
- Worship develops a worship service most helpful with preschool families and prayer resources for the preschool family as a whole.
- Education selects some of its best teachers for the nursery and preschool classes and starts one or two new adult groupings for preschool parents.
- Church and society discovers the specific societal issues with which preschool families are wrestling in the community and vigorously addresses them.
- Trustees develops a nursery (and preschool facilities) that looks more like a 1990s nursery than a 1950s one. (That is, the board will look at the nursery through the eyes of a mother and father who are having their firstborn child in the 1990s. I see too many recently redecorated 1950s nurseries; the persons on the committee had their children in the 1950s.)
- Pastor-parish delivers whatever future staffing makes best sense.
- Finance advances a solid component of the budget toward this major priority.
- Communications distributes excellent publicity with preschool families in the community.

The core group functions as a team contributing to the advancement of the whole. In a flexible, wholistic, integrative, dynamic way, the team—as a whole—contributes to the central missional priority that the team has identified as most crucial for the mission and well-being of the whole. (Note that the central priority may not be preschool families. I help churches in Florida, Arizona, and New Mexico where there is no one in the community under sixty-five years of age.) Furthermore, the core group may have more than one central priority, but it will *not* have eight or nine. The range will look more like one to four. In a wholistic approach, the core group has the following look:

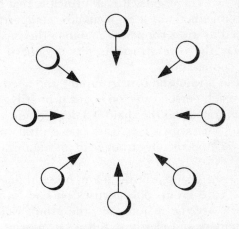

Organizational Focus on the Whole

In the second approach—the segmentalist—the core structure looks more like the following:

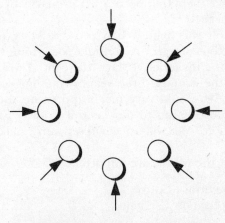

Organizational Focus on the Parts

In a departmental structure, each work area primarily focuses on its own agenda. Mission does its own work. Evangelism and worship do their own work. Education does its work, and so forth. It is like a collection of individuals living under the same roof who have not yet become a family.

In this second approach, the value of cooperation is frequently emphasized. Why? The organizational principle that brought the core structure together was a segmentalist, compartmental one. Hence, the need to stress cooperation among the various departments. The way the core structure gets organized creates the need to stress cooperation.

By contrast, in a wholistic core grouping, the need is lessened. Why? Because each person came on board primarily as a member of the team, not initially as the chair of a department, *and* because of the unifying character of at least one central priority. The sense of unity is immediately stronger in an organizational focus on the whole.

A wholistic core group will do many other things. I am not suggesting the core group only focuses on one to four central priorities. These are the majors. Yes, the group will achieve its fair share of minors and electives. But what informs and orders the work of the group are the majors that the core group has in common. It is not the case that *each* part is a major each year.

Key Point: **How you ask someone to come on board shapes how they will participate.** Their original perception shapes their behavior. You give them that perception primarily by the way you invite them on board.

This suggestion will help. When you ask Mary (or John) to become part of the core group, consider something like this as a way of sharing the invitation. "Mary, the central priority for the council during the coming three years is our mission with preschool families. We would very much appreciate your being on the team and contributing to our central priority as the team's leader in education." You will use whatever words make best sense to you.

The steps, not the words, are important:

1. Share the central priority.
2. Share appreciation for them.

3. Affirm that their participation is *on the team*, contributing to the central priority.
4. Indicate that they are the team's leader in education.

Note that they are *not* education's leader on the core team.

In the second approach, the invitation is usually shared like this. "Mary, we would appreciate your being willing to chair the work area on education this coming year. That would also mean that you would represent education on the council." You get what you ask for. It is *not* simply a matter of words. People live forward or downward to our expectations of them.

It will be helpful for nomination committees to consider how they ask persons to come on board. The nature of the invitation influences the leadership behavior.

In coming years, it is important for local churches to develop organizational and missional structures that focus on the whole. This invites changes in perspective, structure, and practice. Indeed, some local church councils have already achieved these advances. Many are in the process of doing so. On a mission field, the quality of the whole *is* decisive.

LONG-RANGE PERSPECTIVE, NOT REACTION

Persons learn leadership best in an organizational and missional structure wherein the quality of a long-range perspective is strongly present. Many organizations have a perspective best illustrated as follows:

That is, their behavior pattern is to react to whatever has emerged *in the present moment* and to head immediately to a quick-closure resolution.

An organization's response time is important. A few organizations have tried a behavior pattern as follows:

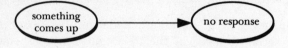

Such organizations generally do not last very long. Their lack of response finally calls into question the "being" and value of their existence.

Fortunately, few local churches have this "no response" behavior pattern. The majority tend to have a "reactive → quick closure" pattern. The meetings of their core structure frequently wrestle with "immediate problems and quick-closure solutions." I am not being critical of this. They are, in fact, trying to achieve something.

I have worked with some churches who have developed a "something comes up → no response" behavior pattern. As a result of such a pattern, sustained over a period of time, they have created for themselves enormous problems. Many of those problems could have been resolved earlier and easier. At least, "reactive → quick closure" churches are avoiding that pitfall.

The healthiest organizational and missional structures include both of the following:

- a reactive → quick closure perspective
- a long range → short term perspective

The former without the latter creates a ship without a rudder. A "long range → short term" perspective informs and guides an organization's "reactive → quick closure" pattern. The long-range perspective provides a sense of direction, growth and development, accomplishment and achievement. In developing a long-range planning perspective for your local church, several guidelines are important.

Purpose

The purpose of long-range planning is immediate action. In a more specific way, this type of planning is best referred to as long-range short-term planning. The purpose of long-range planning is short-range action. We look ahead to achieve now.

Some persons have emphasized primarily the end results of long-range planning. They have focused predominantly on the objectives to be achieved five years from now. Actually, we look long range to know what to accomplish short term.

We set up the long-range objective; then we work backward from there to decide the short-term steps that will help. Most people set the date for the wedding and then work backward from that date. Given the wedding date, they now know what needs to be accomplished the week before the wedding, the month before, two months before, and so on, and therefore they know what needs to be achieved *this week*. An important point: Until most people set the date for the wedding, they tend not to get married.

Someone decides to build a house. They generally set the target date for when they plan to move in—say, fourteen months from today. Once they know the target date, they know what to achieve this week. Another person may have a target date of twenty months. That will make a strong difference in what they focus on this week. Someone else may have a date of nine months.

Without a date for the wedding, the marriage does not usually happen. Without the "move in" date for the house, it does not usually get built. The purpose of the long-range target date is to help one know what to achieve now.

Horizon

The best time horizon for long-range planning is three years, sometimes five years. The more chaotic and confusing and the more ambiguous and changing the terrain, the more important long-range short-term planning is.

The value of long-range planning is direction, not control. Some persons have imagined that a long-range plan will enable them to control their future. No, it gives the person (and the local church) a strong sense of direction.

In sailing, the variables are considerable—wind, rain, tide, current, reefs, shore, gusts, sun, moon, heat, cold, and other ships. The storms are many. The reefs are near. The sailor has no control over these.

The sailor's course serves as a guide. It is this sense of direction—given the variables of the moment and those on the horizon—which helps the sailor to decide the heading important now. There will be many tacks. The compass headings, from hour to hour, will vary. It is the course that provides direction.

To be sure, in an earlier time, persons in the field of long-range planning thought of ten-year plans. They were confident of their planning. The seas may have been calmer then. Then, the thought of seven years made sense. In more recent times, there has been a focus on five years.

Given the emerging trends of these times, the enormous variables that are in motion, and the character of our mission field, the best way forward is to work with an *operational* time horizon of three years, sometimes five. That is, help the day-to-day operations of your work and mission to have a three-year time horizon. Do what you do today, looking forward this year and two more.

On some matters we will certainly look from five to ten, twenty, or thirty years ahead. In helping a church think through whether it makes sense to relocate, we certainly look long, long range. And in something as central and vital as growing forward a specific, concrete missional objective, we will want to look five, seven, or ten years ahead.

Most local churches need to quit looking only one year ahead. Their mistake is *not* in looking long range. Their mistake is in looking no more than a year. Their mistake is a "reactive → quick closure" annual behavior pattern.

In their operational planning, they look only one year ahead. Then they look another year ahead. Their operational behavior is a series of one-year plans. The difficulty is that their ability to develop a strong sense of momentum in mission is minimal.

In something as simple as professional football, we know it takes five years to build a winning team. In something as complex as mission—helping persons with their lives and destinies—it may take three to five years to build a strong missionary congregation.

In many ways, we look ahead. People buy a car, thinking three years. They buy a house, thinking five to ten years. People enter college, thinking four years. People plant a forest of pine trees, thinking ten years. In building a new sanctuary, people think ahead twenty-five years or more. In relocating a church, people think ahead thirty years or more.

In something as important as mission, however, many local churches think only one year ahead. The excuse is that there are too many variables. Yet we do all of the above "lesser things," looking more than one year ahead.

Consider the creativity, energy, time, and long-range planning that a building committee invests in developing a blueprint for a building: the revisions of the plans; the meetings held, frequently every week; the care taken to see that every wall and every room are in the right place.

A church's "blueprint for mission" deserves the same creativity, energy, time, and long-range planning. A mission planning committee is as important as a building planning committee.

God invites us to look more than one year ahead on the greater things as well as the lesser things. Encourage your mission team to develop the sense of direction for its operational, day-to-day mission, looking to the coming three years.

THE PROCESSIVE APPROACH

Develop a processive approach to long-range planning, not a block approach. The block approach is a rigid, static methology— and no longer useful. It looks like the following diagram:

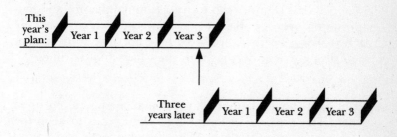

The grouping creates a three-year (or five-year) plan. Then, toward the end of the third year, they create another three-year plan. There are too many variables in our time for this approach to work.

The processive approach is more developmental and dynamic and has a more flexible spirit. We could diagram this approach as follows:

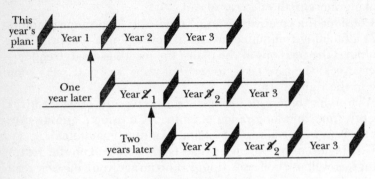

Advance and improve; add new third year.

That is, toward the end of the first year, accomplish two steps:

1. Advance, improve, add, change, modify, or delete the objectives for year 2 and year 3 of the original plan.
2. Add the new third year.

Thus, in a processive way, with considerable flexibility, you can build the momentum for significant mission.

The council that continues to focus on annual planning is generally presiding over a stable and declining mission. As best one can, each year work with a three-year time horizon. Your mission will more strongly help persons with their lives and destinies.

Options

The art of long-range planning is to keep as many options open as possible. The purpose of long-range planning is to keep the future open, not close it down. The mistake some make is to develop a unilateral long-range plan that they are going to follow "come hades or high water." They will be disappointed.

Do not try to "lock everything down." It is not so much that you have a backup plan. Rather, it is a matter of moving forward with your plan, knowing:

1. Many objectives will be well achieved.
2. Some objectives will be excellent mistakes from which we learn.

3. Some objectives will not work.
4. We will discover new objectives as we move forward.

It is important to build into your planning a flexible set of objectives that keep your future open.

The Planning Team

Develop a long-range planning team for your local church. In our time, most local churches benefit from having a specific team whose primary task is to help the church look long range.

Two points will help. First, create an on-going, working team. Do not fall into the trap of having a long-range planning committee help to formulate a plan and then disbanding the group. It is important that on a consistent, ongoing basis, some team help the local church have a long-range vision.

Second, create a team of persons who do *not* have many annual program responsibilities. To be sure, all key leaders now look three years ahead, not just one. At the same time, it is not fair to ask the person who is delivering major work *now* to focus also on long-range planning. The long-range planning steering committee has a major task in its own right.

This team may be called "the long-range planning steering committee" or whatever is deemed appropriate. *Twelve Keys to an Effective Church: The Leaders' Guide* will provide you with considerable resources on the ways in which a long-range planning team goes about its work.

As we look to the future, it will take the best efforts of missionary pastors, mission team leaders, and missionary congregations together to advance the church's mission. The development of local-church leadership and missional structures will be decisive, both in the mission and in helping persons to learn leadership for the mission.

It is important that these local-church structures, which appropriately will take many forms, live out the criteria for structures, the principles of organization, and the qualities in missional structures.

As a missionary pastor, help your local church to discover a simple structure that advances your mission. Begin today. The mission is now.

17. Church Development

GROUPINGS FOR DEVELOPMENT

Missionary pastors have a strong, urgent interest in church development, that is, in planting and developing increasingly effective mission outposts. Missionary pastors do *not* have an interest in perpetuating "churched culture" churches who had their best day in the long-ago churched culture of the late 1940s and 1950s and who have turned blatantly or passively inward on themselves. Such churches have closed their door to the world. They have hung out a sign that reads, "No room in the inn for you." Fortunately, there are fewer and fewer churches like this left.

The best way forward in church development is to *discern the current strengths of your church.* As a missionary pastor, think through whether you are serving a First Third, a Middle Third, or a Third Third local church.

A group of local churches (whether called a mission area, a presbytery, a district, or a diocese) can be divided into these three kinds of local churches. Each local church in the larger group can be placed into one of these specific groupings on the basis of the strengths and competencies that that local church has well in place.

I recognize that some persons would suggest the designations of top, middle, and bottom third. I am reluctant to use the terms *top* and *bottom.* They suggest a more hierarchical order than is appropriate. I recognize that "Third Third" is awkward, but I prefer it over the alternative. *Bottom* and *top* imply a more permanent situation, when in fact these specific groupings constitute stages of church development.

Note that the focus of the three groupings is on strengths, not size. Dividing a group of churches by size is an all-too-common mistake in the "fading denominations." They think in categories of "large" and "small" and sometimes "medium" and divide their list of churches accordingly. That creates the illusion, the myth, that what is needed is more large churches. No, what is needed is *stronger, more vital* churches.

For the missionary pastor, strength is of more consequence than size in developing a local church. Some churches large in membership size may rank as Middle Third churches in terms of the number of central characteristics they have well in place. Some medium-sized churches and some small-sized churches, by contrast, may rank as First Third churches on the basis of the number of central characteristics they have well in place. *Think strength, not size.*

THE FIRST THIRD

The First Third grouping includes those churches that have well in place nine of the twelve central characteristics of effective churches. That is to say, in evaluating those churches they would score as an 8, 9, or 10 on at least nine out of the twelve characteristics that effective churches have in common. (See the chart of central characteristics in chapter 3 above.)

To be sure, each church will have its own distinctive rankings for these twelve characteristics. And for each church, the strengths will be evident in a distinctive configuration of nine characteristics.

What distinguishes First Third churches is that each has intentionally developed the nine that match with their current strengths and that match with the mission field they are seeking to serve. They have "tailor made" their nine lead strengths to correspond with what they do best and to correspond with the people to whom they are reaching out.

During over thirty years as a consultant with local churches, I have had the privilege of working with many churches—some small, some medium, some large in size—who have put well in place nine of the twelve. They have become strong, solid First Third churches. Their contributions in mission have been amazing to behold.

THE MIDDLE THIRD

The Middle Third grouping includes those churches that have five to eight of the twelve central characteristics well in place.

Again, it will be whichever five to eight characteristics each church has grown forward from among the twelve.

A Middle Third church is "almost" a First Third church. That is, it is in a solid, midrange position of strengths for mission. It has the potential to move into the First Third. The tendency, regrettably, in some of the fading denominations has been to focus primary attention on the very weak and very strong local churches, to the neglect of the churches with a middle range of strengths. The art is to grow the Middle Third churches to First Third, that is, to help them to add new strengths to their current strengths, building from five, six, seven, or eight central characteristics to achieve nine characteristics well in place.

This Middle Third grouping of churches holds the strongest promise for church development. It is possible to help a Middle Third local church grow itself to the First Third in three to five years. By contrast, to help a Third Third church become a First Third is usually a pilgrimage, of many more years.

It is important not to rush a Middle Third church. Its development to First Third must be solid and steady, sound and sure. Avoid the temptation to rush toward quick closure—the temptation to move too swiftly and therefore too shallowly. Develop realistic objectives with steadfast timetables toward firm, solid development. (See my discussion of the Leadership Development Principle of the Middle Third in *Twelve Keys to an Effective Church: The Leaders' Guide*, pp. 84–93.)

THE THIRD THIRD

The Third Third grouping includes those churches that have from zero to four of the twelve central characteristics well in place. Over the years, I have worked with many churches that have had none of these central characteristics well in place. In one church, the best strength we could discover ranked as a -6. The church had been in existence for ninety-three years and had had forty-seven pastors.

More often than not, churches in the Third Third have from one to four of the central characteristics well in place. These churches often underestimate the strengths they really have. I have worked with many churches who thought they had only one or two of the central characteristics well in place, but upon closer examination they discovered that they really had three or four.

Third Third churches commonly run themselves down and feel apologetic about themselves. They have a tendency to look down on themselves, to think more poorly of themselves than they have a right to. They suffer from low self-esteem.

They do not need someone to come in and say, "Oh, it's all right. It's all going to be all right." They do not need romanticism. They need a realistic assessment of their current strengths and weaknesses, not a romantic assurance that "one day everything will be all right." Third Third churches do not need the mixed blessing of passive dependency as someone feels sorry for them. What they need is to discover their strengths and weaknesses.

Two key principles will be helpful to you. First: *In church development, positive reinforcement any day helps more churches forward than negative reinforcement every day.* Some denominations could learn this lesson.

Point first to the strengths, however few, that are well in place. Do so in the spirit of a realistic assessment, not as an ingratiating ploy. In the first practice of the season as the players show up, the wise football coach looks the team over and asks "What do we have going *for* us this year? Is this the year of power, blocking, and a running game? Or is this the year of speed, quickness, and a passing game?"

Second: *Face the weaknesses constructively.* Do not grieve over the areas that are not strong. It does no good to beat your chest and wail, "Woe is us! We have so many weaknesses." Instead, accept the reality of a low rating on some characteristics and be thankful for opportunities to make changes. See the weaknesses as excellent weaknesses. Say, "We do these weaknesses well." Be thankful for God's ever-present love and forgiveness. A characteristic that was rated as a 2 may be improved over time to a 5 or 6, and later, to an 8 or 9.

It is not constructive to try to develop a Third Third church immediately and instantaneously into the First Third. Regrettably, when missionary pastors try to move them quickly to the First Third grouping, this unrealistic effort has negative results—the church experiences yet another dismal failure. The art is to help a church in the Third Third to see the realistic potential to grow its way forward to the Middle Third. That is constructive help.

THE SIMPLE MISTAKES

BEING NAIVE AND IDEALISTIC

Missionary pastors intent on developing local churches would do well to watch for pitfalls. Several simple mistakes can be predicted and therefore avoided. First, watch out for the mistake of being innocently naive and idealistic about the task of developing a church. It is not something that can be accomplished by applying a simple formula.

Some pastors, naive and idealistic, blithely skim the surface—like toothy, smiling glad-handers intent on keeping their shoes clean, never stepping in the muck or the mud. Their suggestions for the future are more like superficial slogans than real help.

It takes a detached "appreciation" for the complex messes into which churches can sometimes become enmeshed. It takes a certain wisdom and judgment, a certain experience and research, a certain gentle cynicism and confident hope to be helpful with local churches. It takes a corporate, not just an individualistic, understanding of sinfulness and of forgiveness and resurrection. It takes a deep sense of compassion.

To the other extreme, some well-intentioned pastors will become overwhelmed by the mess they discover. They get caught up in the mire of that mess and get sucked in and stuck. They are overcome.

As a missionary pastor helping develop a local church, the art is both to "stand with" the church and at the same time to keep sufficient "distance" (objectivity) that one can be helpful.

THINKING IT WILL BE EASY

A second pitfall is the mistake of thinking that developing a church will be easy. The missionary pastors who are prone to this mistake are primarily those new to church development. They bring an enthusiastic eagerness. They are fresh and not yet scarred or battle weary.

They are new and may have a natural anxiety in the strangeness of their new position. But frequently the combination of a brash eagerness and a low-grade anxiety leads the person to the belief that local church development will be easy. This assumption functions to reinforce the eagerness and allay the anxiety.

Church development is never easy. It can be most satisfying and is certainly most worthwhile. But it is never easy.

Churches who have invested forty years getting themselves into their current plight have key leaders who have learned well the understanding of the nature of leadership, the behavior patterns, and the values and objectives that worked well in the churched culture of the late 1940s and 1950s. As their churches have become more stable and declining in recent years, these key leaders have redoubled their efforts in the *old* behavior pattern. They have simply dug the hole deeper.

They really want to hear your commendation for their hard work in the old behavior patterns. As a missionary pastor, the art is helping them learn a new understanding of leadership, a new set of behavior patterns, and a new set of values. Then help them claim objectives that are important and urgent for the current mission field on which we all now live. Church development work is not easy.

PERFECTIONISM

A third pitfall is the mistake of allowing a compulsiveness toward perfectionism to confuse you. For whatever reasons, some persons have cultivated in themselves a meticulous, detailed commitment toward perfectionism. In some ways, they may have gotten as far as they have because of that compulsiveness, or so they sometimes conclude. Sometimes they may have gotten as far as they have in spite of their perfectionism.

Their compulsiveness toward perfectionism confuses them in two ways:

- They overcoach the team. They send in more plays than the team can run. They create too many objectives for that local church to complete successfully. They set up failure, not success.
- They send in the plays they think the team *should* run, ought to run, must run—not the plays the team *can* run. They fail to match the plays with the players.

As a missionary pastor, the art is to send in the plays the team *can* run, and not too many at that. The art is to help the local church discover the objectives it *can* achieve and, when that church is tempted to create too many, to help it focus on a realistic range of objectives.

MORE MONEY

A fourth pitfall is the mistake of assuming that more money is the solution. Certainly, money is one of the values of this culture, and the culture does influence our behavior patterns and values. More money is not the solution to church development.

In developing new local churches, a denominational office often provides a subsidy to a new church to get it started. It is amazing to me the number of "new" churches that continue to request money from the denomination, even after those churches have been in existence for five, ten, or sometimes fifteen years. "We're almost able to support ourselves, but we've had a couple of difficulties. Just a little more money this next year will help." And they have been saying that same thing for five, ten, and fifteen years.

Moreover, some of these so-called new churches work very hard to maintain their classification as a new church. There is usually more money in the denominational pot for new churches than there is for "old" churches.

Regrettably, underlying this gamesmanship is the assumption that more money will help. It does not. **Mission, not money, will help a church to become stronger.** That local church needs to discover its mission in the world, rather than seeing itself as a mission of the denomination. God calls a local church to be *in* mission, not to be the mission.

TREATING DESPAIR WITH SUCCESS

A fifth pitfall is the mistake of emphasizing success over against despair. It is an interesting phenomenon. On a mission field, we will have our rich, full share of despair, depression, and despondency. These "old friends" come with the terrain.

As some persons become part of the Christian life, however, they assume that, now that they are Christian, life will be better. And once they become missionary pastors, they are certain life will be better! Oh, there will be some bumps and bruises, some tough, tight times. There will be, now and then, a dark valley.

Then a time comes when things really do get very bad. As things worsen, they sense their despair growing. To counter the despair, they try to create success (mostly as the world defines success) with quick closure and results of immediate satisfaction.

These superficial forms of success do give us just enough of a "fix" to cover up the despair. But then we get hooked. The "drug" of quick closure, immediate-satisfaction success takes over. The drug temporarily covers up the despair, but we still ache in our bones. There is a kind of haunting shallowness to a string of manufactured successes. Yet we press on because we are hooked, and our despair grows worse.

The missionary pastor discerns that *what helps one with despair is mission, not success.* At bottom, despair has to do with whether one's life will count. The string of quick successes is used to create the illusion that one's life does count. But what is eternal is the mission of God, not the fleeting successes of humankind. As a missionary pastor, the art is to discover constructive ways in which you can participate in God's mission in this world. Stay the course in that mission. Then one's life does count, in enduring and abiding ways.

CONSTRUCTIVE HELP

DEPENDENCY

Missionary pastors too frequently invest too much help with a Third Third local church—because they are interested in being helpful. Frequently, a Third Third church, sensing its weaknesses, "stews" over what is wrong. They blame the preacher. They blame the denomination. They "scapegoat" their problems. They bicker and fuss, and before long a "grass fire" gets started.

Missionary pastors, out of their own concern and desire to be helpful, come running to help put out the grass fire. They become the volunteer fire department. They deliver attention, affection, recognition, reward, and dependency—and they teach that one of the next best things that church can do is to start another grass fire.

Someone will come running to help put it out again, and that person will deliver to them attention, affection, recognition, reward, and dependency. And a cycle is created of grass fires and people who come running to put them out. Indeed, for many churches in the Third Third, that cycle has been going on for twenty or more years.

As we have moved from a churched culture to an unchurched culture, many of these Third Third churches have found themselves in an even more desperate plight. In the churched culture, they had perhaps only three of the twelve central characteristics well in place. And they came to depend on the churched culture to deliver to them a range of "new" churched people.

When the culture shifted to unchurched, their plight worsened. New people were no longer showing up. They could no longer depend on the culture to sustain them. Hence, they turned to the pastor or the denomination. They had depended on the churched culture. Now they would depend on the pastor or the denomination. They simply shifted the focus for their dependency.

When such a church gets into a grass fire, a missionary pastor comes running to put it out. All too frequently, the person who comes running "needs" to have people dependent on him or her. That person is the codependent in the relationship. The church is dependent, the helper is codependent. That parasitic relationship does not create strong churches. Both the church and the helper need to learn new patterns of behavior.

It is fair to distinguish between a grass fire and a forest fire. When in doubt, however, it is appropriate to give the Third Third church the chance to learn from its own mistakes, rather than protecting it from failure.

Pain is one of the best friends and teachers a person struggling with alcoholism has available. When someone else steps in and quickly relieves all of the pain, the alcoholic no longer has available that excellent good friend and teacher. It is the same with dependent churches. When someone runs to help a Third Third church put out a grass fire, that helper removes one of the most constructive friends and teachers that church has available, namely, the pain associated with learning from one's mistakes.

It is important to not teach churches a dependent pattern of starting grass fires, confident that others will come running to help put them out. The pattern of investing more help than would be helpful with Third Third churches creates reactive, organizational, passive, institutional churches, because the pastor comes running to deliver attention, affection, recognition, reward—and dependency.

To be sure, the biblical text invites us to feed the hungry, clothe the naked, and share water with the thirsty—to be in mission with the poor and the powerless, the lonely and the downtrodden. Indeed, that is what mission is about. "Even as you have done it unto the least of these. . . ."

But it is not appropriate for Third Third churches to use this biblical invitation as an excuse for their own dependency patterns. Christ's invitation describes what he invites local churches *to do,* not to have done for them. In the parable, the church is called to be the Samaritan, not to be the man in the ditch.

Do not miss the key point. I am *not* suggesting that Third Third churches be ignored. In all my days of coaching, I have followed the policy that whoever shows up for practice, plays. You normally go with the team you have and coach them forward. But the danger of investing too much help with a Third Third church is that it creates a pattern of dependency and passivity.

This is the best way forward:

1. Invest solid, minimal help with First Third churches. Say, "Thank you for effectively sharing mission with the community." Share gratitude and prayer, not rules and regulations. Stay out of the way. Give them encouragement.
2. Invest strong help with the Middle Third churches. Indeed, intentionally help these churches to develop themselves in strength to First Third.
3. Invest moderate help with the Third Third churches. Help them to grow themselves in strength to the Middle Third. Avoid any pattern of dependency or codependencey.

This investment of church development helps the Middle Third, the Third Third, and the First Third. Five years from now, the character and quality of these churches will thereby be substantially advanced.

CONSTRUCTIVE HELP

One of the primary reasons some missionary pastors are drawn to investing so much of their efforts with Third Third churches is that they have the best intentions and genuinely want to be helpful. Four guidelines for *constructive* help are important.

First, constructive help *is alert to avoiding a pattern of dependency.* Recognize and avoid the way some persons regrettably offer their help, namely, because they find value and meaning in life when a specific church becomes dependent on them. They need to be needed and wanted—and who would criticize the "selfless" way they give help to "those poor churches"? They create dependent churches, not mission churches. Avoid delivering coddling instead of caring. The focus of help is best directed to advancing that local church's mission, not satisfying the helper's need to be needed.

When helping people need, rely on, and count on the church being dependent on them, the relationship is much like the dependent/codependent dynamic found in various addictive behavior patterns. Should that local church show signs of constructive advance, the codependent helper may sabotage the growth process in order to keep the church dependent. Both must change their behavior patterns for permanent growth to be possible.

Second, constructive help *does not cause harm.* It is evident that too much "help" is more harmful than helpful. The art is to share almost enough help to be helpful—almost, but not so much that the church fails to draw upon its own resources, gifts, and competencies.

Third, constructive help *does not allow itself to be controlled by the church that is being helped.* Years ago, while working with people who were struggling with alcoholism, I learned that a person who needs help has many ploys to control whoever is helping. It is ironic that someone who cannot control his or her own behavior can manage to exert so much control over the behavior of another. This is a parallel pitfall to avoid when helping churches that have become dependent.

I am not comparing Third Third churches and alcoholics. I am comparing the codependent behavior—what helping persons tend to do with both Third Third churches and alcoholics. They allow their helping to be controlled by what the local church wants, rather than by what it may truly need. They pander to that local church's symptoms and wish list, rather than focusing on the deeper causes and substantive components for health. The art is to share one's help with wisdom, judgment, vision, common sense, and prayer.

Fourth, constructive help *provides positive reinforcement and recognition to those persons in the local church who are advancing and developing their mission.* Sadly, some pastors are preoccupied with persons in their stable and declining or dying church who demonstrate a dependency pattern. The focus of energy and resources is on them. As a result, they overlook or neglect to boost along the persons who are developing some strength and vitality.

Oh, to be sure, growth and development are spotlighted from time to time. Success stories appear, now and then, in the local church's publications. But the preponderant emphasis is on illness, not wellness. We would be well advised to consider an emerging development in the medical health field. In recent years, the research has increasingly focused on the components that contribute to wellness, as opposed only to a focus on how to correct illness.

As a matter of fact, the twelve central characteristics are the components that contribute to the wellness of a local church—to its strength, soundness, and mission. It will become increasingly vital that missionary pastors focus more fully on giving positive reinforcement and recognition to their healthy sources of strength.

The parable of the steward is a helpful text for church development. The good steward, when given five talents, developed five more. The Lord said, "Well done, thou good and faithful servant. You have been faithful over a little. I will make you steward over much." And it was the same with the steward given two talents.

But it was the steward who buried the talent in the ground who needed the flashlight. He claimed that it was buried in order to conserve, hold, protect, and preserve it. His master rebuked him, saying, "You didn't even invest it so that it would earn interest." This was the steward cast into outer darkness. If you have ever been in outer darkness, you know the value of a flashlight to find your way back.

Good stewardship of our churches implies advancing and developing them. Good stewardship is not conserving and holding, protecting and preserving these churches as they are. The constructive help of missionary pastors advances the mission outpost's strengths for mission.

As a missionary pastor, consider these possibilities. First, when you are serving on a mission field with a Third Third church, do not reinforce their passive, dependent behavior with your co-dependent behavior. It will only make matters worse. Avoid being in a passive, dependent relationship with your denomination. That will only confirm the same in your church. Develop a strong, proactive, missional spirit in your leadership work.

Second, focus on helping a Third Third church become a Middle Third church. Do not try to force them to go too far too quickly.

Third, when you are serving with a Middle Third church, choose well the central characteristics you plan to expand and add. Focus only on as many of the central characteristics as will help the church move forward to First Third.

Fourth, stay long enough to have the fun of seeing the church progress in strength and mission. Your next strong church might best be the one you are already serving and developing. You are more likely to grow a strong church by serving the same church for a number of years than you are by moving frequently.

Fifth, when you serve as missionary pastor with a First Third church, maximize the mission outreach you and your church have in the community. Your church is in an extraordinary position to help people with their lives and destinies. Remember that the stronger the church, the stronger the mission. The stronger the mission, the stronger the church.

PART FIVE.
CONCLUSION

18. The Way Forward

FROM THE GROUND UP

The nature of leadership is missional, not institutional. The task is not to focus on revising old structures, having more effective meetings, developing better goals, and involving more people in more committees. It is no longer as simple as that.

We must began again from the ground up. We have tried for thirty years to strengthen various denominations from the top down. If that approach has not worked in the past thirty years, it is not likely to work in the coming thirty years. We should have learned better after the first ten years of effort at the top-down approach. Frankly, we are smarter than that.

We must begin as though this is a mission field, because that is precisely what it is. And we must begin with the grass roots of those persons who are not now participating in churches and, with and among them, help to create missional communities of reconciliation, wholeness, caring, and justice. This work will simply not move forward by focusing solely, or even primarily, on those persons who are already participating in current local churches.

Indeed, those persons who have spent the better part of the past thirty years active in local churches will want to begin again from the ground up in developing a new understanding of the foundations for leadership on a mission field. Many of us have spent the past thirty years with an institutional understanding of leadership, with its related values, behavior patterns, and objectives. A reactive, organizational, passive, institutional understanding will no longer work. All of us—unchurched and churched—will learn new ways in the days to come. This can best be achieved from the ground up.

NEW CONGREGATIONS

If you and I were to have the privilege of starting a new congregation this coming year, we would look for many unchurched persons to become participants. We would want many un-churched persons to be *early* participants in this new missional community of reconciliation, wholeness, caring, and justice.

It would not be helpful for the founding participants to consist solely or even primarily of already longtime churched persons. Mostly, their experience will have been in stable and declining or dying churches. They will have learned well how to build stable and declining and dying churches, having learned the behavior patterns that focus on the functional, institutional approach to the local church.

Instead we would gather a substantial number of our new participants from among the unchurched on our mission field. As they discover fulfillment in their foundational life searches with us, they will become part of the mission team, bringing yet other persons *new to the Christian life*. We will build, thereby, a stronger new community. This new congregation will begin by forming community, not committees.

The primary focus in the first and the second years is on helping people to discover a sense of mission, involving shepherding and visitation; worship and prayer; and roots, place and belonging, sharing and caring. In this new emerging community of the faith, mission teams would be encouraged and *would be the major value*. Small, short-term organizational task forces would do modest work.

Perhaps toward the end of the second or third year, some of the energy of the leadership will focus on forming specific committees. The early agenda is mission, shepherding, worship, and community, not committees.

Some will say, "But won't some things go undone?" That is precisely the point. Some things will not get done. Mostly, what will *not* get done is focusing on the tenth, eleventh, and twelfth characteristics—land and parking, space and facilities, and financial resources and money. Standing committees, organized in the first and second years, inevitably focus most of their energies on those matters.

We have, for too long, put the cart before the horse. We have been concerned about the tasks that might not get done unless we quickly form committees in a new congregation. The quicker we form the committees, the more the focus of the grouping is drawn away from the missional community and toward a functional, organizational, institutional church.

The art is to focus first on that which is primary, not secondary. That which is primary is the development of the relational characteristics. In doing so, many people will discover new sources of fulfillment for their foundational life searches. Once the relational characteristics are strongly developed, then that which is secondary—developing specific functional characteristics—will move ahead yet even more strongly.

NOT A NEW CHURCH

The art is to grow a new congregation, not start a new church. We need to start more missionary congregations and fewer local churches. And the art of starting a new congregation (or renewing a present congregation) is to focus on the first four relational characteristics:

1. specific, concrete, missional objectives
2. pastoral and lay visitation in the community
3. corporate, dynamic worship
4. significant relational groupings

The bureaucratic mentality would focus on the tasks that "the new church has to achieve." Indeed, they have traditionally focused on the last three of the twelve central characteristics of an effective church—land and parking, space and facilities, and financial resources. The bureaucratic mentality seeks to build a new church building. No, we are growing a new congregation. There is a vast difference.

I cannot emphasize strongly enough that when the focus is on committee, the development of community does not occur. Some bureaucratic persons think that development of community happens naturally and automatically, but that is not the case. It requires tending, nurturing, growing and developing, advancing and building—thoughtfully, intentionally, purposefully.

We need missionary pastors of new congregations to create new missional communities, not form old committees. The focus is radically different. The nature of the grouping is decisively distinct. The strength, well-being, and nurturing that persons discover from a community of reconciliation, wholeness, caring, and justice is extraordinary. They do not discover that same strength and nurturing from a committee. Our task is to grow missionary leaders more than it is to recruit committee volunteers.

Someone may argue that some committees serve as community. That is exactly true. Some *few* committees may serve as community. They do so insofar as their primary origin is community, not committee.

A committee that has spent its earliest time together focusing on functional, organizational, and institutional matters has a tough pilgrimage to grow into a missional community of reconciliation, wholeness, caring, and justice. It is easier first to help a new grouping discover a strong sense of community and then also to do some of the tasks of a committee.

The mother-daughter church modality of starting new congregations has precisely that flaw within it. The mother churches are typically stable and declining churches. The members who leave that mother church to become the founding core of the new daughter church have generally learned how to build a stable and declining church.

The new daughter church will experience a blush of growth during the first three to four years because of the newness, the enthusiasm, and the pioneering spirit that attracts persons to a new church. But usually about the fourth or fifth year, the church will bump up against some tough, hard decisions. And in its decision making, it will fall back on the conserving, holding, protecting, preserving behavior patterns of stable and declining churches. It will become preoccupied with the functional characteristics. Like mother, like daughter.

It will make decisions that in about the tenth year will lead to a nearly new but now stable and declining congregation, plateaued and leveled out. And it will plateau and level out because the solutions to the problems were primarily functional, institutional, and organizational solutions. In our time, people are not drawn to or attracted by groupings who live out their existence primarily on the basis of a functional, institutional, and organizational understanding of leadership values and behavior patterns.

EXISTING CONGREGATIONS

What is true for new congregations is true for existing congregations. The way forward is to help existing congregations to a new sense of mission and a new understanding of the nature of leadership. We need more missionary congregations and fewer churched-culture local churches.

The way forward is not to pour money into shoring up the functional characteristics of our existing congregations or to try to re-create the busy programs and activities of the churched culture or to develop "better professional ministers." The way forward is to have missionary pastors and missionary congregations.

NEW COMMUNITIES

The way forward is to focus in relational, person-centered, and Christ-centered ways on the construction of new missional communities of reconciliation, wholeness, caring, and justice. New communities with the unchurched, new communities with the churched, and existing congregations can become new missional communities. Some already are. Many are on the way.

RECONCILIATION

These new communities are missional communities in which people discover reconciliation. In these communities, we discover reconciliation within ourselves and reconciliation with one another. All of us have sinned and fallen short of the glory of God. Each of us has our own private, personal sins of omission and commission. Each of us longs for, hopes for, yearns for forgiveness and reconciliation. We also have our corporate and societal sins of omission and commission. These equally well keep us awake late at night with anxiety, fear, and dread. In this community of reconciliation, we will discover that sense of forgiveness as well.

It is not simply that we come to this community for brief, brisk friendships, nodding acquaintances, almost knowing one another's names. It is that we bring to this community our sense of alienation, our sense of loneliness, our sense of sinfulness—and we look for and hope for a sense of forgiveness, a sense of reconciliation.

WHOLENESS

These communities are communities of wholeness. They take seriously the whole person, not simply the spiritual dimension of who we are or the physical dimension. Some churches have focused on food; some churches have focused on salvation. Some churches have thought we were primarily emotional beings and have focused, more often than not, on sentiment.

These new communities help the whole person, whether physical food or spiritual food is needed, whether the help is emotional or vocational. These missional communities focus on helping each person with the wholeness of each one's foundational life searches.

Furthermore, these communities function one with another in a sense of wholeness. To be sure, there exists a variety of subcultural groupings that have their own distinctive sociological, economic, cultural, vocational, and theological dynamics, all of which will be present. And persons will understand, appreciate, and value the relativity, the unimportance, and the lack of significance of these varied socioeconomic, cultural, vocational, and theological distinctions. People live with one another in a sense of wholeness, as a whole community. The whole is considered more important and stronger than the parts.

CARING

These communities have about them a sense of caring: caring in the world and caring with one another, primarily the former. It is not simply that this community has about it a spirit of caring within itself. That is not what will distinguish this community, as important as that may be.

Yes, some people will say, "See how they love one another." Far more important, people will say, "See how they love the world." See how they love people with specific human hurts and hopes. See how their compassion for persons in trouble and need is extraordinary, amazing, and beyond all recognition—especially so, considering the values of this world.

These are communities whose people are self-giving, not self-seeking. They are committed to a theology of service, not a theology of survival; their abiding contribution will be a "living in the world" with persons who are hurting and hoping.

JUSTICE

These communities have an abiding, strong focus on justice. They are not communities of pleasant generalities and pious statements. They are missional communities that take seriously the difficult ambiguities of societal and ethical concerns in our time. These communities wrestle with those concerns.

These communities are more interested in societal issues than social graces; more interested in poverty than platitudes; more interested in inequities in the culture than in study committees in the church. These communities live out compassion and courage, not timid, calculating pieties.

These communities live out the discovery of a new humanity, not a pattern of idealism. I encourage us to renounce any effort to make this community spiritualistic over against earthly, in the old docetic dualism. I encourage us to set aside the thought that structures are primarily sinful and evil. We are created in the image and likeness of God. In the discovery of our new humanity, structures live out both the origin of who we are and the demonic character we sometimes express.

It is not simply that structures are sinful and evil and that we somehow are not. Even as we are sinful, we are created in the image and likeness of God. When, with Christ, we discover our best, true selves, we share the amazing generosity and grace that God has shared with us. And with Christ, new missional communities arise who are more of grace than of sin, more of power than of powerlessness, more of belonging than of lostness, more of meaning than of cynicism, and more of hope than of despair.

THE CHURCH AND THE CULTURE

To be sure, these missional communities live in relation to the culture in which they emerge. They will customarily have some affinity to a particular cultural setting. It is decisive that this *not* be too cozy a relationship. These communities best relate to the structures of the culture when they stand over against them.

Some of the fading denominations are at a theological and societal cul-de-sac. (*Cul-de-sac* is the appropriate term because, unlike *dead end* or *end of the road*, it relates to the suburbs, which have been the predominant focus of some denominations ever since suburbs began springing up.) Some denominations have identified themselves too cozily with a very limited number of socioeconomic, vocational, theological, and subcultural groupings in this country. And some of these subcultural groupings are diminishing. There is a simple fact we hardly even remember. The white-collar, upper middle-class in this country is shrinking. It is not surprising, therefore, that some denominations are also declining.

THE LEADER'S TASK

The way forward is with missionary pastors and mission team leaders. The way forward is to understand the nature of leadership, which is proactive, relational, intentional, and missional in the mission of God in the world. Today, you can live this understanding of leadership.

Life is a search. Leadership is discovery. The way forward is to help persons discover fulfillment in their foundational life searches for individuality, community, meaning, and hope in the cause of Christ and the kingdom. Cynicism and careerism are the foes. Today, compassion and courage are your friends.

The way forward is for missionary pastors and mission teams to achieve these four central leadership tasks:

- Help persons rediscover power in their own lives and destinies.
- Construct new missional communities of reconciliation, wholeness, caring, and justice—in the name of Christ.
- Create a new theological direction of specific, shared purposes.
- Launch and lead intentional missional teams to meet specific, concrete human hurts and hopes—both societal and individual—in the world.

Today, these tasks are decisive.

The way forward is to develop strong, effective practices in:

1. leadership values
2. leadership environment
3. constructive perspective
4. evaluation process
5. leadership structures
6. missional structures
7. church development

Such a focus helps missionary pastors and mission team leaders develop themselves. Do not wait for these practices to come from the top. Today, begin implementing these emphases where you are—on the mission field God has given to you. Be at peace. Know that my prayers and the prayers of many are with you. There will be grace and strength for the times.

This final analogy will help. A denomination is not like a huge ocean liner that must be turned slowly, ever so slowly, to a new course over a long period of time. A denomination is better understood as a flotilla, a fleet, a convoy of many ships of different sizes and shapes.

The art is to help now this ship, now that ship, and another, and yet another to chart a new course. As enough ships chart the new course, the rest of the fleet will see the new direction.

Without a vision, the people perish. Hope is stronger than memory. We are the Easter people. We are the people of hope.

God be with you as a missionary pastor, as a mission leader.

Appendix

These are the two to four key action objectives I planned to accomplish this past year.

Objective 1

Objective 2

Objective 3

Objective 4

As succinctly and as accurately as possible, these are the results that have been achieved for each.

Objective 1

Objective 2

Objective 3

Objective 4

These are the principal strengths and weaknesses of each.

	Strengths	*Weaknesses*
Objective 1		
Objective 2		
Objective 3		
Objective 4		

These are the new insights and discoveries related to each.

Objective 1

Objective 2

Objective 3

Objective 4

These are the one or two specific competency growth objectives I chose to develop this past year. This is the current status of each.

Specific Competency   *Status of Development*

1.

2.

These are the three principal areas in which I would appreciate help from my consultive team.

1.

2.

3.

These two to four key action objectives will be important for my work in the coming year.

Objective 1

Objective 2

Objective 3

Objective 4

These one or two specific competency growth objectives are important to my growth and development in the coming year.

1.

2.